SUSTAINABLE DEVELOPMENT GOAL
AND
NATIONAL EDUCATION POLICY 2020

About the Editors

Dr. Ahmad Mujtaba Siddiqui is an Educator and Administrator presently working as an Assistant Professor, Department of Geography, Aligarh Muslim University, Aligarh. He has been working in the field of education for more than 17 years. He has several papers presentations in National and International Conferences and Seminars. He has contributed 12 papers and 10 articles in National and International reputed Journals andpublished2 research publication.

Dr. Sayyed Muhammad Usman presently serving as executive member of Al-Barkaat Educational Society. He is a young, dynamic and dedicated Researcher and Administrator with a strong work on ethic and commitment to excellence in teaching and administration. He has completed his Ph.D in Urdu from Aligarh Muslim University,He has presented several papers in National and International Conferences and Seminars andcontributed research papers in National and International reputed Journals.

Dr. Rubina Shahnaz presently serving as Principal in Al-Barkaat Institute of Education.Dedicated SeniorEducator and Administrator with a strong work on ethic and commitment to excellence in teaching.She has been serving in the field of education for more than 15 years. More than 34 paper presentations in National and International Conferences and Seminars. There are 21 papers published in National and International Journals,6 chapters inedited books and also published 1 book to her credit.

As anTeacher and Educator, **Dr. Saba Anees**, presently working as an Assistant Professor in Central University of Kerala. She has been working in the education sector for more than 12 years. She has presented several papers in National and International Conferences and Seminars. Her 13 research papers and articles published in National and International reputed journals, books, proceedings and magazines. She has also developed the academic learning material in the form of e-content, video lectures, moodlé course and convened an online short-term course.

Dr. Tabassum Qamar is a Teacher and Educator presently working with Al-Barkaat Institute of Education, an affiliated Institute of RMPSSU, Aligarh.She has several paper presentations in National and International Conferences and Seminars. There are about 7 papers published in National and International reputed Journals, books and magazines.

SUSTAINABLE DEVELOPMENT GOAL AND NATIONAL EDUCATION POLICY 2020

Edited by
Ahmad Mujtaba Siddiqui
Syed Mohammad Usman
Rubina Shahnaz
Saba Anees
Tabassum Qamar

CONCEPT PUBLISHING COMPANY PVT. LTD.
NEW DELHI - 110059

ISBN: 978-93-5594-659-1

First Published 2024

Published and Printed by

Concept Since 1974

Concept Publishing Company Pvt. Ltd.
A/15-16, Commercial Block, Mohan Garden
New Delhi-110059 (India)
T: +91-11-41101460
E: publishing@conceptpub.com, *W*: www.conceptpub.com

Cataloging in Publication--Courtesy: D.K. Agencies (P) Ltd. <docinfo@dkagencies.com>

Achieving SDG 8 Through Education 4.0: Across the Globe and Beyond the Disciplines (Conference) (2022 : Online)
Sustainable development goal and national education policy 2020 / edited by Ahmad Mujtaba Siddiqui [and four others].
pages cm
"... outcome of the papers presented and contributed in the 3 days multidisciplinary international conference on the theme 'Achieving SDG 8 Through Education 4.0: Across the Globe and Beyond The Disciplines' held from 24th-26th November 2022"--Preface.
Includes bibliographical references and index.
ISBN 9789355946591

1. Education--India--Congresses. 2. Education and state--India--Congresses. 3. Educational technology--India--Congresses. 4. Sustainable development--India--Congresses. I. Siddiqui, Ahmad Mujtaba, editor. II. Title.

LCC LA1151.A24 2022 | DDC 370.954 23

Preface

Global sustainability and development have always been a major agenda of preference among all nations with the commencement of 21st century (The 8 Millennium Developmental Goals, 2000). In 2016, these broad MDGs were segmented into 17 more focused SDGs (Sustainable Development Goals) for a better world. The onset of the COVID-19 epidemic caused a spike in the unemployment rate and a worldwide economic closure. As a result, it becomes urgent to concentrate efforts on sustaining SDG 8, which aims at fostering sustained, inclusive economic growth, full and productive employment, and decent work for all.

The proposed target of SDG 8 majorly focuses on achieving higher levels of economic productivity through diversification, technological upgrading and innovation, including through a focus on high-value added and labour-intensive sectors, promoting development-oriented policies that support productive activities, decent job creation, entrepreneurship, creativity and innovation, and encourage the formalization and growth of micro-, small- and medium-sized enterprises, including through access to financial services, by 2030, achieve full and productive employment and decent work for all women and men, including for young people and persons with disabilities, and equal pay for work of equal value, by 2020, substantially reduce the proportion of youth not in employment, education or training, taking immediate and effective measures to eradicate forced labour, end modern slavery and human trafficking and secure the prohibition and elimination of the worst forms of child labour, including recruitment and use of child soldiers, and by 2025 end child labour in all its forms, protecting labour rights and promote safe and secure working environments for all workers, including migrant workers, in particular women migrants, and those in precarious employment, by 2030, devise and implement policies to promote sustainable tourism that creates jobs and promotes local culture and products, by 2020, develop and operationalizing a global strategy for youth employment and implement the Global Jobs Pact of the International Labour Organization etc.

Improvements brought about by Industrial Revolution, such as Internet of Things (IOT), Virtual and Augmented Reality, Artificial Intelligence (AI), Machine Learning (ML), and Robotics have drastically changed the current workplace and the labour market across a variety of industries.

The future era is going to witness a drastic change in the roles, responsibilities and work profile medicos, engineers, entrepreneurs, investors, corporate houses, trade & commerce, tourism, business world and teachers as well. Since, every nation's educational system focuses on preparing students as per future social and civic requirements; education is indispensible for all academic disciplines in order to meet these worldwide technologically driven personnel demands and achieving Sustainable Development Goals by 2030.

The Education India initiative aims to use Fourth Industrial Revolution technologies to enhance learning and reduce inequalities in India and globally. According to a 2021 **World Economic Forum** Paper, '**Shaping an Equitable, Inclusive, and Sustainable Recovery: Acting Now for a Better Future**', at least 24 million children, predominantly girls, may never return to school. Hence, urgent action is needed to overcome these learning losses and to scale up solutions that will not only address these gaps but also create sustainable learning environments.

Digital learning can address these challenges effectively and ensure that no one is left behind on the educational journey.

The National Achievement Survey of 2021 found nearly half of primary school students to have learning levels lower than appropriate for their grades, a situation that the pandemic has intensified. This has far-reaching implications for young Indians' readiness for the 21st century workplace and India's preparedness for the Fourth Industrial Revolution. **The Knowledge and Information Network for Digital Learning and Education (KINDLE)** is an initiative to utilize digital and other technologies to address learning gaps and make education accessible to all.

Present book is a significant outcome of the papers presented and contributed in the 3 Days Multidisciplinary International Conference on the theme '**Achieving SDG 8 Through Education 4.0: Across the Globe and Beyond The Disciplines**' held from 24th-26th November, 2022. The areas of the chapters covered the following sub-themes: Future requirements for skilled professionals in the various fields including education across the globe post pandemic, Revolution across sectors (Business, Commerce, Trade, Health care, Technology, Education, Economy etc.). A way forward of transforming different sectors to, COVID-19 pandemic and its impact on economic growth and various sectors of economy, ILO manpower requirement trends pre & post pandemic across the globe, Ways and means to generate more employment opportunities in different sectors of an economy with special reference to education, Evolving and generating employment opportunities due to artificial intelligence, machine learning, robotics etc., Evolution of education from web 1.0 to 4.0, OER, MOOCs etc. as tools for globalization of education, Education and multidisciplinary researches, Transforming India into a 'Global Education Hub' as envisioned by NEP, 2020 and Pros and Cons of Education post pandemic.

The book 'Sustainable Development Goal and National Education Policy 2020' seems to be of utmost importance for academicians and policy makers in the following areas of work.

Firstly, it offers a comprehensive exploration of the complex issues surrounding SDG and the role of education in achieving its targets. The United Nations has recognized SDG as a critical global goal, and it is essential to understand the challenges and opportunities associated with achieving it. This book provides a broad and interdisciplinary approach to understanding SDG, drawing on insights from fields such as education, economics, and technology.

Secondly, New Education Policy 2020 aligns well with the goals of Sustainable Development Goal 8 by emphasizing skill development, holistic education, research, innovation, and inclusive learning. By equipping individuals with relevant skills, knowledge, and values, NEP 2020 can contribute to creating a workforce that supports sustainable economic growth, productive employment, and decent work for all. This book explores how NEP 2020 can support the achievement of SDG 8, making it an essential resource for anyone interested in the intersection of education, technology, and economic development.

Finally, the book's interdisciplinary approach and global perspective make it a valuable resource for readers interested in these topics across different fields and regions. The authors draw on examples and insights from around the world to provide a comprehensive understanding of the challenges and opportunities associated with achieving SDG. This makes it an essential read for policy-makers, educators, students, and anyone interested in working towards a more sustainable and equitable future.

Overall, 'Sustainable Development Goal and National Education Policy 2020' is a must-read for anyone interested in understanding the complex issues surrounding SDG and the role of Education in achieving its targets. With its interdisciplinary approach, global perspective, and innovative insights, this book provides a valuable resource for anyone committed to promoting sustainable economic growth and social justice around the world.

We acknowledge the sincere efforts of the organizing committee members.

Editors

Acknowledgements

It is our privilege to express my profound sense of gratitude and indebtedness to all the esteemed Paper Contributors who contributed their valuable piece of knowledge in the form of chapters for the successful compilations of present edited book. We are grateful to them to give up their precious time and expertise throughout the progress of this book. Without their support, this book would not have become a reality.

We express our gratitude to all the members of the **Advisory Committee** for their expert guidance, constant encouragement, keen interest, untiring efforts, indispensable support and constructive criticism.

We would also like to acknowledge the significant contribution made by our **International & National Paper Review Committee** for the valuable contributions as the reviewers regarding the improvement of quality, coherence and content presentation of chapters.

It is our extreme pleasure to thank **Prof. Syed Muhammad Amin (President)** & **Mr. S.M. Ashraf (Vice-President)**, of the **Al-Barkaat Educational Society** for helping us in countless ways during the preparation of this book.

It is our pleasure to thank all the **Mr. S.M. Aman (Executive Committee Member)** & **Dr. F.U. Siddiqui (Coordinator)** of Al-Barkaat Educational Society for their enormous technical help and support during the compilation of present book.

We extend our heartfelt thanks to the members of the **Editorial Team** for their deep hardwork, dedication, sincere efforts, unconditional and splendid cooperation offered for the enrichment of this book.

We are also thankful to all the **teaching staff members** of Al-Barkaat Institute of Education for their consistent contribution and all the cooperation.

Our acknowledgement would remain incomplete without making special mention for the funding received from **ICSSR.** We sincerely acknowledge the board of **ICSSR** for considering the proposal worth to sponsor.

Aligarh **Editorial Team**

Contents

Section IV
Ensuring Sustainable Development to All

List of Contributors

Afshan Anees, Assistant Professor, Al-Barkaat Institute of Education, Aligarh. **Email:** afshan.anees1@gmail.com

Amit Ahuja, Faculty, University School of Education, Guru Gobind Singh Indraprastha University, Dwarka, Delhi. **Email:** dr.amitahuja1975@gmail.com

Archana Anil, Trainee Teacher, School of Education and Humanities, Manav Rachna University.

Asma Ishaque, Research Scholar, ILSR, Department of Law, Mangalayatan University, Aligarh. **Email:** advocateasmaishaque1@gmail.com

Atin Das, Research Scholar, Hospitality Management, Sanskriti University, Chatta, Mathura, Uttar Pradesh. **Email:** atin.das70@gmail.com.

Dyutima Kesar, Research Scholar, Department of Education, University of Jammu. **Email:** dyutimakesar1991@gmail.com

Hena Naaz, Assistant Professor, Al-Barkaat Institute of Management Studies, Aligarh. **Email:** naazalig278@gmail.com

Himanshoo Kumar Sharma, Research Scholar, Sanskriti University Mathura, U.P. **Email:** himanshookumarsharma@gmail.com

Jwel Hoque, Research Scholar, Department of Education, Aligarh Muslim University. **Email:** jwelwb5@gmail.com

Mahfooz Alam, Research Scholar, Department of Education, Aligarh Muslim University. **Email:** mafoozalam150988@gmail.com

Manju, P.K., Research Scholar, Research Centre in Education, NSS Training College, Ottapalam, Affiliated to University of Calicut, Kerala. **Email:** manjupappully@gmail.com

Mini Kumari, D., Research Centre in Education, NSS Training College, Ottapalam, Affiliated to University of Calicut, Kerala. **Email:** minidevu1976@gmail.com

Mohd Mubashshir Ali, Coordinator to Libraries, Al-Barkaat Educational Institutions & Librarian, Al-Barkaat Institute of Education, Aligarh. **Email:** mohdmubashshirali@gmail.com

Mohd. Nadeem Khan, Ex-Research Scholar, Centre for Women's Studies, AMU, Aligarh.
Email: mohdnaddemkhan2509@gmail.com

Mubeen Zehra, Research Scholar, Teacher Training and Non-formal Education (IASE) Faculty of Education, Jamia Millia Islamia New Delhi. **Email:** mubeen.zr@gmail.com

Nakul Barman, M.A in Education, Raiganj University, West Bengal. **Email:** nbarman836@gmail.com

Ozma, Assistant Professor, School of Education, Sharda University
Email: ozma.1@sharda.ac.in

Prasenjit Das, Ph.D. Scholar, Department of Education, Raiganj University, West Bengal. **Email:** pdas1534@gmail.com

Prathistha Tandon, Research Scholar, Sanskriti University.
Email: prathistha.tandon23@gmail.com

Rajani Upadhyay, Research Scholar, University School of Education, Guru Gobind Singh Indraprastha University, Dwarka, Delhi. **Email:** rju.2285@gmail.com

Rubina Shahnaz, Principal in Al-Barkaat Institute of Education, Aligarh. **Email:** drrubinashahnaz@gmail.com

Saba Anees, Assistant Professor in Educational Studies, Department of Education, Central University of Kerala.
Email: dranees.saba7@gmail.com

Sachi Jain, Trainee Teacher, School of Education and Humanities, Manav Rachna University. **Email:** sachijain821@gmail.com

Saleha Zaini, Senior Faculty, Al-Barkaat Educational Institutions, Aligarh. **Email:** dr.salehazaini@gmail.com

Sana Hashmi, Assistant Professor, Al-Barkaat College of Graduate Studies, Aligarh. **Email:** hashmisana2@gmail.com

Shafeeqa Bano, Assistant Professor, Al-Barkaat College of Graduate Studies, Aligarh. **Email:** bshafeeqa@gmail.com

Shagufta, Assistant Professor, Al-Barkaat Institute of Education, Aligarh. **Email:** shaguftamubeen2006@gmail.com

Soram Sonia, Assistant Professor, Department of Teacher Education, Manipur University.
Email: soramsonia82@gmail.com

Syed Wajahat Ali, Research Scholar, Sarojini Naidu Centre for Women's Studies, Jamia Millia Islamia, New Delhi.

Syeda Ayeman Mazhar, Assistant Professor, Department of TahaffuziwaSamaji Tib, Rajasthan Unani Medical College, Jaipur. **Email:** syedaayeman@gmail.com

Tabassum Qamar, Assistant Professor, ABIE, Aligarh.
Email: drtabassumqamar@gmail.com

Umesh Sharma, Associate Professor, Hospitality Management, Sanskriti University, Chatta, Mathura, Uttar Pradesh.
Email: umeshsharma.mgmt@sanskriti.edu.in

Umme Kulsoom Zaidi, Assistant Professor, Al Barkaat College of Graduate Studies, Aligarh. **Email:** u.k.zaidi@gmail.com

Section I
Education and Teaching Learning Process

1
Education
Opportunities and Challenges

Hena Naaz

Introduction

Education has undergone several transformations over the years. The shift from traditional classroom learning to online and blended learning has resulted in the emergence of Education. Education is an innovative approach to education that integrates technology, personalized learning, and critical thinking to prepare students for the future workforce (Hong and Ma, 2020). The concept of Education has gained traction in India, with many educational institutions embracing it to enhance the quality of education. However, the implementation of Education in India faces several challenges, including inadequate infrastructure, teacher training, and lack of access to technology. This empirical research paper explores the concept of Education in India, the factors driving its adoption, and the challenges educators face in implementing it. Education represents a new era in education, one that is characterized by the use of digital technology, artificial intelligence, and immersive technologies (Miranda *et al.*, 2021). It has the potential to transform the learning experience and to prepare learners for the jobs of the future. Education can bring a range of benefits, including closing the skills gap, improving learning outcomes, and democratizing education (Joshi, 2021). However, it also presents several challenges, including the digital divide, the need for ethical and transparent use of AI, and the need to strike a balance between digital technologies and traditional forms of education (Miao *et al.*, 2021). To realize the potential of Education, it is important to address these challenges and to ensure that digital technologies are used in a way that benefits all learners. This requires a concerted effort by educators, policymakers, and technology developers to ensure that Education is inclusive, equitable, and effective. With the right approach, Education has the potential to revolutionize education and prepare learners for the challenges of the future (Rachmadtullah, 2020).

Literature Review

Education is an emerging concept that is gaining momentum worldwide. According to Jankowski (2019), Education is a paradigm shift that integrates technology, personalized learning, and critical thinking skills. The concept of Education is built on the foundation of the previous three industrial revolutions, which have transformed the way we live and work. Education is characterized by the use of digital technologies such as artificial intelligence, big data, and the Internet of Things (IoT) to enhance the learning experience. In Education, learning is personalized, interactive, and student-centred, with an emphasis on developing critical thinking skills and problem-solving abilities (Jankowski, 2019). The adoption of Education in India is driven by several factors. According to (Moid, 2020), the increasing use of digital technologies in education, the need to prepare students for the future workforce, and the demand for personalized learning are the key drivers of Education in India. The Indian government's initiatives such as Digital India, National Education Policy 2020, and Atmanirbhar Bharat have also played a significant role in promoting the adoption of Education in India (Pulicherla *et al.*,

2022). The National Education Policy 2020 emphasizes the need to leverage technology to enhance the quality of education and prepare students for the future workforce (Ahmad, 2020). Despite the potential benefits of Education, its implementation in India faces several challenges. According to (Abrol and Jain, 2020), the lack of infrastructure, inadequate teacher training, and the digital divide are the key challenges in implementing Education in India. The digital divide is a significant challenge, with many students lacking access to digital devices and the internet, especially in rural areas. The lack of infrastructure, such as power supply and high-speed internet connectivity, also hinders the adoption of Education in India.

Opportunities

Education refers to the integration of emerging technologies such as artificial intelligence, machine learning, virtual and augmented reality, and the Internet of Things into the educational system (Halili, 2019).

Here are some of the opportunities that Education can provide:

Personalized Learning: Education can provide personalized learning experiences for students by analyzing their performance data and adapting the curriculum to their learning styles and abilities.

Improved Access to Education: Education can provide access to education for students who are unable to attend traditional schools due to geographical or financial constraints.

E-learning platforms, virtual classrooms, and mobile applications can provide an opportunity for students to learn from anywhere in the world.

Collaborative Learning: Education can provide opportunities for collaborative learning, allowing students to work together in real time, share their knowledge, and build upon each other's ideas.

Enhanced Learning Experience: Education can provide an immersive and interactive learning experience through the use of virtual and augmented reality, gamification, and simulations. This can make learning more engaging, enjoyable, and effective.

Data-Driven Insights: Education can provide educators with data-driven insights into student performance, enabling them to identify areas of improvement and tailor their teaching methods accordingly.

Lifelong Learning: Education can provide opportunities for lifelong learning, enabling individuals to acquire new skills and knowledge throughout their lives. This can help them to adapt to changing job requirements and stay relevant in the job market.

Student-Centred Learning: Education provides personalized learning opportunities that cater to individual student needs and preferences, allowing students to learn at their own pace and style.

Digital Technologies: Education promotes the integration of digital technologies, such as artificial intelligence, virtual and augmented reality, and gamification, to enhance learning experiences and engagement.

Workforce Readiness: Education prepares students for the future workforce by equipping them with the skills and knowledge required to succeed in a technology-driven world.

Overall, Education has the potential to transform the way we learn and teach, making education more accessible, engaging, and effective.

Challenges

While Education offers many opportunities, it also presents several challenges that need to be addressed to ensure its successful implementation.

Here are some of the challenges of Education:

Inadequate Infrastructure: The success of Education in India depends on adequate infrastructure, such as high-speed internet connectivity, digital devices, and power supply (Dhanabalan and Sathish, 2018). However, many schools in India lack access to these resources, making it challenging to implement Education effectively.

Lack of Teacher Training: Educators need to be trained to integrate technology into teaching effectively. However, many educators in India lack the skills and knowledge required to use digital technologies effectively, making it challenging to implement Education (Hariharasudan and Kot, 2018).

Digital Divide: The digital divide refers to the gap between those who have access to digital technologies and those who do not. The digital divide in India is a significant challenge that needs to be addressed to ensure equitable access to education.

Cost: The cost of implementing Education can be a significant challenge for schools in India, particularly those in rural areas. Schools need to invest in infrastructure and digital devices, which can be costly, making it challenging for them to implement Education effectively.

Conclusion

The increasing adoption of digital technologies and the demand for personalized learning indicate a shift towards student-centred learning in India. However, the challenges of inadequate infrastructure, lack of teacher training, and the digital divide need to be addressed to ensure the success of Education in India. The government's initiatives such as Digital India and Atmanirbhar Bharat provide a favorable environment for the adoption of Education. However, more needs to be done to address the challenges faced by educators. The government could provide incentives for schools to invest in infrastructure and provide teacher training programmes to equip educators with the skills and knowledge required to integrate technology into teaching. This chapter explores the concept of Education in India, the factors driving its adoption, and the challenges faced by educators in implementing it. Overall, while Education presents several opportunities to transform education in India, it also poses significant challenges that need to be addressed to ensure its success. The government, educators, and stakeholders in the education sector need to work together to address these challenges and ensure that all students have access to quality education that prepares them for the future. The results indicate that Education is gaining momentum in India due to the increasing adoption of digital technologies, the need to prepare students for the future workforce, and the demand for personalized learning. However, the challenges of infrastructure, teacher training, and lack of access to technology need to be addressed to ensure the success of Education in India. The government could play a crucial role in addressing these challenges by providing incentives for schools to invest in infrastructure and providing teacher training programmes to equip educators with the skills and knowledge required to integrate technology into teaching. Education has the potential to transform education in India by promoting student-centred learning, personalized learning, and the integration of digital technologies in education. However, the success of Education in India depends on addressing the challenges faced by educators, such as inadequate infrastructure, lack of teacher training, and the digital divide. The government's initiatives such as Digital India and Atmanirbhar Bharat provide a favorable environment for the adoption of Education, but more needs to be done to address these challenges. This study recommends that the government should provide incentives for schools to invest in infrastructure, such as high-speed internet connectivity, digital devices, and power supply, to enable the effective implementation of Education. Furthermore, the government should provide teacher training programmes to equip educators with the skills and knowledge required to integrate technology into teaching. The findings of this study can guide policymakers, educators, and stakeholders in the education sector to make informed decisions and investments to ensure the success of Education in India. Further research is needed to explore the impact of Education on learning outcomes, student engagement, and teacher effectiveness in India. This will provide a better understanding of the potential benefits and challenges of Education and guide future investments and policies in the education sector.

References

Ahmad, T. (2020). A scenario-based approach to re-imagining the future of higher education prepares students for the future of work. *Higher Education, Skills and Work-Based Learning, 10*(1), 217-238.

Abrol, S., & Jain, M.K. (2022). Digital Transformation of Higher Education in India. In *Technology Training for Educators From Past to Present*, pp. 59-72. IGI Global.

Dhanabalan, T., & Sathish, A. (2018). Transforming Indian industries through artificial intelligence and robotics in industry 4.0. *International Journal of Mechanical Engineering and Technology, 9*(10), 835-845.

Halili, S.H. (2019). Technological advancements in Education 4.0. The Online *Journal of Distance Education and e-Learning, 7*(1), 63-69.

Hariharasudan, A., & Kot, S. (2018). A scoping review on Digital English and Education for Industry 4.0. *Social Sciences, 7*(11), 227.

Hong, C., & Ma, W.W. (2020). Introduction: Education: Applied degree education and the future of work. *Applied Degree Education and the Future of Work: Education*, 1-13.

Joshi, S. (2021). The rising importance of remote learning in India in the wake of COVID-19: issues, challenges and way forward. *World Journal of Science, Technology and Sustainable Development, 18*(1), 44-63.

Jankowski, E., Dreßler, C.A., & Tran Anh, D. (2019). Education in the context industry 4.0 at the Brandenburg University of Technology Cottbus-Senftenberg. ZarzadzaniePrzedsiebiorstwem, *22*(3).

Miao, F., Holmes, W., Huang, R., & Zhang, H. (2021). *AI and education: A guidance for policymakers*. UNESCO Publishing.

Moid, S. (2020). Education: Future of Learning with Disruptive Technologies. In *Promoting Inclusive Growth in the Fourth Industrial Revolution*, pp. 181-200. IGI Global.

Miranda, J., Navarrete, C., Noguez, J., Molina-Espinosa, J.M., Ramírez-Montoya, M.S., Navarro-Tuch, S.A., & Molina, A. (2021). The core components of Education in higher education: Three case studies in engineering education. *Computers & Electrical Engineering*, 93, 107278.

Pulicherla, K.K., Adapa, V., Ghosh, M., & Ingle, P. (2022). Current efforts on sustainable green growth in the manufacturing sector to complement "make in India" for making "self-reliant India". *Environmental Research*, 206, 112263.

Rachmadtullah, R., Yustitia, V., Setiawan, B., Fanny, A.M., Pramulia, P., Susiloningsih, W., & Ardhian, T. (2020). The challenge of elementary school teachers to encounter superior generation in the 4.0 industrial revolution: Study literature. *International Journal of Scientific & Technology Research, 9*(4), 1879-1882.

2
Awareness about Education among Educators

Ozma

Introduction

Education is the main element in shaping the attitudes and behaviour of humans along with enhancing knowledge, and skills while encouraging creativity and innovation. It is rapidly changing with the present dynamic world. Its journey from 1.0 to 4.0 was not simple. In education 1.0, where educators spoke and students listen as they were passive listeners. There was no collaboration of technology with classrooms. Education was in form of textbooks, notes, handouts, etc. It was a start for Education 2.0 when both students and teachers started to use technology in basic way. Technology was used in a most basic way such as Wikipedia, blogs, personal websites, and podcasts enabling learners to directly approach the content available. As this technology advanced Education 3.0 came into existence. There was an increment in the available chances to learn virtually. There were platforms to which you can connect easily with the faculty and other students as well. It was no longer delimited to learner and tutor but rather involved a broad framework where anyone anywhere could learn from anyone who is an expert in the field (learning virtually). With a more network approach, students could directly connect to new information resources. Learning was encouraged because of flexibility from every corner of the world in any field. Even the educators were transformed into a supporter, resource guides, coaches, and advisors providing our learners with tools, techniques, methods, and directions to create, reframe, and apply their own ideas in the digital world and beyond it.

We are now heading towards a new chapter of this phase, which is called Education which aligns itself with industrial revolution 4.0. Smart technologies, augmented reality, artificial intelligence, robotics, icloud, gamification, evaluation by teacher and self-evaluation by student, big data, and digital platforms usage are to name a few in Education. We need to embrace and adapt with our learners to enable them to develop the skills that they would need in the future in order to effectively and appropriately use these technologies for their benefit.

The industry is in synchronization with education as we have seen that the revolution of the industry from 1.0 to 4.0 has paralleled with Education from 1.0 to 4.0 (Pangandaman, H.K., *et al.* 2019). India is putting all its efforts into aligning the education system with global trends. Here we really need to take a pause and think carefully if we are really prepared to take this upcoming challenge. How much are our students and teachers aware of and prepared for? It is to submerge ourselves into new upcoming technologies to enhance the learning process. As educators, we need to be aware of the digital transformations taking place to encourage learning. It has proved to be a process of optimizing and transforming institutional operations, strategic directions, and value prepositions. Our educational organizations and their stakeholders are putting their best efforts in this direction. Education is destined to make shifts in institutional culture and workforce due to its flexibility and ease of availability.

Literature Review

Aldo Vladimir Sabando Barreiro (2022), the effect of technical transformations on education. The pace of change is remarkable with the introduction and application of these technologies creating a paradigm shift in education. As educators, we need to prepare teaching strategies that can unlock the skills of our students. It is a big concern to prepare students who are ready for revolutionary industry 4.0 (Tandon, R., & Tandon, S., 2020). Therefore, it is of utmost importance that our educators must be not only aware and well-equipped with the emerging technologies but also know the application and effect of using them. Zabidin, N.S., *et al.* (2021) stressed on change of educational pedagogy. Nor Azizah, J. *et al.* (2019) and Avelino, N.M., & Ismail, H.H. (2022) found that the integration of 4IR elements into teaching practices is affected by level of respondent's knowledge. Srivani, V., Hariharasudan, A., Nawaz, N., Ratajczak, S. (2022) in their research proved that English language efficiency of engineering students was improved by usage of Education.

A complete understanding is required for Education ten technological pillars: integration systems, internet of things, artificial, robotics, cloud, big data, simulation of the virtual environment, cyber security, augmented reality, and additive manufacturing (Martinic, S., & Villalta, M., 2015).

Research Objectives

Following are the objectives of present study:

1. To determine the demographic variables of the educators in different universities of Delhi and NCR.
2. To explore the level of teachers' awareness, knowledge, and beliefs in dealing with Education.

Research Methodology

This study is based on using a descriptive survey method for collecting data by stratified random sampling survey. Educators from different departments of colleges and universities from Delhi NCR were taken as the sample of study.

Population and study sample

The present study was conducted on educators from different departments of colleges and universities from Delhi NCR. The sample for the study consisted of 400 educators from five different Universities in Delhi and NCR through a stratified random sampling technique. These educators belong to different types of Universities such as Government and private. There were 50% (n=200) educators from the government and 50% (n=200) educators from private universities.

Research tools

A self-designed questionnaire which was validated and reliability was calculated before collection of data was used. It consists of two sections A and B. Section A includes demographic details such as age, gender, no. of years of teaching experience. Section B was divided into 3 parts in which Part I included questions identifying the awareness level of educators about Education, Part II included questions to explore the level of knowledge of educators, and Part III included questions to explore educators' beliefs in the usefulness of Education.

Results

Objective 1: *To determine the demographic variables of the educators in different universities of Delhi and NCR.*

Age of educators

There were educators who belonged to the following age groups: 21-30 years 96 (24%), 31-40 years 146 (37%) 41-50 years 101 (25%), and 51 and above 57 (14%) females in the sample. In the current study, the age group 31-40 years has comparatively higher number of individuals.

Table 2.1: Age distribution of educators

S. No.	Age Group	Frequency	Percentage	Cumulative frequency
1	21 - 30 Years	96	24%	14
2	31 - 40 Years	146	37%	47
3	41 - 50 Years	101	25%	76
4	50 and above	57	14%	100

Gender of educators

There were 177(44%) males and 223 (56%) females in the sample. In the current study, the female number is comparatively higher.

Table 2.2: Gender distribution of educators

S. No.	Gender	Frequency	Percentage	Cumulative frequency
1	Male	177	44%	44
2	Female	223	56%	100
3	Other	0	0%	100

Teaching Experience of educators

There were educators who had teaching experience as follows: 1 - 5 years 63 (16%), 6 -10 years 198 (50%), 11-15 years 169 (42%), and 16 and above 83 (21%) in the sample.

Table 3: Teaching experience of educators

S. No.	Teaching Experience (years)	Frequency	Percentage	Cumulative frequency
1	1 - 5 years	49	12%	14
2	6 - 10 years	168	42%	47
3	11 - 15 years	129	32%	76
4	16 and above	54	14%	100

Objective 2: ***To explore the level of teachers' awareness, knowledge, and beliefs in dealing with Education.***

Educators' level of awareness about Education

There were five categories in which educators' level of awareness about Education was divided, namely (a) not at all, (b) a little, (c) some, (d) a lot, and (e) completely. Most of the educators which are 49% have little awareness of Education while only 2% know everything about Education

Table 2.4: Educators' level of awareness about Education

S. No.	Level of Awareness	Frequency	Percentage	Cumulative frequency
1	Not at all	58	15%	15
2	A little	196	49%	64
3	Something	121	30%	94
4	A lot	17	4%	98
5	Everything	8	2%	100

Educators' level of knowledge in dealing with Education

There were five categories in which educators' level of knowledge regarding the Education was divided, namely (a) not at all, (b) a little, (c) some, (d) a lot, and (e) completely. Most of the educators which are 40% have little knowledge of Education while only 3% know everything about Education

Table 2.5: Educators' level of knowledge of Education

S. No.	Level of Knowledge	Frequency	Percentage	Cumulative frequency
1	Not at all	92	23%	23
2	A little	161	40%	63
3	Something	113	28%	91
4	A lot	23	6%	97
5	Everything	11	3%	100

Educators' beliefs in the usefulness of Education

There were five categories in which Educators' beliefs in the usefulness of Education, was divided, namely (i) Strongly Agree, (ii) Agree, (iii) Neutral, (iv) Disagree, and (v) Strongly Disagree

Table 2.6: Educators' beliefs of Education

S. No.	Beliefs in the usefulness of Education	Frequency	Percentage	Cumulative frequency
1	Strongly Agree	181	45%	45
2	Agree	128	32%	77
3	Neutral	72	18%	95
4	Disagree	19	5%	100
5	Strongly Disagree	0	0%	100

Impact of Education on our Education System

Sharma, P. (2019) suggests that the Education is very helpful for teachers and educators as it helps to meet the specific need of the student. It permits educators to modernize their teaching and learning methods and also improves their skills. Identification of the strengths and weaknesses of students will be easy. Education facilitates learning beyond boundaries where each and every individual learner is equally important and appreciated. It benefits students by initiating and enhancing problem-solving skills, critical analysis, scientific attitude, observation, collaborative skills, time management skills, etc. Education aims to build a self-capable and self-reliable independent individual who can overcome future challenges. Moreover, Himmetoglu, B., Aydug, D. & Bayrak, C. (2020) highlighted that having technical and guidance skills along with lifelong learning skills and some personal characteristics are expected from educators.

Challenges encountered and efforts taken by educators to implement Education

A survey was conducted through an open-ended questionnaire in order to collect the views of educators working in educational institutes. A new approach is required by human resource in order to compete successfully in this technical age. Most educators are well aware of the shift in the whole education system that is currently taking place. Although they do not hold a high level of understanding of the different pillars of Education, their enthusiasm and willingness to put extra effort into getting familiar with these are appreciable. There are almost 80% of educators, who are very comfortable in teaching through digital mode, while around 50% of these are very good with different digital platforms of the teaching-learning process, and the other 20% understand and try to do the same looking at the need of the hour. As self-directed learning, and virtual learning Education are benefits provided by Education along with fast and easy access to information, it can be defined as Systematic Computer Assisted Learning and Environment.

The challenges that educators encounter in the implementation of Education are:

(a) self-knowledge and understanding of Education
(b) level of Technical knowledge
(c) Connectivity with distant students
(d) Comfort level in using different applications of computers such as google meet, google classroom, google sheets, etc.
(e) Interacting with passive students
(f) Evaluation of learning
g) Time challenge
(h) 100% engagement of students.

Although different challenges persist, educators do not sit and hold back. Zulkipli, N.H. & Musa, M. (2022) conducted a study and the results revealed that irrespective of the age, gender, or grade level they taught teachers have a positive attitude towards the use of technology. Pardiñan, E.G. & Loremia, R.A. (2020) mentioned that the competencies of the students are developed by computer-assisted learning environment.

The efforts made by these educators in enhancing the education system with reference to Education are remarkable. Some of them include:

(a) taking regular Faculty Development Programmes, and online courses
(b) there is a need to restructure course content using pedagogical approaches
(c) a need to modify the pedagogy of the subject
(d) building digital skills
(e) upgrading classrooms with technology.

Discussion and Conclusion

It is evident from the current study that there is a need to make our educators not only aware but also an expert on Education such that they are able to prepare our future generations that hold practical applicability of the skills involved. There is a need for them to get familiarised with the new applications running in our system and to know how to best apply them. In order to prepare our young generation to face the challenges of upcoming digital world we need to integrate Education in our classroom teaching learning practices. For this to occur, there is a need to have (a) easy access to and availability of learning materials for students at any place and at any time, (b) availability of a comfort zone to achieve information, (c) focus on the model and project-based learning, (d) encourage students' participation and entitlement to responsibilities, and (e) process of evaluation to be enhanced and skill-based.

References

Aldo Vladimir Sabando Barreiro (2022). *Education 4.0 and its impact on the educational system during the pandemic and post-pandemic Covid 19 in Ecuador*. Universidad de Oriente, México, ISSN-e: 2661-6661, Vol. 7, No. 1. http://portal.amelica.org/ameli/jatsRepo/382/3822817007/index.html

Avelino, N.M., & Ismail, H.H. (2022). Teachers' Levels of Knowledge and Readiness in Integrating 4IR Technologies: The Primary ESL Classroom Context. *International Journal of Learning, Teaching and Educational Research,* Vol. 21, No. 3, pp. 415-433, March 2022 https://doi.org/10.26803/ijlter.21.3.22

Alakrash, H.M., & Razak. N.A., (2020). Towards the Education 4.0,

Readiness Level of EFL Students in Utilising Technology-Enhanced Classroom. *International Journal of Innovation, Creativity and Change.* Volume 13, Issue 10. www.ijicc.net

Himmetoglu, B., Aydug, D. & Bayrak, C. (2020). Education: Defining the Teacher, the Student, and the School Manager Aspects of the Revolution. Turkish Online *Journal of Distance Education-TOJDE* ISSN 1302-6488 IODL-Special Issue Article 2

Martinic, S., & Villalta, M. (2015). Classroom time management and school performance in full-day schools in Chile. *Perfiles Educativos*, 37(147), 28-49. https://doi.org/10.1016/j.pe.2013.03.001

Mudgil, S. (2021). Challenges and Implementation of Education in the Education Sector, *International Research Journal of Modernization in Engineering Technology and Science.* Volume 3, Issue 10, October-2021 Impact Factor- 6.752

Nor Azizah, J., Tuan Mastura, T.S., Diyana, S.N.M., & Zanaton, H.I. (2019). Science Teacher's Knowledge, Understanding and Readiness in Dealing with the Education Transformation of the 4th Industrial Revolution. *Science Teacher*, 7, 102-119. https://www.ijicc.net/images/vol7iss11/71107_Junid_2019_E_R.pdf

Pardiñan, E.G. & Loremia, R.A. (2020). Digital Pedagogy Analysis On Technology Trend Relevant To Education. *International Journal of Scientific & Technology Research*, Volume 9, Issue 8, August 2020.

Panagiotopolos, G.A., & Karanikola, Z.A. (2020). Education 4.0 and Teachers: Challenges, Risks and Benefits. *European Scientific Journal, ESJ*, *16*(34), 114. https://doi.org/10.19044/esj.2020.v16n34p114

Pangandaman, H.K., *et al.* (2019). Philippine Higher Education Vis-s-Vis Education: A Scoping Review. *International Journal of Advanced Research and Publications*, *3* (3), 65-69.

Sharma, P. (2019). Digital Revolution of Education. *International Journal of Engineering and Advanced Technology (IJEAT)* ISSN: 2249-8958 (Online), Volume 9, Issue 2.

Srivani, V., Hariharasudan, A., Nawaz, N., Ratajczak, S. (2022). Impact of Education 4.0 among engineering students for learning English language. *PLOS ONE 17*(2): e0261717. https://doi.org/ 10.1371/journal.pone.0261717

Singh, D. & Tilak, G. (2020). Implementation of Education Model 4.0: Developing Industry 4.0 Skills in Graduates Engineers for Improving Employability Skills. *Humanities & Social Sciences Reviews*, Vol. 8 No. 2.

Tandon, R., & Tandon, S. (2020). Education 4.0: A New Paradigm in Transforming the Future of Education in India. *IJISET - International*

Journal of Innovative Science, Engineering & Technology, Vol. 7, Issue 2, February 2020 ISSN (Online) 2348-7968 | Impact Factor (2019) – 6.248 www.ijiset.com

Zabidin, N.S., *et al.* (2021). Awareness and Barriers of Industry 4.0 and Education 4.0 between Construction Players and Academicians in Malaysia. *Journal of Technology Management and Business*. Vol. 8, No. 2 (2021) 26-37 http://penerbit.uthm.edu.my/ojs/index.php/jtmb

Zulkipli, N., H. & Musa, M. (2022). Education 4.0: An Analysis of Teachers' Attitude towards the Use of Technology in Teaching Mathematics. *International Journal of Information and Education Technology*, Vol. 12, No. 7, July 2022.

3
Socio-Emotional Competence among Teachers

Manju, P. K. and *Mini Kumari, D.*

Introduction

Education has always been a difficult endeavour that occasionally goes through changes as a result of growing social responsibility. The aim of education in general is to develop people who are generally good in physical, mental, and moral health and who are aware of their obligations and rights. Quality education envisions a society with well-adjusted individuals persistently hungry to better their performance for the upliftment of the quality of life everywhere. The requirements of a teachers' profession in the 21st century go beyond the demonstration of technical and professional skills to include social and emotional skills due to the unprecedented events happening all around the world. Socio-emotional skills of a teacher are vital for managing a range of classroom scenarios, including handling difficult situations, solving learning challenges, fostering inclusion and many more (Carmen *et al.*, 2022). The COVID-19 pandemic has exacerbated the situation demanding educators to imbibe socio-emotional competence in their own teaching practices. This can only be attained by teachers' understanding of SEL practices and improving their own socio-emotional competence. Socio-emotional competence of teachers can assist them in mastering the social and emotional challenges inherent in their profession and to build positive teacher-student relationships. It's critical for educators to realise that they can strongly influence their students' learning and behaviour. Schonert-Reichl (2017) suggests that classrooms with pleasant teacher-student interactions promote in-depth learning and the healthy development of students' social and emotional skills. Since teachers are the ones who can make social and emotional learning (SEL) practises and programmes happen in classrooms, their own social-emotional well-being and competence have a significant impact on their students. However, when teachers struggle to balance the social and emotional demands of the classroom, both the academic performance and behaviour of the students suffer. Students exhibit lower performance and less focused behaviour when teachers fail to effectively manage the social and emotional demands of teaching. It is obvious that teachers' effectiveness in the classroom determines the development of students' socio-emotional competence. Widespread research evidence currently supports that socio-emotional competencies can be taught and assessed, the fact that they encourage growth and decrease problematic behaviours thereby achieving sustainable development goals in education.

Literature Review

Socio-emotional Learning

According to SEL Framework adopted by the Ministry of Education in Singapore, the five Socio-emotional competencies are self-awareness, social awareness, self-management, relationship management and responsible decision making (Liem *et al.*, 2017). "Social and emotional learning" (SEL) is the term used to describe the process by which children and adults develop these competencies (NEP, 2020). School-based socio-emotional learning (SEL) can increase students' emotional and cognitive resilience and foster positive social interaction (NEP, 2020). By enhancing socio-emotional competencies in children, they will be able to easily acquire the skills, knowledge and dispositions that help them to face future challenges. Higher level of socio-emotional competence was seen associated with stronger self-control, responsible decision-making and good relationship skills in students (Durlak & Wells, 1998). Prosocial conduct encourages human flourishing, which is crucial for achieving the sustainable development goals.

Socio-emotional Competence in Teachers

For teachers to effectively prepare their students for the 21st century, they must have the proper mindset (Ee & Cheng, 2013). Teachers' classroom management techniques, their interactions with students, and their capacity to execute social emotional learning curricula all heavily depend on their social emotional competence (Schonert-Reichl *et al.*, 2017). Teachers who have excellent social emotional skills are more self-aware, demonstrate prosocial attitudes, and set up their classrooms to offer strong emotional and educational support and foster a positive learning environment (Schonert-Reichl *et al.*, 2017). Teachers' social-emotional well-being is an essential element of a prosocial classroom, successful student outcomes, and teacher well-being (Tom, 2012). In order to achieve sustainable social development, teachers who have received training in socio-emotional competencies have a significant role to play in promoting these skills among students (Elias *et al.*, 2017).

Objectives of the Study

1. To find out the level of socio-emotional competence of teachers.
2. To study the significant difference in the socio-emotional competence of teachers with respect to the background variables, gender, age, type of school/institution and category of teaching.

Methodology

Participants

The participants were 142 teachers, 27 persons (19.01%) male and 115 persons (80.98%) female, randomly chosen from different schools of Thrissur, Malappuram and Palakkad districts. They were categorised based on age, type of schools and category of teaching. There were 38 teachers (26.76%) aged below 30; 76 teachers (53.52%) aged between 30 to 40 and 28 teachers (19.71%) aged above 40. 25 teachers (17.60%) were from government service, 22 teachers (15.5%) from aided schools and 95 teachers (66.90%) from private schools. There were 35 (24.64%) primary school teachers,14(9.86%) middle school teachers, 26 (18.30%) high school teachers, 38 teachers (26.76%) from higher secondary, 14 (9.85%) from degree/PG department and 15 teachers (10.56%) engaged in professional training.

Design

Present study's design is quantitative in nature and includes both descriptive and inferential elements. A sample of teachers from three districts of Kerala participated in the survey. An online survey using an adapted questionnaire was utilized to better understand the teachers' socio-emotional competence and to collect demographic information including gender, age, type of schools/institutions and category of teaching. The participants were requested to complete the questionnaire honestly and their identities were kept secured. JAMOVI software was used for data analysis.

Tools Used

The instrument used to measure socio-emotional competence was an adapted version of Forcina Survey Instrument developed by Forcina, Leslie Carole (2012). This tool is valid and reliable and describes the theory of socio-emotional competency which is divided into the following four dimensions: Self-awareness, Self-regulation, Social-awareness, Relationship skills and Decision making skills. It comprises of 24 items, each of which is scored on a 5-point Likert scale that went from strongly disagree (1) to strongly agree (5). To avoid participants responding in generalised ways based on the survey language, reverse-scored items were also used. By using Jamovi software version 2.3.18, an analysis of item reliability was determined through the reliability coefficient test. The acceptable value of Cronbach Alpha was 0.717 which shows acceptable consistency of reliability.

Analysis

The data provided by 142 participants in this study were analysed using the Jamovi software; the Shapiro-Wilk test was used to determine whether or not the data had a normal distribution; parametric tests were then run since the data had been found to have a normal distribution; assumption of homogeneity of data is also met by the Levene's test of homogeneity of variance. Independent samples t-test and one-way analysis of variance (ANOVA) with Tukey post-hoc tests (variances for all variables were homogeneous) were utilized to find the significant difference in the mean scores of socio-emotional competence of teachers with respect to the background variables, gender, age, type of school and category of teaching. The results of the analysis were evaluated at the "0.05" level of significance.

Results and Discussion

Table 3.1: Descriptive Statistics of the scores of Socio-Emotional Competence of Teachers

Variable	N	M	M_d	M_o	SD	Shapiro-Wilk W	Shapiro-Wilk p
Socio-emotional competence	142	87	86.9	85	6.48	0.986	0.153

As can be seen in Table 3.1, the three measures of central tendency viz., mean, median, and mode of the scores of socio-emotional competence of teachers are almost equal. The p value of the Shapiro-Wilk Test is 0.153 ($p > 0.05$) and hence the distribution of scores of socio-emotional competence of teachers follow approximately a normal distribution.

Table 3.2: Percentage-wise distribution of sample according to different levels of Socio-Emotional Competence

Variable	Group	Score	n	%
Socio-emotional competence	High	≥ 93.48	23	16.20
	Average	93.48-80.52	102	71.83
	Low	≤ 80.52	17	11.97

The different levels of socio-emotional competence of teachers were determined by classifying the whole sample into three groups–high, average and low in the conventional procedure of finding σ distance from mean μ. The standard deviation (σ) and mean (μ) of the scores are found to be 6.48 and 87 respectively. From the Table 3.2, it is evident that 16.20 per cent of the total sample has high socio-emotional competence, 71.83 per cent has average socio-emotional competence and 11.97 per cent has low socio-emotional competence.

Table 3.3. Test of Significance of Difference in the Mean Scores of Socio-Emotional Competence of Female and Male Teachers

Variable	Gender	N	M	SD	t	P
Socio-emotional competence	Male	27	87.1	5.69	0.144	0.886
	Female	115	86.9	6.68		

The results shown in Table 3.3 reveals that the obtained t-value (t=0.144) is not significant (p>.05). This indicates that there exists no significant difference between male (M=87.1, SD=5.69) and female (M=86.9, SD=6.68) respondents in terms of socio-emotional competence.

From Table 3.4, it is seen that the obtained F-value (F=0.552) is not significant (p >.05). Hence, there exists no significant difference in the mean scores of socio-emotional competence of teachers aged below 30, between 30 and 40 and above 40 years. So it can be concluded that age has no influence on socio-emotional competence of teachers.

Table 3.4: Test of Significance of Difference in the Mean Scores of Socio-Emotional Competence of Teachers Based on Age Groups

Age groups	Test of homogeneity of variance		ANOVA			
	Mean	Std. Deviation	Levene Statistic	Sig.	F	Sig.
Below 30	86.3	7.15	1.64	0.199	0.552	0.557
30-40	87	6.58				
Above 40	88	5.22				

Table 3.5: Test of Significance of Difference in the Mean Scores of Socio-Emotional Competence of Teachers Based on Type of Schools

Type of school	Test of homogeneity of variance			ANOVA		
	Mean	Std. Deviation	Levene Statistic	Sig.	F	Sig.
Government	87.2	6.12	0.132	0.876	0.580	0.564
Aided	88.2	5.82				
Private	86.7	6.74				

From Table 3.5, it is seen that the obtained F-value (F=0.580) is not significant (p >.05). Hence, there exists no significant difference in the mean scores of socio-emotional competence of teachers working in government, aided and private schools. So it can be concluded that type of school has no influence on socio-emotional competence of teachers.

Table 3.6: Test of Significance of Difference in the Mean Scores of Socio-Emotional Competence of Teachers Based on Category of Teaching

Category	Test of homogeneity of variance		ANOVA			
	Mean	Std. Deviation	Levene Statistic	Sig.	F	Sig.
Primary	85.8	6.97	0.132	0.876	0.580	0.564
Middle school	85.6	5.84				
High school	89.6	6.00				

(*Contd.*)

Category	Test of homogeneity of variance		ANOVA			
	Mean	Std. Deviation	Levene Statistic	Sig.	F	Sig.
Higher secondary	88.0	6.78				
Degree/PG	83.1	5.43				
Professional courses	87.7	4.81				

From Table 3.6, it is seen that the obtained F-value (F=2.62) is significant at 0.05 level. Hence, there exists significant difference in the mean scores of socio-emotional competence of teachers based on the category of teaching.

Table 3.7. Group Differences in the Mean Scores of Socio-Emotional Competence of Teachers Based on the Category of Teaching

Category of Teaching	Group Differences	
	Mean Difference	Sig
High school-Degree/PG	6.54*	P<05

In order to check for individual differences between groups, Tukey Post-Hoc Test was conducted. The results given in the Table 3.7 indicates that the mean scores of high school teachers (M=89.6, SD=6.00) is significantly different from degree/PG teachers (M=83.1, SD=5.43) at 0.05 level. However, no significant differences were detected between and among other groups.

Major Findings

1. Majority of teachers have average level of socio-emotional competence. There exists no significant difference between male and female teachers in their socio-emotional competence.
2. There exists no significant difference in the mean scores of socio-emotional competence of teachers with respect to age and type of school.

3. There exists significant difference between high school teachers and degree/PG level teachers in their socio-emotional competence.

Conclusion

The study revealed that majority of teachers has an average level of socio-emotional competence. It was also found that gender, age and type of school have no influence on socio-emotional competence of teachers. But the study identifies significant difference in socio-emotional competence of teachers teaching in high schools and in degree/PG levels. Since a majority of research findings consistently report a lack of social and emotional intelligence in offenders and criminals, growing demand for the enhancement of socio-emotional competence among youth is highly crucial. This can only be made possible through teachers building their own socio-emotional competence. Building emotional and intellectual intelligence in students through social and emotional learning is an urgent need of the hour. It can play a pivotal role in the development of peaceful and sustainable societies. Teachers can intentionally enhance the socio-emotional competence of their students by providing good model behaviours. And hence strategies for developing socio-emotional competence of teachers need serious consideration.

References

Carmen, R.G., Olga, B.G., & Beatriz, M. (2022). Socio-Emotional Competence and Self Efficacy of Future Secondary School Teachers. *Education Sciences, 12*(3), 161. MDPI AG. Retrieved from http://dx.doi.org/10.3390/educsci12030161

Durlak, J.A., Wells, A.M. (1998). Evaluation of indicated preventive intervention (secondary prevention) mental health programmes for children and adolescents. *American Journal of Community Psychology, 26*(5), 775-802. https://doi.org/10.1023/A:1022162015815

Ee, J. & C., Quek. (2013). Teachers' Perceptions of Students' Social Emotional Learning and their Infusion of SEL. *Journal of Teaching and Teacher Education: An International Journal, 1*, 59-72. 10.12785/jtte/010201.

Elias, M., Zins, J.E., Weissberg, R.P., Frey, K.S., Greenberg, M.T., Haynes, N. M., & Shriver, T.P. (2017). *Promoting Social and Emotional Guidelines for Educators*. Alexandria, Virginia: Association for Supervison and Curriculum Development. Retrieved from http://www.casel.org/what-is-sel/

Forcina, Leslie Carole, "Social Emotional Competence and Teacher Stress" (2012). *Electronic Theses and Dissertations*. 798.https://digitalcommons.georgiasouthern.edu/etd/79

Liem, Gregory Arief & Chua, Bee & Seng, Yvonne & Kamarolzaman, Khairyani & Cai, Elaine. (2017). *Social and Emotional Learning in Singapore's Schools: Framework, Practice, Research, and Future Directions*. 10.1007/978-981-10- 3394-0_10.

National Education Policy. (2020). https://www.mhrd.gov.in/sites/uploadfiles/mhrd/files/nep/ NEP Final English.pdf

Schonert-Reichl, K.A. (2017). Social and Emotional Learning and Teachers. *The Future of Children, 27*(1), 137-155. http://www.jstor.org/stable/44219025

Schonert-Reichl, Kimberly & Kitil, M. & Hanson-Peterson, Jennifer. (2017). *To Reach the Students, Teach the Teachers: A National Scan of Teacher Preparation and Social & Emotional Learning*. Retrieved from http://www.researchgate.net

Tom, K.M. (2012). Measurement of teachers' social-emotional competence: Development of the social-emotional competence teacher rating scale. In *BMC Public Health*, Vol. 5, Issue 1. Retrieved from http://www.researchgate.net

4

Education and IR 4.0

Transforming Teachers for IR 4.0 Challenges

Saleha Zaini

Introduction

With the quick and simple access to information provided by the tools at their disposal, instructors face a variety of challenges and difficulties. IR 4.0 is an era of advanced markets, industry, and technology with linkages between the revolutions, and eras in which they occurred, serve as their foundation. The "Machine Age", "Electricity Age", "Electronics Age", and "Internet Age" are the names given to the first four Industrial Revolutions (Peters, 2017, p.34). Implementation is challenging due to the rapid pace of information availability and changes in technology, systems, and legislation. The emergence of new industrial technology, or IR 4.0, is a change that makes it possible to collect and analyse data from multiple machines, enabling quicker, more adaptable, and more efficient production processes that result in higher-quality products at lower costs. The revolution will boost productivity, alter economics, promote industrial development, and alter workforce demographics, altering the competitiveness of businesses. The growth of cyber-physical systems known as "industry 4.0". In order to compete and build an industry basis for IR 4.0, which leads to 5.0 IR, these changes in education must follow a hierarchy of operational and administrative processes that demand intelligent decision-making in liaison.

Let there not be an instance where "learners of the industrial age 4.0, learning in industrial space 3.0, and taught by industry teachers of 2.0, or even 1.0" emerge, according to Nababan *et al.* (2020, p. 220)

Literature Review

In view of the existing education challenges, newer methods of utilising human labour and abilities have emerged as a result of the industry's remarkable evolution and the influence of technology. Industries have been affected by IR 4.0 in many ways (Ellahia, Khaub & Saha, 2019, Karag, Karagözolu, 2017). Rapid change is necessary to keep up with the market, but smart decision-making and the process of evaluating how that change will function are rarely given much thought. Change is required to keep up with the pace and demands of the market, and its impact is visible in the imbalance, inconsistency, and instability that are evident at every level. It has become ever challenging for teachers to understand their expectations and prove relevant in the 4.0 educational era. With technology advancements and its influence on education with apps like chatGPT, the teacher has to outperform and have hands on experiences with the pros and cons of such functions. The 'millennial generation' (Nababan, *et al.*, 2020) that the teachers are exposed to, have an unstable and eccentric worldview because of the disturbing temperament that the reels, YouTube, and other social media platforms have cultivated. It is a pendulum swinging from soft skills to cyber-physical skills.

Understanding Cyber-Physical Systems

The application of digital technology in the learning process defines the 4.0 IR. Making virtual platforms available to continually learn without regard to space or time constraints. The standard of instruction in learning environments should correspond to the performance and abilities required for the fourth industrial revolution. The establishment of objectives that integrate human-centric, digital economy with advanced automation can be a crucial function for teacher training institutions (Oztemel & Gursev, 2018). Increased automation, better communication and self-monitoring, and the deployment of intelligent machines that can analyse and diagnose problems without human involvement are all outcomes of integration. It is an era of embedded connectedness, one in which technology is widely and ubiquitously used in society (such as the metaverse); changing how people see and understand their surroundings. In contrast to only using their natural senses and industrial prowess, it asserts that we have built and are entering an enhanced social reality.

The Internet of Things (IoT) is largely what drives and underpins the elusive IR 4.0. It establishes a connection between actuators and sensors that are built into physical objects. These are then connected via networks so they can communicate (Kipper, 2013). Devices, sensors, actuators, smartphones, and smart appliances can all be connected through the internet (Talari *et al.*, 2017). Technologies associated with IoT and cyber-physical systems include virtual reality, augmented reality, artificial intelligence, cloud computing, 3D printing (Bloem *et al.*, 2014, p. 11; Peters, 2017, p. 36) others including but not limited to robotics, nanotechnology, quantum computing, genetic innovations, etc. Keeping the disparities in skills, and not being skilled enough for the emerging industry, this emergence of being with the times is increased rates of unemployment and underemployment as a result of skill innovation trends fall out of proportion. It is still uncertain whether the skills needed and those that are already accessible would be industrious in the future or not.

Preparing young people for the IR 4.0, the education sector is vital in adapting to the needs, future prospects and working demands that are essential to build educational goals. Because of technology's utility, responsiveness, intelligence, and connectedness, automation is adopted by all occupations (Oztemel & Gursev,

2018). Human-centred task demand teamwork and other 21st Century Skills. The workforce preparation programme must be flexible to accommodate different skill sets. Reflecting this, teaching and learning requirements of young people as well as the educational institutions, designed to prepare them, are always impacted by the realities of future job (Van Laar *et al.*, 2017).

It is uncertain how IR 4.0 will affect education in general, how teaching and learning processes are built in particular, and how new technologies will define skill demands and eventually influence how educational systems construct curriculum (Ellahia *et al.*, 2019). It is expected that teachers and students must be conversant with technological difficulties that are correlated with 21st-century competencies (Binkley, *et al.*, 2012, p. 18). A teacher is required to investigate the abundance of information, make effective decisions from the wide variety of options, and apply the knowledge to a person's life both professionally and personally (Van Laar *et al.*, 2017). The procedures, even so, show the degree of complexity that workers will need to maintain their relevance and competitiveness (Lamb & Doecke, 2017, National Skills Commission, Australia, 2020).

The Job Market

The fastest growing occupations for the future based on future jobs, are computer engineers, computer specialists, database administrators, data processing and equipment repairs, dental hygienists, desktop publishing specialists, medical assistants, paralegals, personal care and health aides, residential counsellors, securities and financial sales workers, system analysts to name a few. For the development of skills, the teachers that are responsible for the teaching and learning process, need to upskill themselves in multiple faculties for upgradation into the 4.0 IR.

Education and skills for IR 4.0

With the advent of IR 4.0 changes, utilising technology to engage teachers has become essential for all global educational systems

(National Council for Accreditation of Teacher Education, 2011; Pedersen, 2003; AITSL, 2014; Council for the Accreditation of Education Preparation, 2014; Kelentric *et al.*, 2017). A teacher's function in imparting information, knowledge, and wisdom used to be crucial, as opposed to the teacher's current modified role as a facilitator and motivator, who can, 'secure them in a virtual environment and guide them' (Himmetolgu *et al.*, p. 20). The IR 4.0 education is geared at a generation that is far ahead of its teachers' ability and even questions their subject matter expertise. Here, the teacher is intended to lay the foundation for the student's learning preferences and speed. Naban *et al.*, 2020 refers to this generation as the 'millennial generation'. Digital technology integration with education, seamless learning environments, individualised education, exploratory education, and lifelong learning are all part of the basic skills need for teachers.

The evolving nature of work has grown more collaborative, nonroutine, and cognitive. Therefore, both Teacher Training Institutes (TTI) and Teacher Educators (TEs) must commit time to address the effects of pedagogy centred on cooperation, dialogue, efficient formative assessment, and feedback. Action research conducted studies available (Arfandi, 2019) on ICT skills of teachers and TPD reflect that although teachers can effectively use offline technology in the classroom, there is always room for improvement in the creation of mind maps, instructional videos, and visual arts. The teachers had used online learning technology into lessons. Otherwise, they must develop the skills needed for the learning process that supports the industrial era, which include using databases, online learning, online video, online data storage, and online data sharing 4.0.

According to research by Oner's (2020), virtual environments (VEs) can be created to foster teaching ability and critical thinking. This idea aids students by using virtual "rooms" that focus on human-centric activities including conversation, feedback, and social constructivist methods.

Education and Administration for IR 4.0

The support of the administrative bodies goes in hand with the teaching and learning process. Ministry of Education, boards and administrating bodies are responsible for change in the education system. Ministry of Education (MoE), National Council of Education Research and Training (NCERT), State and Union Territory Administration, Governing Boards and affiliations, Teacher Education Departments and Training Centres—the primary competencies of school managers in the Education paradigm can be categorised under the following categories: guidance skills, technological skills, learning skills, and technical abilities. In the study conducted by Hariharasudan & Kot (2018, p. 6), it was underlined that Education school managers should possess learning abilities including creative thinking, possess technological abilities of Education because it is defined as a technology-based learning and teaching system This makes it possible to claim that the outcome that Education administrators should use technology wisely and keep up with new advances. One of the leadership philosophies that is stressed in the 21st century is technological leadership, which is described as the person's responsibility for enhancing the interface between people and information technology components (Scanga, 2004, p. 5).

The most important Education competencies, according to the research, are creativity, critical thinking, sensitive communication, and cooperation (Saimon, 2019, p.109).

Discussion

Since its existence, revolution 4.0 in education is yet unknown, it is challenging to describe and investigate due to the wide range of individual approaches it is characterised by. There are many conceptual studies in the literature but empirical research is scarce (Wallner & Wagner, 2016, p. 157). It can only be empirically examined when it is put into use. Digital technology integration with education, seamless learning environments, individualised education, exploratory education, and lifelong learning are all part of the basic skills need. The learning environments powered by technology are "globalised, automatized, virtualized, networked, and flexible" (Wallner & Wagner, 2016, p.155). These qualifications are condensed by Fisk (2017) into nine categories. Personalized learning, free choice, project-based learning, field experience, data interpretation, various assessment kinds to test knowledge application, student involvement in curriculum development, and last but not least, teachers as mentors are some of these (Hussin, 2018, pp. 92-93).

The primary competencies of teachers in Education are examined in the studies available are under the areas of technology skills, guidance skills, lifelong learning skills, and personal qualities including being inquisitive, patient, and fostering Sustainable Development Goals (SDG).

Kilic (2018) stressed that in Education, mentor teacher figures will be crucial in place of the traditional authoritarian teacher figure. Because pupils have easy access to a wealth of knowledge, instructors' guidance abilities are becoming increasingly important. The conclusion is that instead of being a subject matter expert, Education teachers should act as a mentor to help students acquire and make use of this new information (Wallner, & Wagner, 2016, p.157). Students will be able to identify correct information from the incorrect from a variety of information sources as a result.

Lifelong learning abilities were discovered in the study to be another set of requirements for teachers in Education. Since instructors have a role in more than just disseminating knowledge in the twenty-first century, their lifelong learning abilities have become crucial and demonstrating how to have access to them. Teachers who pursue lifelong learning are receptive to learning and have a learning mindset (Yaman & Kilic, 2015, p. 1555). Teacher education and training programmes have a vital role to play for upskilling the existing and future teachers with ITC skills. This requires teacher educators to be well equipped and use integrated approaches to cover applicable technologies, programmes and apps.

Additionally, it is anticipated that teachers in the Education movement will be proficient in using technology and integrating it into their lesson plans. The students' propensity to utilise technology in class is one of the factors that Cagiltay *et al.* (2007, p. 209) claim is responsible. One possible explanation for these demands is that 21st century students are members of generation Z, who were born and reared in the digital era (Prensky, 2001, p. 1).

There are also neither assessment criteria nor student participation in the curriculum creation process that are specified, as the planning and execution are witnessing gaps. Even though education outlined by the SDG Education 4 emphasises education for all, it is now available for everyone, anytime, and anywhere; school boundaries are no longer setting the pace for learning.

The advancements in technology are changing the world of human perception. The recent available technological challenge awaiting to be addressed is chatGPT, a chatbot developed by OpenAI. The apps detailed responses and articulate answers are presented by large language models which are tuned with learning techniques. Teachers need to address the emerging tools available and how they can be used for teacher and instructional purposes. Therefore, research on the curriculum's subject matter with SDG goals, incorporating technology in teaching instruction and strategies, and evaluation procedures might also be advised in order to attain Education. goals. Additionally, research should be done to gauge the readiness levels within the NEP (National Education Policy) framework of the qualifications identified in this chapter, Transforming Teachers for Education.

References

Arfandi, A. and Sampebua, O., 2018. The Study of Vocational Higher Education Graduates Skills That Requires in Industry. *Advanced Science Letters, 24*(5), pp. 3632-3635.

Arfandi, P.A., (2019) states, "Teachers Ability on Information and Communication Technology in Industry 4.0 Era". Advances in Social Science, Education and Humanities Research, volume 481, 3rd

International Conference on Education, Science, and Technology (ICEST 2019), pp. 161-164.

AITSL (Australian Institute for Teaching and School Leadership) (2011a). Australian Professional Standards for Teachers, updated 2014. Melbourne, VIC: AITSL, Australian Government. Retrieved from http://www.aitsl.edu.au/australian- professional-standards-for-teachers/Standards/list

Binkely, M., Estad, O., Herman, J. Raizen, S., Ripley, M., Ricci, M.M., *et al.*, (2012). Defining twenty first century skills. In P. Griffin, B.Mc. Graw. & E. Care (Eds.), *Assessment and Teaching of 21st Century Skills*, pp. 17- 66. Dordrecht: Springer.

Bloem, J., Van Doorn, M., Duivestein, P., Excoffier, D., Maas, R. & Van Ommeren, E. (2014). The fourth industrial revolution. Things to tighten the link between IT and OT. SOGETI: VINT Research Report 3 of 4.

Council of Accreditation of Education Preparation (2014). Guide to CAEP accreditation: The continuous improvement (CI) pathway. Retrieved from hhtp://www.ctc.ca.gov/educator-prep/accred-files/guide-caep-accred.pdf.

Ellahia, R.M., Khanb, M.U.A., & Shaha, A. (2019). Residing curriculum in line with industry 4.0. *Procedia computer science*, 151, 699-670.

Fisk, P. (2017). *Education 4.0... the future of learning will be dramatically different, in school and throughout life*. Retrieved from: https://www.thegeniusworks.com/2017/01/futureeducation-young-everyone-taught-together

Gulicheva, E., Lisin, E., Osipova, M., & Khabdullin, A. (2017). Leading factors in the formation of innovative education environment. *Journal of International Studies,* Vol. *10*(2), 129-137.

Hariharasudan, A., & Kot, S. (2018). A scoping review on Digital English and Education for Industry 4.0. *Social Sciences*, *7*(11), 227, 1-13.

Harkins, A. M. (2008). Leapfrog principles and practices: Core components of education 3.0 and 4.0. *Futures Research Quarterly*, *24*(1), 19-31.

Himmetoglu, B., Aydug, D., & Bayrak, C. (2020). Education 4.0: Defining the Teacher, the Student, and the School Manager Aspects of the Revolution. Turkish Online *Journal of Distance Education*, 21, 12-28. https://doi.org/10.17718/tojde.770896

Cagiltay, K., Yildirim, S., Aslan, I., Gok, A., Gurel, G., Karakus, T., Saltan, F., Uzun, E., Ulgen, E., & Yildiz, I. (2007). Ogretim teknolojilerinin universitede kullanimina yonelik aliskanliklar ve beklentiler: Betimleyici bir calisma. Akademik Bilisim' 07 - IX. Akademik Bilisim Konferansi Bildirileri, Kutahya, Dumlupinar Universitesi, 31 Ocak-2 Subat 2007.

Hussin, A.A. (2018). Education made simple: Ideas for teaching. *International Journal of Education and Literacy Studies*, *6*(3), 92-98.

Karagozoglu, B. (2017). Technology and its aftermath. In B. Karagozoglu (Ed.), *Science and Technology from global and historicl perspectives* (1st ed.), Cham: Springer International Publishing.

Kelentri´c, M., Helland, K., & Arstorp, A.T. (2017). Professional digital competence framework for teachers. https://www.udir.no/globalassets/filer/in-english/pfdk_framework_en_low2.pdf

Kelentric, M., Helland, K. & Asstorp, A. (2017). Professional digital competence frameworks of teachers. The Norwegian Centre for ICT Education.

Kipper, G. (2013). Vision of the furture in G. Kipper, & J. Rampolla (Eds.), *Argumented reality* [pp. 129-42] Syngress.

Kilic, T. (2018). Hezarfen egitim modeli. Istanbul: AZ Kitap.

Lamb, S.M. & Doecke, E. (2017). *Key Skills for the 21st century: An evidence-based review*. New South Wales: NSW Department of Education.

Nababan, T.M., Purba, S., Subirian, P. (2020). The Challenges of being a teacher in Industrial revolution 4.0. [Seminar proceeding] 5th Annual International seminar on transformative education and education leadership. 488, 219-223. http://creatiVecommons.org/licenses/by-nc/4.0/.

National Council for Accreditation of Teacher Education (2011). Technology and the new professional teacher. Preparing for the 21st century classroom (Washington, DC).

National Skills Commission (2020), The shape of Australia's post COVID-19 workforce, Commonwealth of Australia, Canberra, Australia.

Oner, D. (2020). *Education Policy Outlook 2019: Working together to help students achieve their potential.* Paris: OELO publishing. https:// doi.org/10.1787/2b8ad56e-en.

Oztemel, E., & Gursev, S. (2018). Literature Review of Industry 4.0. and related Technologies. *Journal of Educational Technology, 36*(2).

Palmer, P.J. (1998). *The courage to teach: exploring the inner landscape of a teacher's life.* San Francisco, Calif: Jossey-Bass.

Pedersen, S., and Liu, M. Teachers' Beliefs about Issues in the Implementation of a Student Centred Learning Environment. *Educational Technology Research & Development, 51*(2): 57-76, 2003.

Peters, M.A. (2017). Technological unemployment: Educating for the fourth industrial revolution. *Journal of Self-Governance and Management Economics, 5*(1), 32-41.

Prensky, M. (2001). Digital Natives, Digital Immigrants Part 1. *On the Horizon, 9*(5), 1-6.

Scanga, D. (2004). *Technology competencies for school administrators. Unpublished Dissertation of Doctor of Philosophy*. Florida, USA: South Florida University.

Salmon, G. (2019). May the fourth be with you: Creating Education. *Journal of Learning for DevelopmentJL4D*, *6*(2), 95-115.

Talari, S. Snatie-Khan, M., Stano, P. Lota, V., Tommasetu, A. & Catalao, J. (2017). A review of smart cities based on internet of things concept. *Energies, 10*(4).

Teo, T., Siobhan, U., Ronny, S. and Veronica, G. (2021). Initial teacher training for twenty-first century skills in the Fourth Industrial Revolution (IR 4.0): A scoping review. *Computers & Education, 170*(4):104223. https://doi.org/10.1016/j.compedu.2021.104223

Van Laar E., Van Deursen A.J.A.M., Van Dijk J.A.G.M., De Haan, J. (2017). The relation between 21st-century skills and digital skills: A systematic literature review. *Computers in Human Behavior*, 72, 577-588. https://doi.org/10.1016/j.chb.2017.03.010

Wallner, T. & Wagner, G. (2016). *Academic Education.* Proceedings of the international conference on education and new developments END 2016 icinde, pp. 155-159. Ljubljana, Slovenia, 12-14 Haziran 2016.

5
Smartphone Addiction and its Impact on Academic and Learning Achievements

A Cross-Sectional Observational Study among Senior Secondary Students

Syeda Ayeman Mazhar

Introduction

Smartphone has potentially replaced the features provided by computers and laptops including internet browsing, gaming, listening to music and watching videos and thus has become an inevitable need, rather than a luxury in a person's life, becoming pervasive. This has led to a new kind of health hazard among young population termed as smartphone addiction. Mobile phone technology is predominantly used for better calling and receiving services. India's smartphone market is the second largest in terms of active smartphone users which is next to China. With the amount of users crossing 220 million in February 2016, as per a report by Counterpoint Research, it's reached all segments of population from all parts of the society. Among young adults, the usage of smartphone has risen steeply from 5% in 2012 to 25% rise in 2014 (Katz, 2002).

Significant increase in Smartphone use and their capabilities allow adolescents to access the web, communicate, and entertain themselves anywhere and at any time. Therefore, most teenagers in 10-19 years aged can use the Smartphone as a continuing companion. As more and more adolescents enjoy exploring their Smartphones in their free hours, smartphone abuse is increasing in the 21st Century. (Davey and Davey 2014)

Moreover, little research has been conducted about smartphone use and its consequences. Considering the high rate of smartphone use among Indian adolescents, this area must be further explored attentively on what roles technology plays in fostering fantasies, acting out behaviors. [Seong-Soo Cha and Bo-Kyung Seo, 2018]

Adolescents are defined as children between the ages of 10 and 19 years as per WHO (2014) criteria. Today, 20% of individuals in the world are adolescents, constituting 1.2 billion people worldwide. As per the UNICEF Report (2011) nearly, 243 million adolescents live in India. (Divya *et al.*, 2016)

India has the largest adolescent population in the world. Within India, state-wise highest proportion of adolescents is 24.5% in Uttar Pradesh, 19% in Maharashtra, 16.3% in Kerala and comprising overall 21% for India.

An observational study is defined as the study that does not involve any intervention on the part of the investigator. A cross-sectional study is a study that examines the association between diseases or other health related characteristics and other variables of interestas they exist in defined population at a particular time. Smartphone Addiction Scale-Short Version (SAS-SV) was used to evaluate level of addiction to Smartphone. It is evident from a number of similar studies that, a higher rate of addiction to Smartphone in students is associated with negative effects on health, social life and may lead to the deterioration in academic performances.

Therefore, this study was designed to evaluate and validate both the harmful and beneficial effects of excessive smartphone usage in this age group in Aligarh area. From management perspective, we feel that future research should focus on changes in Smartphone usage and addiction proneness can be most safely and effectively targeted by school and social interventions.

Material and Methods

Design of the Study

This study was an observational, cross-sectional, non-interventional study to find out the Prevalence of smartphone addiction among adolescent girls students of Senior Secondary Schools of Aligarh Muslim University, Aligarh.

An observational study is defined as the study that does not involve any intervention on the part of the investigator. A cross-sectional study is a study that examines the association between diseases or other health related characteristics and other variables of interest as they exist in defined population at a particular time.

Place of Study

Senior Secondary Schools (Girls) of AMU, Aligarh which included both Senior Secondary School (girls) +2 and AMU Girls School. As the wide range of adolescents' age group is obtainable at school level, therefore, the study was preferred to be conducted in schools.

Duration of Study

The study was conducted for a period of 12 months from March 2020 to April 2021. Besides school holidays and online survey was also avoided during the preparation leaves for examinations.

Methods of Selection of Subjects

Inclusion Criteria

- Students enrolled in Senior Secondary Schools (Girls) of AMU.
- Participants willing to participate and given the consent.

Exclusion Criteria

- Students other than AMU.

- Individuals who do not agree to give the consent.
- Participants who do not complete the questionnaire.

Sample Size

Davey and Davey have reported the overall prevalence of smartphone addiction in Indian adolescents ranges from 39% to 44% in a mixed method approach as per preferred reporting items for systematic review and meta-analysis (PRISMA, 2009) guidelines, done by using Med-Calc online meta-analysis software. (Davey & Davey, 2014)

Taking the average of the prevalence rate, i.e., 42% was used to calculate the sample size for the present study. The error was set at 15% and sample size was calculated by the following formula: (Rao NSN, 2010) (Rao TB, 2010)

n=4pq/L2

Where,

n=required sample size

p=approximate prevalence rate of disease to be studied

q=100-p

L= permissible error in the estimate of p

Taking p=42 and L=15% of p

n= (4×42×58)/(6.3)2

= 245

Rounding it off, final sample size was set at 250.

Ethical Considerations

Ethical Issues

Informed Consent

Informed assent/consent was taken from the individual. The personal information received was kept confidential. Health Education and adequate counselling was provided to all the individuals who were interviewed.

Ethical Clearance

Permission was taken from Institutional Ethical Committee of Ajmal Khan Tibbiya College, Aligarh Muslim University, Aligarh. The committee did not found anything objectionable or unethical in the research proposal. The committee therefore, approved the synopsis for research work.

Study Procedure

Due to the prevailing COVID-19 pandemic situation and nationwide lockdown, students were attending all their classes through online mode only. And, due to the time constrains to complete the study within the stipulated time period, the online mode of survey was chosen to conduct the study. The study was conducted after obtaining permission from respective authorities of the schools through the Chairperson of the Department.

For the students of Senior Secondary School (Girls), the questionnaire was administered through their respective e-mail IDs. More than 850 students of Class XII and around 700 students of Class XI were given the questionnaire individually via e-mails. Very few candidates responded to the e-mails. To remind the students to participate in the online survey, the e-mails were resent after one week to get the responses. After that the e-mails were resent twice a week to get more and more responses.

For the students of AMU Girls School, the questionnaire was administered through already created WhatsApp groups for classroom teachings and updates. The consent/assent and confidentiality statement were made compulsory before proceeding for the next section. Instructions were also explained to them telephonically for those who asked for having any kind of difficulty in filling the form. About 250 students are enrolled in Class XII in both Science and Arts streams and around 200 are enrolled in Class XI in both Science and Arts streams of regular and Self-finance schemes. The URL or web-link of the google form was shared in the particular class and section-wise WhatsApp groups of the AMU Girls School. The students scarcely responded to the questionnaire.

Their teachers also encouraged them and reminded them to fill the questionnaire. The URL or web-link was shared on a weekly basis and later on, biweekly, to ensure more and more participation in the study.

Those who completely filled the consent and confidentiality statement could only proceed further to fill all the sections of the questionnaire. There was a provision to edit the responses, in the questionnaire, if any respondent felt to change their response, they were allowed to do so before final submission. Near about 300 responses were received during the study period. Some participants responded four times, some three times, some did twice. Among the edited responses, the last response was considered for the statistical analysis.

Methods of Data Collection

A pre-structured questionnaire (consisting of socio-demographic details, Smartphone Addiction Scale Short-Version (SAS-SV) and assessment of Mizaj or temperament using CCRUM proforma (on the basis of ajnas e ashrah) and a self-administered questionnaire related to the impacts (both physical and psychological) of smartphone addiction on the health with emphasis on harkatwasukoon e badaniwanafsani were used to assess the smartphone usage and its health impacts among the senior secondary school students after taking their written informed consent.

Outcome Measures

This was a cross-sectional study focused on determining the prevalence rate of smartphone addiction on the study participants. Further, the physical/physiological and the psychological impacts on health due to smartphone addiction were evaluated. Furthermore, the level of addiction in smartphone users were correlated with their Mizaj.

Study Variables

The following variables were studied:

- Independent variable
- Age of the study subject
- School
- Class
- Section
- Stream
- Religion
- Assessment of smartphone addiction
- Assessment of Mizaj

Statistical Analysis

The data analysis were carried out using appropriate statistical procedures comprising Chi-square test and then the results were computed. To test the statistical significance most of the risk factors were compared among addicted and non-addicted groups using Chi Square technique. Consequently, all the risk factors whose "p-value" was found to be less than 0.05 was said to be statistically significant in the category of addiction. The entire estimation was achieved by the assistance of Microsoft excel.

Evaluation of Study

At the end of the study, the collected data were analyzed and studied using appropriate statistical methods.

Method of Study and Research Instrument

A pre-typed semi-structured proforma consisting of several questions were prepared for collection of data from study subjects. The proforma/questionnaire was developed in English language depending upon the convenience of the students. The respondents were also explained in Urdu/Hindi, if having any doub: in understanding any aspect of the online survey and the questionnaire.

The interview session/online survey was based on pre-structured questionnaire which contains different sections comprising general information, socio-demographic (population based) information, smartphone addiction habits and usage pattern, awareness and impacts of smartphone addiction on physical and mental health.

Informed Consent

Informed consent/assent of all students was made compulsory to fill before proceeding to the next section of the questionnaire. It consisted of 9 points.

A confidentiality statement was also made compulsory and keeping the respondents' identity confidential.

Results and Observations

The present study was conducted through the Department of Tahaffuziwasamaji Tib, Faculty of Unani Medicine, AMU, Aligarh, in two schools through online survey. The following results were observed among the enrolled respondents.

Table 5.1: Distribution of respondents according to Schools

Name of School	No. of Respondents Frequency (n)	Percentage (%)
AMU Girls School	128	51.2
Senior Secondary School (Girls)	122	48.8
Total	**250**	**100.0**

As shown in the Table 5.1, 128 (51.2%) respondents belonged to the AMU Girls High School and 122 (48.80%) respondent's belonged to senior secondary School (Girls).

Table 5.2: Age of Students

AGE (in years)	Frequency (n)	Percentage (%)
15	9	3.6
16	58	23.2
17	108	43.2
18	68	27.2

(*Contd.*)

19	7	2.8
Total	**250**	**100.0**
Mean +-S.D. = (17.02+-0.94)		

As shown in Table 5.2, majority of students 108 (43.2%) were 17 years of age, 68 (27.2%) students were 18 years of age, 58 (23.2%) students were of 16 years, 9 (3.6%) students were of 15 years, 5 (2.8%) students were of 19 years of age.

Table 5.3: Distribution of respondents according to Class

Class	Frequency (n)	Percentage (%)
XI	102	40.8
XII	148	59.2
Total	**250**	**100.0**

Table 5.3 shows the distribution of students according to the class. 102 (40.8%) students belonged to class XI and 148 (59.2%) students belonged to Class XII.

Table 5.4: Distribution of respondents according to Stream

Stream	Frequency (n)	Percentage%
Commerce	19	7.6
Humanities (Arts/ Social Science)	57	22.8
Science	174	69.6
Grand Total	**250**	**100.0**

As observed from the Table 5.4, Out of 250 respondents, majority belonged to Science stream 174 (69.6%), 57 (22.8%) were from Humanities (Arts/Social Science) stream, and 19 (7.6%) students were from Commerce stream.

Table 5.5: Distribution of respondents according to Residential status

Residential status	Frequency (n)	Percentage %
Day scholar	166	66.4
Hosteller	84	33.6
Grand Total	**250**	**100.0**

As observed from the Table 5.5, out of 250 respondents, 166 (66.4%) were day scholars and 84 (33.6%) among them belonged to the hosteller group.

Table 5.6: Distribution of respondents according to Religion

Religion	Frequency(n)	Percentage%
Hindu	40	16.0
Muslim	210	84.0
Total	**250**	**100.0**

Table 5.6 shows the distribution of respondents according to their religion. Out of 250 respondents, majority 210 (84%) belonged to the Muslim religion and 40 (16%) respondents belonged to the Hindu religion.

Table 5.7: Smartphone uses by the students

Smartphone You Use Belongs to	Frequency (n)	Percentage%
You	144	57.6
Your parents	85	34.0
Your siblings	16	6.4
Any other	5	2.0
Grand Total	250	**100.0**

Among the 250 students, maximum students 144 (57.6%) were using their own smartphones, 85 (34%) students were using smartphones of their parents, 16 (6.4%) students were using siblings' smartphones, and only 5 (2%) students were using smartphones of any of (their relative or friends) any other Table 5.7.

Table 5.8: Preference between Smartphone or Library among students

Do You Prefer Using Your Smartphone Rather Than Library	Frequency (n)	Percentage%
Maybe	43	17.2
No	73	29.2
Yes	134	53.6
Grand Total	**250**	**100.0**

Majority of the students 134 (53.6%) were in favour of using smartphone rather than the library, 73 (29.2%) did not prefer using smartphone rather than library and 43 (17.2%) were not sure about using smartphone rather than library Table 5.8.

Table 5.9: Reason of using smartphone then the library

If yes, what's the reason?	Frequency (n)	Percentage%
It's convenient to use smartphone	40	16.0
It's faster to use smartphone	58	23.2
Lack of time to visit library	56	22.4
Satisfactory and reliable	26	10.4
(blank)	70	28.0
Grand Total	**250**	**100.0**

70 (28%) respondents were not in favour of using the smartphone rather than the library. 58 (23.2%) said that, it's faster to use smartphone, 56 (22.4%) gave the reason, lack of time to visit library, 40 (16%) respondents agreed with the reason that it's convenient to use smartphone, 26 (10.4%) find it satisfactory and reliable to use smartphone Table 5.9.

Table 5.10: Use of smartphone Before Pandemic

Have You Use Smartphone Before Pandemic	Frequency (n)	Percentage%
Maybe	32	12.8
No	48	19.2
Yes	170	68.0
Grand Total	250	**100.0**

Majority of the respondents were using smartphone before the pandemic 170 (68%), 48 (19.2%) did not used the smartphone before pandemic, 32 (12.8%) were not sure about using smartphone before pandemic Table 5.10.

Table 5.11: Addiction of smartphone

Addiction Non-Addiction	Frequency (n)	Percentage%
Addicted to smartphone	119	47.6
Not addicted to smartphone	131	52.4
Grand Total	**250**	**100.0**

Out of 250, 131 (52.4%) were non-addicted and 119 (47.6%) were addicted to smartphone Table 5.11.

Table 5.12: Reason of using smartphone

Most Self-Perceived Positive Effects of Smartphone on Learning Achievements	Frequency (n)	Percentage %
Academic performance has been increased due to smartphone technology	43	17.2
Can easily contact classmates to get help in studies	45	18.0
Can easily contact the teachers for study purposes	58	23.2
Smartphone has helped to improve the level of quality of education	64	25.6
Students use dictionary/thesaurus/ calculator of smartphone in classes	40	16.0
Total	**250**	**100.0**

In Table 5.12, maximum students responded that 64 (25.6%) Smartphone has helped to improve the level of quality of education, 58 (23.2%) can easily contact the teachers for study purposes, 45 (18%) students can easily contact classmates to get help in studies, 43 (17.2%) students admit that academic performance has been increased due to smartphone technology, 40 (16%) students use dictionary/thesaurus/calculator of smartphone in classes.

Table 5.13: Import of smartphone

Most Self-Perceived Negative Effects of Smartphone in Learning Achievements	Frequency (n)	Percentage %
I purchased the smartphone without the permission of the parents	4	1.6
I waste my time sending/writing SMS during class work	45	18.0
Smartphone has put negative impact on students' moral values	104	41.6
Smartphone is responsible for my low academic performance	68	27.2
Students use smartphone in examination hall as a source of unfair means	29	11.6
Total	**250**	**100.0**

Maximum students are of the opinion that 104 (41.6%) Smartphone has put negative impact on students' moral values, 68 (27.2%) students admit that Smartphone is responsible for their low academic performance', 45 (18%) perceived that they waste their time sending/writing SMS during class work, 29 (11.6%) students think that students use smartphone in examination hall as a source of unfair means, 4 (1.6%) students purchased the smartphone without the permission of the parents.

Table 5.14: Use of smartphone for academic achievements

Respondents' Perceived Usefulness of Smartphone in Academic Achievements	Frequency (n)	Percentage %
I can easily access my e-mail using smartphone due to instant alert	15	6.0
It enables me to take a snapshot of illustration which cannot be memorized at instance for later life	55	22.0
Smartphone has saved me from buying personal laptop for studies	32	12.8
The use of the smartphones in online group discussions	55	22.0
Using the smartphone for learning has enabled me to gain extra skills outside classroom	93	37.2
Grand Total	**250**	**100.0**

Table 5.14 shows that 93 (37.2%) admit that, using the smartphone for learning has enabled me to gain extra skills outside classroom, 55 (22%) students think that the smartphones are useful in online group discussions, 55 (22%) students think that it enables them to take a snapshot of illustration which cannot be memorize at instance for later life, 32 (12.8%) students perceive that smartphone has saved them from buying personal laptop for studies, 15 (6%) can easily access their e-mail using smartphone due to instant alert.

Table 5.15: Use of smartphone by the students of different discipline

Most self-perceived negative effect of smartphone on learning achievements	Commerce	Commerce %	Humanities (Arts/ Social Science)	Humanities (Arts/ Social Science) %	Science	Science %	Grand Total
I purchased the smartphone without the permission of the parents	1	25	1	25	2	50	4
I waste my time sending/writing SMS during class work	5	11	10	22	30	67	45
Smartphone has put negative impact on students' moral values	8	8	27	26	69	66	104
Smartphone is responsible for my low academic performance	5	7	14	21	49	72	68
Students use smartphone in examination hall as a source of unfair means	0	0	5	17	24	83	29
Grand Total	**19**	**8%**	**57**	**23%**	**174**	**70%**	**250**

INFERENCE

25% respondents from Commerce stream, 25% respondents from Humanities stream and 50% respondents from Science stream purchased the smartphone without the permission of the parents.

11% respondents from Commerce stream, 22% respondents from Humanities stream and 67% respondents from Science stream think that they waste the time sending/writing SMS during class work. 8% respondents from Commerce stream, 26% respondents from Humanities stream and 66% respondents from Science stream perceive that Smartphone has put negative impact on students' moral values. 7% respondents from Commerce stream, 21% respondents from Humanities stream and 72% respondents from Science stream perceived that Smartphone is responsible for their low academic performance. 17% respondents from Humanities stream, 83% respondents from Science stream and no student from Commerce stream perceived that students use smartphone in examination hall as a source of unfair means.

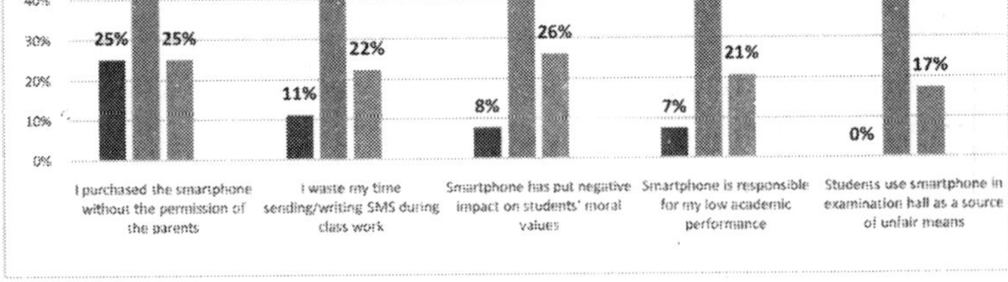

Table 5.16: Most self-perceived negative effect of smartphone on learning achievements

Respondents' perceived usefulness of smartphone in their academic activities	Commerce	Commerce %	Humanities (Arts/ Social Science)	Humanities (Arts/ Social Science) %	Science	Science %	Grand Total
I can easily access my e-mail using smartphone due to instant alert	1	7	5	33	9	60	15
It enables me to take a snapshot of illustration which cannot be memorize at instance for later life	6	11	10	18	39	71	55
Smartphone has saved me from buying personal laptop for studies	2	6	10	31	20	63	32
The use of the smartphones in online group discussions	5	9	8	15	42	76	55
Respondents' perceived usefulness of smartphone in their academic activities.	**Commerce**	**Commerce %**	**Humanities (Arts/ Social Science)**	**Humanities (Arts/ Social Science) %**	**Science**	**Science %**	**Grand Total**
Using the smartphone for learning has enabled me to gain extra skills outside classroom	5	5	24	26	64	69	93
Grand Total	**19**	**8**	**57**	**23**	**174**	**70**	**250**

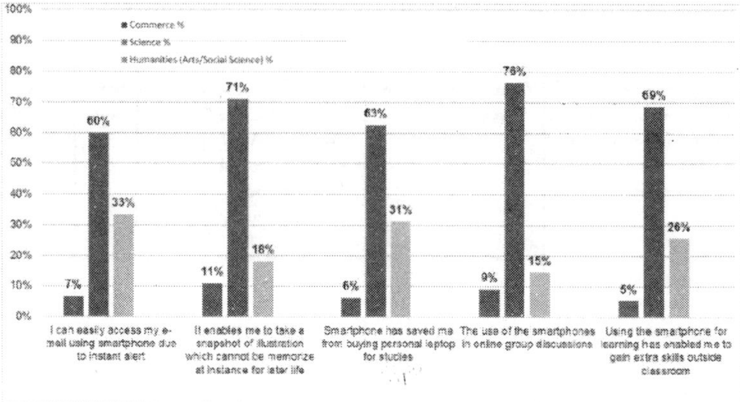

Table 5.17: Most self-perceived positive effect of smartphone on learning achievements

Most self-perceived positive effect of smartphone on learning achievements	**Commerce**	**Commerce %**	**Humanities (Arts/ Social Science)**	**Humanities (Arts/ Social Science) %**	**Science**	**Science %**	**Grand Total**
Academic performance has been increased due to smartphone technology	3	7	10	23	30	70	43
Can easily contact classmates to get help in studies	5	11	12	27	28	62	45
Can easily contact the teachers for study purposes	4	7	12	21	42	72	58
Smartphone has helped to improve the level of quality of education	4	6	12	19	48	75	64
Students use dictionary/thesaurus/ calculator of smartphone in classes	3	8	11	28	26	65	40
Grand Total	**19**	**8**	**57**	**23**	**174**	**70**	**250**

TR and FR shows the most self-perceived positive effects of smartphone on learning achievements. 7% candidates in the Commerce stream, 23% in the Humanities and 70% in the science stream, admit that their academic performance has been increased due to smartphone technology.

11% respondents in the Commerce stream, 27% in the Humanities stream and 62% in the Science stream say that they can easily contact classmates to get help in studies.

7% in the Commerce stream, 21% in the humanities stream, 72% in the Science stream say that they can easily contact the teachers for study purposes.

6% in the Commerce stream, 19% in the Humanities stream, and 75% in the Science stream said that smartphone has helped to improve the level of quality of education.

8% students in the Commerce stream, 28% in the Humanities stream, and 65% in the science stream, admit that they use dictionary/thesaurus/calculator of smartphone in classes.

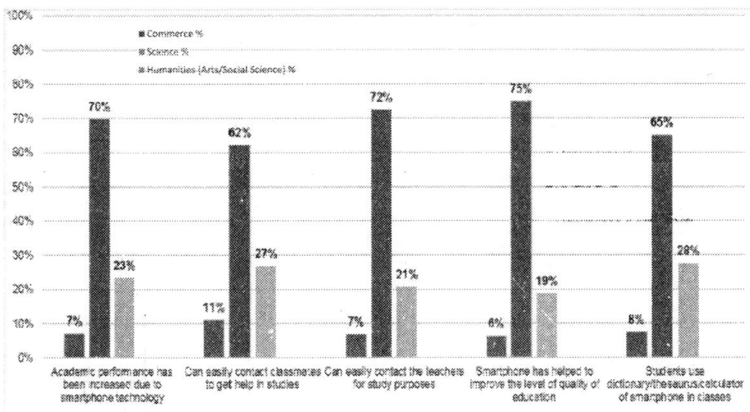

Do you think most self-perceived positive effect of smartphone on learning achievements that excessive use of smartphone?

Discussion and Conclusion

The Smartphone Addiction Scale-Short Version (SAS-SV), (Kwon, Kim, et al., 2013): Was used to detect the addicted individuals. Our study delineated that, out of 250 respondents, 131 (52.4%) were non-addicted and 119 (47.6%) were addicted to smartphone. According to Leonard (2015), the smartphone usage has become a serious addiction phenomenon. As per his study findings, on an average, college going female students uses phones for ten hours a day. It was found in an another survey, that, three out of five smartphone users can't resist more than 60 minutes without peeping their phones. A new phobia known as NOMOPHOBIA, i.e., fear of being without a phone, has now been established. Additional health associated problems due to smartphone addiction, such as backache, nerve problem, depression and anxiety are seriously concerned. (Leonard 2015)

A similar study carried out by Arora, observed that children handle smartphones habitually for long hours for playing games etc. So, non-stop use and exposure can lead to detrimental effects such as tumour due to harmful radiation, disturbed brain activity, inappropriate media and academic malpractice. (Arora 2018)

Maximum students 64 (25.6%) responded that Smartphone has helped to improve the level of quality of education, 58 (23.2%) can easily contact the teachers for study purposes, 45 (18%), students can easily contact classmates to get help in studies, 43 (17.2%) students admit that academic performance has been increased due to smartphone technology, 40 (16%) students use dictionary/ thesaurus/calculator of smartphone in classes. Concluding that the students enrolled in our study used the smartphone for enhancing their academic performances.

In our study, maximum students 104 (41.6%) are of the opinion that Smartphone has put negative impact on students' moral values, 68 (27.2%) students admit that Smartphone is responsible for their low academic performance, 45 (18%) perceived that they waste their time sending/writing SMS during class work, 29 (11.6%) students think that students use smartphone in examination hall as a source of unfair means, 4 (1.6%) students purchased the smartphone without the permission of the parents. Kendra (2018) expresses that the too much usage of smartphone can aggravate thumb arthritis by undue texting on smartphones.

Arora (2018) reveals that it has been observed that children are handling smartphones regularly for long hours playing games etc. So, continued use and exposure can lead to harmful effects viz tumour (radiation effects), disturbed brain activity, inappropriate media and academic malpractice. Domoff *et al.*, established that addictive phone usage associated with poorer academic performance. These results indicate that addictive use of smartphones may be a risk factor for decreased academic performance. (Domoff, S.E., 2020)

Our findings are consistent with research examining excessive phone use and academic outcomes in young adults (e.g., Felisoni & Godoi, 2018; Giunchiglia *et al.*, 2018; Paul *et al.*, 2012; Wentworth & Middleton, 2014). That is, prior research has revealed that greater dependence on Smartphones is associated with lower GPA in college students. Similarly, we found that it is the nature of adolescents' Smartphone use (e.g., dependence), and not solely hours of social media use that best associates with academic performance. Similar findings have been reported when examining problematic media use in younger children and psychosocial outcomes (Domoff, S.E. *et al.*, 2019), (Felisoni, D.D., 2018), (Giunchiglia, F., *et al.* 2018), (Paul, J.A., *et al.*, 2012) and (Wentworth, D.K., *et al.* 2014).

Thus, from the above discussion, it can be concluded that, there is no uncertainty of smartphones' detrimental impacts on students' health whether physical or mental. However, in our study it is evident that majority of the students used the smartphone as a means to enable them to get better cognitive, learning opportunities and academic achievements.

References

Arora, T., Broglia, E., Thomas, G.N., Taheri, S. (2018). Associations Between Specific Technologies and Adolescent Sleep Quantity, Sleep Quality, and Parasomnias. *Sleep Med.* 2014; *15*(2): 240-7.

Divya Rani Singh, Vandana Goswami, (2016). Impact of Mobile Phone Addiction on Adolescent's Life: A Literature Review, *International Journal of Home Science, 2*(1): 69-74.

Domoff, S.E., Foley, R.P., Ferkel, R. (2020). Addictive Phone Use and Academic Performance in Adolescents. *Human Behaviour & Emerging Technology*. 2:33-38. https://doiorg/10.1002/hbe2.171. Printed By [Wiley Online Library - 027.060.149.191 - /DOI/e-pdf/10.1002/Hbe2.171]

Felisoni, D.D., & Godoi, A.S. (2018). Cell Phone Usage and Academic Performance: An Experiment. *Computers & Education*, 117, pp. 175-187.

Giunchiglia, F., Zeni, M., Gobbi, E., Bignotti, E., & Bison, I. (2018). Mobile Social Media Usage and Academic Performance. *Computers in Human Behaviour*, 82, pp. 177-185.

Katz, J.E., & Aakhus, M. (Eds.). (2002). Perpetual Contact: Mobile Communication, Private Talk, *Public Performance*. Cambridge University Press..

Kendra, K. (2018). *The Effects of Smartphones on the Brain*. Retrieved From https://www.verywellmind.com/how-do-smartphones-affect-the-brain-2794892

Kwon, M., Kim, D.J., Cho, H., Yang, S. (2013). The Smartphone Addiction Scale: Development and Validation of a Short Version for Adolescents. *Plos One*. *8*(12): E83558.

Leonard, J. (2015). *16 Seriously Damaging Side Effects of Your Smartphone Addiction*. Retrieved from https://www.naturallivingideas.com/16-seriously-damaging-side-effects-of-yoursmartphone-addiction/

Paul, J., Baker, V., Cochran, J. (2012). Effect of Online Social Networking on Student Academic Performance. *Computers in Human Behavior*, *28*(6), 2117-2127.

Rao, N.S.N., Murthy, N.S. (2010). *Applied Statistics in Health Sciences*, 2nd Ed. New Delhi, Jaypee Brothers Medical Publishers (P) Ltd., p. 105.

Rao, T.B. (2010). *Methods of Biostatistics—Principles and Concepts*, 3rd Ed. Hyderabad, Paras Medical Publishers, p. 107.

Sanjeev Davey and Anuradha Davey (2014). Assessment of Smartphone Addiction in Indian Adolescents: A Mixed Method Study by Systematic-Review and Meta-Analysis Approach, *International Journal of Preventive and Social Medicine*, 2014 Dec; *5*(12): 1500-1511.

Seong-Soo Cha and Bo-Kyung Seo (2018). Smartphone Use and Smartphone Addiction in Middle School Students in Korea: Prevalence, Social Networking Service, and Game Use; Health *Psychology Open*; https://pubmed.ncbi.nlm.nih.gov/29435355/

UNICEF Annual Report (2011). Available online through: UNICEF annual report 2011. UNICEF.

Wentworth, D.K. and Middleton, J.H. (2014). Technology Use and Academic Performance. *Computers & Education*, 78, 306-311. http://dx.doi.org/10.1016/ j.compedu.2014.06.012

World Health Organization (2014). Available online through: www.who.int/adolescent/second-decade Health for the World's Adolescents, A second chance in the second decade, Department of Maternal, Newborn, Child and Adolescent Health, 20 Avenue Appia 1211 Geneva 27, Switzerland Website: www.who.int/maternal_child_adolescent

Section II
Current Trends in Education

6

Education and Emerging Trends in Teaching

A Way Forward

Saba Anees and *Tabassum Qamar*

Introduction

Education refers to the latest phase of the education system, which has been heavily influenced by the digital revolution and technological advancements. It completes the phenomenon of digital integration where human beings and machines are aligned and discover new theory of innovation. In Education, information is available ubiquitously and teaching and learning process has become dynamic. It has dramatically changed the economic use of information.

As a result, the demands of education have also changed significantly. The traditional methods of teaching like teacher centred and subject centred approaches have become outdated and are significantly replaced with the child centred and personalized learning approaches. With the help of technology, it has become possible to create customized learning experiences for each student. This approach is far more effective than the traditional one-size-fits-all approach; as it takes into account each student's strengths, weaknesses, and learning style.

With the advent of time, the focus on skill development is more emphasized. The constructive learning approach and Education also lay emphasis on the development of skills such as creativity, critical thinking, problem-solving, and collaboration. These skills are considered essential for success in the modern workplace, where automation and artificial intelligence are rapidly changing the nature of work.

Education recognizes that learning does not end with formal education. Rather, it is a lifelong process, and individuals must continue to learn and develop new skills throughout their lives. It also emphasizes the importance of hands-on and experiential learning. Present approach allows students to apply their knowledge in real-world situations, which helps them to develop a deeper understanding of the subject matter.

Technology with the introduction of the concept of 'blended learning' has made it possible to combine traditional classroom teaching with online learning. It allows students to learn at their own pace and from anywhere, while still benefiting from the guidance of a teacher.

Besides lifelong learning, a special emphasis has also been placed on estimating the gig workforce in India, which has otherwise been confounded by methodological issues in identifying gig workers. As per the NITI Aayog Report 2022 on 'India's Booming Gig and Platform Economy: Perspectives and Recommendations on the Future of Work' in the education sector, the expansion of gig workers in India is more than one lakh (1,00,000) by 2019-20.

The 4 Core Components of Education

The 4 core components as proposed in a study suggests four core components that shape the proposed concept of Education. These components are (i) *Competencies* (training and development of desirable critical competencies in today's students), (ii) *Learning Methods* (incorporation of new learning methods), (iii) *Information and Communication Technologies (ICTs)* (implementation of current and emerging ICTs), and (iv) *Infrastructure* (use of innovative facilities, services, and systems to improve learning processes) (Minada, J. *et al.*, 2021).

Fig. 6.1 summarizes the concept of Education and its four core components. This figure also shows relevant examples of implementations of the proposed components (Minada, J. *et al.*, 2021).

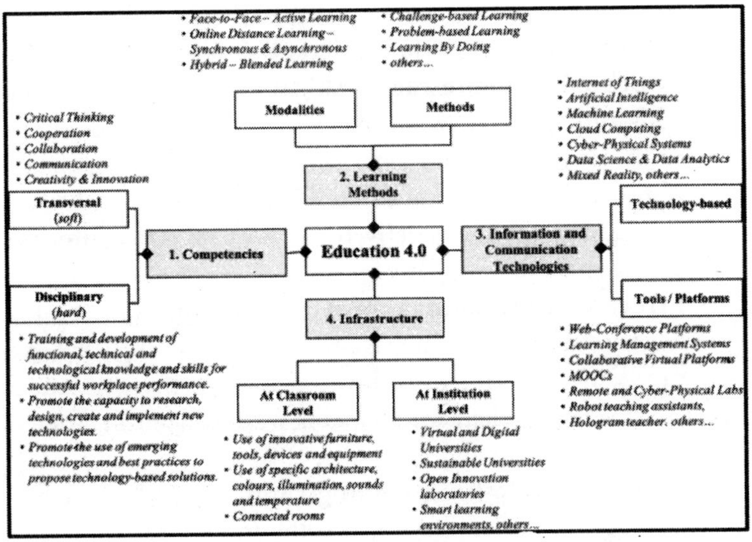

Fig. 6.1: Showing the 4 Core Components of Education.

Source: Miranda, J. *et al.* (2021). The core components of Education in higher education: Three case studies in engineering education. *Computers & Electrical Engineering, 93*.

Paradigm shift of teaching skills during and post-COVID scenario

The COVID-19 pandemic has brought about a paradigm shift in the way education is delivered. With the closure of schools and universities, educators have had to quickly adapt to new teaching methodologies that enable remote learning. The following are some of the changes in teaching skills that have emerged during and post-COVID scenario:

- **Proficiency in online teaching tools:** The shift towards remote learning has necessitated a mastery of online teaching tools such as video conferencing software, learning management systems, and digital collaboration platforms.
- **Adaptability and flexibility:** Educators have had to be adaptable and flexible in their teaching styles to ensure they can cater to the needs of all learners, regardless of their individual learning styles and home situations.
- **Improved communication skills:** With remote learning, communication between educators, students, and parents has become more important than ever. Educators have had to improve their communication skills to ensure that they can convey information effectively and keep everyone informed of any changes or updates.
- **Effective time management:** Educators have had to master effective time management skills to ensure that they can deliver lessons on time and manage their workload effectively, especially when dealing with students in different time zones.
- **Creativity in lesson planning:** With the shift to remote learning, educators have had to be more creative in their lesson planning to ensure that their lessons remain engaging, interactive and effective in a virtual environment.
- **Empathy and emotional intelligence:** The COVID-19 pandemic has been a stressful and uncertain time for many students, and educators have had to demonstrate empathy and emotional intelligence in their interactions with students, providing support and guidance where needed.

Skill for the Future of Work in Education

As the fourth industrial revolution takes shape, education is once again undergoing a revolution of its own, focusing on a more flexible, broader, and integrated lifelong learning approach to better prepare students for a workplace where adaptability, innovation, and flexibility will be essential skills. According to various organisations' differing definitions of "twenty-first century skills", the following fundamental competences and capabilities serve as the foundation for future success in the workplace and in a globalised society (ILO Report, 2021):

- creativity and innovation;
- critical thinking, problem-solving and decision-making;
- learning to learn, metacognition;
- information literacy;
- ICT literacy;
- communication;
- collaboration (teamwork);
- citizenship, both local and global;
- life and career; and
- personal and social responsibility, including cultural awareness and competence.

The following skills have become increasingly important in the teaching and learning process for educators:

- **Digital literacy:** As technology continues to be integrated into the education sector, digital literacy has become a necessary skill for educators. This includes knowledge of basic computer operations, software, and online tools that are used in the classroom.
- **Learning management systems (LMS):** LMSs are software applications that allow educators to manage and deliver content to learners. Educators must be proficient in using LMSs to create and deliver course content, manage student records, and track students progress.
- **Coding and Programming Skills:** With the increasing importance of technology and computer science, coding and programming skills are becoming more relevant in the education sector. Educators with these skills can help teach students about the importance of coding and can also create engaging lesson plans that incorporate coding and programming activities.

- **Multimedia content creation:** Educators must be able to create multimedia content, such as videos, images, and podcasts, to enhance the learning experience for students.
- **Data Analysis and Visualization Skills:** Data analysis and visualization skills are becoming more important as educators are able to track and analyze student data to improve learning outcomes. This includes using tools such as data dashboards and data analysis software to make informed decisions about teaching and learning.
- **Mobile learning:** With the increasing use of mobile devices in education, educators must be proficient in creating and delivering mobile-friendly content and using mobile learning apps.
- **Online Teaching Skills:** With the rise of online learning due to the COVID-19 pandemic, online teaching skills have become essential for educators. This includes proficiency in video conferencing software, digital collaboration tools, and online assessment tools.
- **Soft Skills:** Soft skills such as empathy, adaptability, communication, and critical thinking are also essential for educators. These skills help create a positive classroom environment and can enhance the teaching and learning experience.
- **Cybersecurity:** Educators must be aware of cybersecurity risks and implement measures to protect student data and maintain the privacy of their online activities.

Areas of transformation in Education

1. **Curriculum and teacher training:** A focus on efficient and pertinent learning may necessitate a review of the frameworks for existing curriculum, as well as the topics, pedagogy, materials, and classroom teaching practises. It may also necessitate teacher preparation and professional development. The content of the curriculum, assessments, teacher preparation, and leadership and management of the

school must all be in sync for the curriculum to be holistic and coherent. Evaluation of learning results: Focusing on efficient and pertinent learning calls for more flexible assessment practises as well as more equitable and balanced methods of assessing knowledge, skills, and competencies across a wider range of users and abilities. Focus on the effective acquisition of competencies and the relevance of learning for the world of work and civic life requires the establishment or the strengthening of national quality assurance and qualification frameworks.

2. **Learning Modalities:** Learning delivery modalities include, but are not limited to: online courses and programmes, virtual labs, blended learning and blended instruction. Learning delivery modalities include traditional classroom, blended learning, flipped classrooms and MOOCs.

   Learning delivery modalities have a broad range of benefits to students and teachers. They include traditional lessons within a classroom, e-learning programmes accessed on a computer or other device, self-paced courses that allow students to complete homework or exercises on their own schedule and virtual learning environments designed specifically for adult learners.

   The use of audio and video learning delivery modalities has become the preferred method for higher education institutions. This is mainly because it provides the learners with an opportunity to experience and interact with concepts in a more meaningful fashion. By providing students with more opportunities to learn, choose and apply these modalities are more likely to be retained.

3. **New pedagogical approaches:** It takes a range of instructional techniques to impart 21st century abilities. Teaching methods like "crossover learning" for bridging formal and informal learning, "learning through argumentation" for honing scientific argumentation skills, "incidental learning" by embracing unplanned or unintentional learning, and

"context-based learning" by taking the context that shapes the learning process into account are examples of flexible and personalised pedagogical styles.

Additionally, educators are using other pedagogical practices including the following:

i. **Learning by doing** is an experience-based learning method that relies on real-world scenarios to train and enhance the knowledge, skills, and techniques of learners. This method helps participants gain a deeper understanding of their subject area as they practice it in a safe environment.

ii. **Flipped classrooms** is a pedagogical approach where the class time is left free for activity purposes and the reading material is provided to the students prior to the class. This leads to the development of higher order mental capabilities of students like creativity, collaboration, integration, mind mapping of concept, analysis and synthesis etc.

iii. **Play-based learning** provide opportunity to the students to engage in the activities in various ways and participate enthusiastically in the process of learning. Implementing the learning-in-play continuum, educators balance providing time for uninterrupted free play and embedding or extending academic content in different ways with play-based activities to support children's learning.

iv. **Challenge-based learning** to provide students with the opportunity to challenge themselves in a safe environment, while learning how to solve problems, analyze and evaluate information, think critically and creatively.

v. **Problem based learning** is an innovative pedagogy that emphasizes the importance of real-world experience and hands-on learning. By focusing on a particular problem or issue, PBL creates a collaborative environment where students learn to carry out inquiry with each other while they are actively engaged in solving problems together.

vi. **Gamification-based learning** is a powerful technique for engaging students and improving their learning. The experience of being rewarded for doing well motivates people to take on challenges, achieve goals and learn tasks. This can be applied to many of the areas in education, including: Mathematics, Science and History.

4. **Child centred teaching style:** The process of "individuals acting on their own, either alone or with the help of others, in identifying their learning needs, formulating learning goals, identifying human and material resources for learning, choosing and implementing suitable strategies for learning, and evaluating learning outcomes" is popularly referred to as self-directed learning. The role of the instructor has changed to include finding the greatest resources on the subject or skills in the students' areas of interest, utilising possibilities for large-scale learning experiences, and linking students from different cultures and viewpoints.

Conclusion

Education has brought about significant changes in the education system, and these changes are likely to continue as technology continues to evolve. The focus is now on preparing students for the challenges of the future, rather than simply imparting knowledge. The COVID-19 pandemic has brought about a paradigm shift in the way education is delivered, requiring educators to master new teaching skills such as proficiency in online teaching tools, adaptability, flexibility, improved communication skills, effective time management, creativity in lesson planning, and empathy and emotional intelligence. Hence, IT skills are essential for educators in the 21st century. Digital literacy, proficiency in LMSs and online teaching tools, multimedia content creation, data analysis, cybersecurity, and mobile learning are all essential skills that educators must possess to deliver effective and engaging teaching and learning experiences to students.

Thus, digital literacy, coding and programming skills, data analysis and visualization skills, online teaching skills, and soft skills are all current skill trends that are becoming increasingly important for educators to possess. By developing these skills, educators can help improve learning outcomes and better prepare students for the future.

It can thus be inferred that the evolution of education from traditional teaching methods to EdTech has revolutionized the way students learn, providing personalized and adaptive learning experiences that cater to individual student needs and learning styles. EdTech tools and platforms have become essential for educators and have helped improve learning outcomes while adapting to changing circumstances.

References

Barreiro, A.V. (Vol. 7, No. 1, 2022). *Education and its impact on the educational system during the pandemic and post pandemic Covid 19 in Ecuador, ISSN-e: 2661-6661.* Retrieved from http://portal

Bettinger, E., W Fairlie, R., Kapuza, A., Kardanova, E., Loyalka, P., & Zakharov, A. (2020). Does Edtech Substitute for Traditional Learning? Experimental Estimates of the Educational Production Function. *National Bureau of Economic Research, NBER Working Paper No. 26967.*

Gulati, C., & Thakur, A. (2022). Current Trends in Education: A Literature Review. *International Engineering Journal For Research & Development* *7*, 14.

Higher Education—Trends and Future Perspectives for Teaching and Learning. (2014, March).

Himmotoglu, B., Aydug, D., & Bayrak, D.C. (July 2020). Education: defining the Teacher, The students, and the School Manager aspects of the Revolution. *Turkish Online Journal of Distance Education, ISSN 1302-6488*, 12-28.

Hussain, A.A. (2018). Education Made Simple: Ideas for Teaching. *International Journal of Education and Literacy Studies, ISSN:2202-9478, 6* (3), 92-98.

Kasih, R., Hanafi, N., & Amin, M. (2019). Education 4.0 and the 21st Century Skills: A Case Study of Smartphone Use in English Classes. *Advances in Social Science, Education and Humanities Research, 465*, 48-51.

Kesar, H., & Semerci, A. (2019). Technology trends, Education 4.0 and beyond. *Contemporary Educational Researches Journal, 9* (3), 39-49.

Miranda, J., Navarrete, C., Noguez, J., Molina-Espinosa, J.M., Ramírez-Montoya, M.S., Navarro-Tuch, S.A., *et al.* (2021). The core components of Education in higher education: Three case studies in engineering education. *Computers & Electrical Engineering, 93.*

Organization, I.L. (May 2021). *The Future of Work in the Education Sector in the context of Lifelong Learning for all, Skills and the Decent Work Agenda.* Geneva: ILO.

P.S. & Karthikeyan, R. (2021). Industry 4.0 Challenges and Implementation in Education Sector in India. *International Journal of Research: Granthaalayah, ISSN:2350-0530, 9* (5), 74.

UNICEF. (October 2022). *Education India: Insight Report.* India: World Economic Forum.

7
Impact of Covid-19 Pandemic on Education in Indian Context

Mahfooz Alam and *Jwel Hoque*

Introduction

The World Health Organization (WHO) affirmed COVID-19 as a pandemic on 11 March, 2020 but earlier to this the Chinese government confirmed the first outbreak of Coronavirus disease 2019 (COVID-19) in Wuhan on 31December, 2019. The state-wise lockdown, which was imposed in India due to the second wave of the novel coronavirus pandemic, affected people belonging to every economic stratum. Life, was deeply affected by COVID-19 even for the ones who were not infected, due to isolation; contact restrictions and economic shutdown changed the social and economic scenario of India. Vast populations and crowded settlements increased the number of cases in China, Europe, USA and India. This outbreak pandemic was evolved in Wuhan city of China and affected many countries. The pandemic has significantly disrupted the growth of countries where the cases of novel coronavirus were reported. In order to reduce the crowd, countries took various measures such as lockdown, workplace non-attendance, school closure, suspension of transport facilities etc. For controlling the spread of the COVID-19 pandemic, educational institutions were temporarily closed by most of the countries around the world. Over 90 per cent student population of the world were affected by this closure nationwide. India also suffered a lot from the pandemic. In order to control the infection of COVID-19, Indian government took various measures such as on 22 March, 2020, first Janta Curfew was announced by the Prime minister of India. Later on 21 days lockdown was announced by the prime minister of India to control the cases of COVID-19. On 14 April, 2020, further the lockdown was extended by the Indian government till 3 May, 2020. This decision affected the various sectors of the country. The educational sector was also affected by the lockdown which is a critical determinant of the economic future of the country. As per the directives of the government, all schools, colleges and universities were closed. Whole education system was disrupted by the pandemic COVID-19. The researchers, doctors, and virologists across the globe continuously worked to decode the disease pattern, identify potential treatments, therapies, and develop vaccines. Further, despite the availability of advanced health care systems, there had been an escalation in the number of deaths. Also, the roles of doctors and nurses became very risky as the probability to get infected was increased while treating patients. The COVID-19, not only affected people but also resulted in interruption of trade, business, and economic activities. The pandemic brought trade and business into halt and forced the breadwinners to stay indoors. This lockdown acted as a boon for the environment to revive. In addition, this study discusses the impact of COVID-19 on the economy and education particularly in India.

Literature Review

The outbreak of COVID-19 led to the shutdown of all the institutions may it be educational, social, economic, political or any others. Economic and educational institutions are most affected areas that led to irreparable loss to the education system. But along with these challenges, new opportunities also appeared to take off. E-learning tools have played a crucial role during this pandemic, helping schools and universities facilitate student learning during the closure of universities and schools (Subedi *et al.*, 2020). While adapting to the new changes, staff and student readiness needs to be gauged and supported accordingly. The learners with a fixed mind-set find it difficult to adapt and adjust, whereas the learners with a growth mind-set quickly adapt to a new learning environment. There is no one size-fits-all pedagogy for online learning. There are a variety of subjects with varying needs. Different subjects and age groups require different approaches to online learning (Doucet *et al.*, 2020). Online learning also allows physically challenged students with more freedom to participate in learning in the virtual environment, requiring limited movement (Basilaia & Kvavadze, 2020). Broadly identified challenges with e-learning are accessibility, affordability, flexibility, learning pedagogy, life-long learning and educational policy (Murgatrotd, 2020). To this end, the chapter reviews the current state of knowledge regarding COVID-19, the policy responses to it.

Covid-19 and Its Impact on Economy

The COVID-19 pandemic represents an unprecedented disruption to the global economy as production and consumption are scrabbled back. The developing countries like India are not immune to such external shocks and are likely to witness slowdown in economic growth. As such the Indian economy was going through a sluggish phase since implementation of the demonetization and goods and services tax (GST), and government was identifying ways to bring the economy back on track. However, the COVID-19 has put paid to all hopes of revival of the economy in the near term. The sectors such as tourism, hospitality, aviation, textile, agriculture, construction, gems/jewellery, and start-ups which contribute majorly towards economy and employment generation have reported losses in crores during pandemic. The tourism sector has anticipated an overall loss of Rs. 5 lakh crores and job cuts for 4 crore people who are directly and indirectly related to tourism sector. The hospitality sector particularly the hotel chains have projected loss of Rs. 30,000 crore which can lead to job loss of 15 lakh people. Similarly, the aviation sector has an estimated loss of above Rs. 8,200 crore as international and domestic flights stay grounded. The textile sector comprises of micro, small, and medium enterprise and relies on people skills predicts one crore job cuts due to lack of funds, resources, and decline in demand of textiles and ongoing logistic issues due to lockdown. The agriculture sector has also been affected due to COVID-19. There has been an escalation in demand of wheat, vegetables, and other crops during the pandemic. However, the agricultural outputs are unable to reach the consumers due to supply chain issues. Consequently, the farmers are forced to reduce the prices. The tea industries have reported 8% drop in tea exports as they are unable to harvest the first flush. The non-availability of migrant labor to carry harvesting activities and disruptions in supply chains have affected agricultural sector. Furthermore, the closure of hotels, restaurants, sweet shops, and tea shops has also affected sales of crops, pulses, vegetables, and milk. Meanwhile, poultry farmers have been badly hit due to misinformation, particularly on social media, that chicken are the carriers of COVID-19. The construction industry in India employs around 51 million people. With such a scale, the impact of COVID-19 shock is equally massive. Fear of the disease, closure of on-going projects, loss of income, and lack of food has made the migrant workers to flee the sites in which they were engaged.

The manufacturing units are heavily affected due to lockdown and the suspension of public transport services in the country. Automakers, smartphone makers, consumer electronics firms, and many others have ordered shutdowns causing incalculable damage to production of key products which leads to considerable revenue loss. The COVID-19 has forced startup units to close due to cessation of work, lack of funds, and inability to connect and commute with clients. The DEBATA *et al.* 3 of 5 retail sales of gems/jewellery in India are estimated to have tanked 80% in due to COVID-19 pandemic. The declining footfalls in shopping complexes and movie complexes have affected the retail sector by impacting the consumption of both essential and discretionary items. In the current scenario, with all the retailers closing down their services, the jobs of the employees are at a huge risk. The fast moving consumer durables (FMCD) sector providing grocery items, milk, and hygiene products have seen a surge in demand during the pandemic. The impact of the lockdowns will be borne by the unsuspecting employees across sectors impacting lives, livelihood and thereby the overall economy.

The economic impact of corona virus pandemic in India has been hugely disruptive. The temporary halt in economic activities resulting in decline of India's exports by 34.6% and imports by 28.7% as countries sealed their borders, large fall in the equity markets, and limited work carried out in service sectors has triggered the question how the Indian economy will revive? The World Bank and credit rating agencies have downgraded India's growth for fiscal year 2021 with the lowest figures India has seen in three decades since India's 1991 economic liberalization. However, the International Monetary Fund (IMF) projection for India for the financial year 2021–22 of 1.9% GDP growth is the highest among G-20 nations.

COVID-19 and Its Impact on Education

In order to control the spread of the novel coronavirus, state governments started the closure of schools and colleges across the country. It was somewhere announced in the second week of March as a temporary measure to avoid the crowd. Initially, for a month closure of schools was announced by the government but gradually the time of closure was extended and it is uncertain when they will reopen. During this period, there are various activities take place which are very crucial such as competitive exams and entrance tests of various universities, board examination and semester examinations in universities, nursery school admissions as well as admission process in universities. In order to stop the outbreak of COVID-19, no immediate solution is found out. In India, the closure of school and university will not only have a short-term impact on the continuity of learning of young learners but it will have a large effect on the economic growth of the country as well as having large effect on the society.

(a) Impact of COVID-19 on Schools

In order to raise the skills, best public policy tool available is going to school. School is a place where children can have fun and raise social awareness and social skills. The main motive of going school or being in school is that it enhances the ability of the child. Spending a relatively short period of time in school increases skills and ability. On the other side missing the school or not attending the school will have negative effect on the skill growth. The closure of the schools has affected the structure of learning and schooling. Firstly, it affected the teaching and assessment methodologies. Online teaching methods are adopted by the few private schools that are handful in taking online classes. In those schools, children are taking classes online. On the other side low-income private and government schools have complete closure and not having the access to eLearning solution. It is disrupting the learning of students. Parents are facing various issues because of the change in teaching methodology.

(b) Impact of COVID-19 on Higher Education

The shutdown of universities has also affected the student's learning in universities. In order to ensure the continuity in institutes and universities, one immediate measure is essential. To conduct the class smoothly, online teaching methodology is adopted. Learning management software and open-source digital learning solutions are adopted by the universities to run online classes. Higher education is a critical determinant of the economic future of the country and higher education sector has significantly affected by the pandemic as well. Many students from India enroll in universities abroad. Due to the global closure of the institutes and universities, it is expected that it will reduce the demand for the international higher education. The main concern which is coming in the mind of everyone is the effect of the pandemic on the rate of employment. Because of the current situation, graduates who have recently completed their graduation are fearing from the withdrawal of job offers from corporate. Teaching methodology in institutes and universities has also transformed due to the lockdown in India. It has been replaced by the old chalk-talk model with the new technology. E-learning solutions are making teaching and learning possible in this situation but engagement is a big problem attached with the e-learning. The policy makers are trying to solve the problem of engagement of students and tackling the digital divide. In order to manage the crisis in Indian education section, a multi-pronged strategy is necessary in the long term. An effective education and well-rounded practices are needed in India to build the capacity of young minds in this time of crisis. To ensure the overall progress in India, it will drive employability, well-being, health and productivity through the development of skills.

(c) Impacts of COVID-19 on Online Classes and Parents

In order to maintain the attendance or not missing out too much, children are forced to continue their education at home and generally have not been sent out from the home to play. The major inputs into a child's learning are provided by the families as these are treated as a central to education. Parents are facing issues in understanding the new methodology of teaching. Some parents are not very techno-friendly. Thus, they are not able to guide their ward to take classes online. Connectivity of internet is also a big challenge in front of all teachers, students and parents. Many disturbances have to face due to the poor connectivity.

(d) Assessments

The teaching for students is not only interrupted by the closure of schools, colleges and universities, lockdown also affected the assessment of the students all around the world. Many exams and assessments have been cancelled or postponed because of the closure of educational institutions. For both students and teachers, this is a new era of the education. Many colleges and universities have shifted their traditional classes system to the online classes as well as the examination system also has been shifted from offline to online. They are using online assessment tools for evaluation. Online assessment tools are not free from the limitations. There are various errors related to the measurement reported in online assessment tools in comparison to the usual measurement. As shown in a research that educational credentials are used by the employers to assess the applicants such as grade point averages and degree classifications to sort applicants. Thus, the lockdown is also affecting the placement of the new graduates on labour market. Matching efficiency of the new graduates is reducing due to the increment in the disruptions in the signals of the applicants which is leading higher job separation rates and slower earning growth.

(e) Mid-day-Meal

One of the most successful programmes of Indian school education system is Mid-day-meal scheme. A large section of the students of Indian schools get nutritious food along with education in the schools. As there was nationwide complete closure of school took place, children was deprived of both education and food. Therefore, a large section of students face difficulties to get food and learning experiences.

(f) Salary Half-down

In the private institutions, either schools or any colleges or coaching, teachers' salary cut up to 50%. This is because, earning of schools from students decreased. On the other hand, teachers had to perform their duties through online mode or work from home. They don't have relaxation from their duties. In comparison to their assignments, their salary was too much cut, up to half-down. This led to frustration and anxiety among the teachers of private institutions.

(g) Alternative Job

After the announcement of nationwide lockdown, a large section of the Indian workforce lost their job or compelled to leave their respective professions. This crisis also emerged in the field of education. During the lockdown period, teachers working in private schools or any kind of educational institutions, laid off from their respective workplace, or they themselves left. Hence, they were compelled to go in search of alternative jobs.

(h) Uneducated Parents Become Helpless: Remote learning was not available in every family

According to the Global internet network research, just 24% of households had a consistent internet connection, while other remote areas remained unreachable. As a result, the government was forced to ensure that sufficient benefits and monetary funds were provided.

(i) Training of School Going Lost

The infamous COVID-19 Pandemic followed by national lockdown taught everyone the importance of schools and teachers. Though students were engaged through e-learning platform, but the habit of school going and regular practice of learning lost in time. School is place where habit formation take place, students are trained in different social and democratic skills after the contact with teachers and their peers. Due to the lockdown, everything was hampered.

(j) Confusion and Anxiety

At the lockdown period, major issues occurred was confusion and anxiety among the teachers and students. Teachers were given assignment in online work from home and students were bored led by online learning. Students and teachers were compelled to spend their time in home. Over engagement of the learners with different gadgets like mobile and computer or laptop, earphone and other online platform, bring boredom and anxiety among students and teachers.

(k) Closure down of Low Budget schools

Private school with low budget comes to an end their journey. This is because, earning of the school was almost zero. They were forced to shut the school. Most of the students didn't attend school, cut their affiliation from school, and refused to pay any. Hence, due to the economic burden, management with low budget closed the schools. According to studies, the epidemic has denied almost 32 crore students from education. This is being referred to as a national crisis, with an increase in unemployment as a result.

(l) Girl Education Depleted

Let us not ignore the impact on girls, who have recently begun to defy educational conventions and have been seen dropping out of schools in large numbers. In extreme circumstances, the fall rate of poverty was recorded at 8% of GDP, resulting in additional reasons such as unemployed families who couldn't afford fees and resources being forced to stop their children's education due to debts, and so on. Boys were requested to work as daily wage employees, while girls were assigned to home chores, prompting the government to ask a series of questions in order to stimulate emergence.

(m) Lack of Techno-savvy Teachers and Acceptance

COVID-19 Pandemic can affect the children largely as less understanding about the concept of social distancing is a serious issue for educational institutes as well as for parents. COVID-19 is one of the most critical challenges for mankind and affecting global health after the 2nd World War.

The educational institution will be going to face various issues related to managing the learning activities and engaging the students. The online learning is special kind of methodology and will have lack of acceptance from teachers and students as all are not ready for the sudden transition from classroom learning to online. The online platforms like Skype, Zoom and Google Duo are not sufficient for offering the learning and engaging the students. The lack of internet facility, devices and environment for online learning from home or other places will hurt the learning approaches of institutions and influence the knowledge of the students to understand the concepts and content of the course.

(n) Threat of Cyber Security

School time also raises social skills and awareness besides being fun for the children. There are economic, social and psychological repercussions on the life of students while they are away from the normal schedule of schools. Many of these students have now taken online classes, spending additional time on virtual platforms, which have left children vulnerable to online exploitation. Increased and unstructured time spent on online learning has exposed children to potentially harmful and violent content as well as greater risk of cyberbullying. School closures and strict containment measures mean more families have been relying on technology and digital solutions to keep children engaged in learning, entertained and connected to the outside world, but not all children have the necessary knowledge, skills and resources to keep themselves safe online.

(o) Lack of Sufficient ICT Facilities

Approximately, 1.726 billion learners in the world are currently affected due to school closures in response to the pandemic. As per the UNICEF data, more than 134 countries have implemented nationwide closure, and that is having a negative impact on the offering of courses and completion of degrees and class activities. Broadly identified challenges with e-learning are accessibility, affordability, flexibility, learning pedagogy, life-long learning and educational policy (Murgatrotd, 2020). Many countries have substantial issues with a reliable Internet connection and access to digital devices. While, in many developing countries, the economically backward children are unable to afford online learning devices, the online education poses a risk of exposure to increased screen time for the learner. Therefore, it has become essential for students to engage in offline activities and self-exploratory learning. Lack of parental guidance, especially for young learners, is another challenge, as both parents are working. There are practical issues around physical workspaces conducive to different ways of learning. Majority of students do not have access to smartphones or TV at home in addition to poor Internet connectivity. There is no or less income for huge population due to closure of business and offices. The data package (costs) is comparatively high against average income earned, and continuous access to Internet is a costly business for the farming community.

(p) Passive learning by students

The sudden shift to online learning without any planning — especially in countries like India where the backbone for online learning was not ready and the curriculum was not designed for such a format — has created the risk of most of our students becoming passive learners and they seem to be losing interest due to low levels of attention span. Added to this is that we may be leaving a large proportion of the student population untouched due to the digital divide that is part of many developing nations including India. We are now beginning to realize that online learning could be dull as it is creating a new set of passive learners which can pose new challenges.

(q) Changing Format of Student Recruitment

Universities and colleges worldwide are facing a major risk in the area of student recruitment and retention. The risk of losing students is so high that they will need to re-look at their admission practices, admission criteria and the overall recruitment process itself which will include, new methods of outreach and application process itself. The level of academic performance of the students is likely to drop for the classes held for both year-end examination and internal examination due to reduced contact hour for learners and lack of consultation with teachers when facing difficulties in learning/ understanding (Sintema, 2020). The lockdown of schools and colleges has not only affected internal assessments and examinations for the main public qualifications like Central Board of Secondary Education (CBSE), but the levels have also been cancelled for the entire cohort in the India. Depending on the duration of the lockdown, postponement or cancellation of the entire examination assessment might be a grim possibility (United Nations, 2020). Various state-level board exams, recruitment exams, university-level exams and entrance exams have been postponed across India due to the COVID-19 outbreak and national lockdown. Various entrance examinations (such as CLAT, NEET, NET, UPSC, State PCS, CAT, JEE, GATE etc.) have also been postponed/rescheduled. The education system in schools, colleges and universities across the country has been severely impacted due to the ongoing situation Pedagogy available and used for face-to-face learning is not feasible for online learning. Though a range of pedagogy has been devised for online and distance learning, teachers who are technologically backward require proper professional development and training in order to orient themselves towards their students. Domestic violence and child abuse are on the rise as the perpetrators are many a time at home or in the neighbourhood, which is a mental distraction and threat to the learners (Ravichandran & Shah, 2020).

Conclusion

The closure of schools, colleges and universities is interrupting the learning of students and also disrupting the internal assessment and public assessments for qualifications. The traditional method of teaching has been replaced by the online teaching. One side online teaching is providing opportunity to the students for learning another side there are various issues attached with the new methodology of teaching. Education institutions are searching the ways to solve the issues which arose due to the lockdown and putting their efforts to fill the loss of learning. In order to rebuild the loss in learning at the time when they will be reopened, schools need resources. There are many questions in front of the schools such as how to target the children and how to utilize these resources etc. need to be solved. The internal assessment of the students related to the learning should not be skipped. It should be postponed. In order to avoid the longer unemployment period for new graduates, new policies should be formed to support them in their entry to the labour market.

References

Basilaia, G., & Kvavadze, D. (2020). Transition to online education in schools during a SARS-CoV-2 coronavirus (COVID-19) pandemic in Georgia. *Pedagogical Research*, *5*(4), 10. https://doi.org/10.29333/pr/7937

Debata, B., Patnaik P. and Mishra, A. (2020). COVID-19 pandemic! It's impact on people, economy, and environment. *J Public Affairs*. 2020;20:e2372. https://doi.org/ 10.1002/pa.2372

Doucet, A., Netolicky, D., Timmers, K., & Tuscano, F.J. (2020). Thinking about pedagogy in an unfolding pandemic (An Independent Report on Approaches to Distance Learning during COVID-19 School Closure). Work of Education International and UNESCO. https://issuu.com/educationinternational/docs/2020_research_covid-19_eng

Murgatrotd, S. (2020, March). *COVID-19 and Online learning*, Alberta, Canada. doi:10.13140/RG.2.2.31132.85120

Ravichandran P., Shah A.K. (2020 July). Shadow pandemic: Domestic violence and child abuse during the COVID-19 lockdown in India. *International Journal of Research in Medical Sciences*, *08*(08), 3118. https://doi.org/10.18203/2320-6012.ijrms20203477

Sintema E. J. (2020, April 7). Effect of COVID-19 on the performance of grade 12 students: Implications for STEM education. *EURASIA Journal of Mathematics, Science and Technology Education*, *16*(7). https://doi.org/10.29333/ejmste/7893.

Subedi, S., Nayaju, S., Subedi, S., Shah, S.K., & Shah, J.M. (2020). Impact of e-learning during COVID-19 pandemic among nurshing students and teachers of Nepal. *International Journal of Science and Healthcare Research*, *5*(3), 9.

Süt, H.M., & Öznaçar, B. (2021). Effects of COVID-19 Period on Educational Systems and Institutions. *International Journal of Curriculum and Instruction*, *13*(1), 537-551.

Tarkar, P. (2020). Impact of COVID-19 pandemic on education system. *International Journal of Advanced Science and Technology, 29*(9), 3812-3814.

United Nations (2020). *Policy brief: Education during COVID-19 and beyond.* United Nations. https://www.un.org/development/desa/dspd/wp-content/uploads/sites/22/2020/08/sg_policy_brief_covid-19_and_education_august_2020.pdf

World Health Organization (2020). WHO Director-General's opening remarks at the media briefing on COVID-19, 11 March, 2020. Geneva, Switzerland.

8
Revolution in the Indian Education System
Traditional to ICT Mode

Mubeen Zehra and *Syed Wajahat Ali*

Introduction

Every nation's foundation for a person's whole growth is education. It is crucial to the growth of people and helping them realize their full potential. An individual's ability to compete on a global stage is aided by education. The ultimate goal of education is to stimulate the intellect, foster curiosity, and foster logical thinking, which in turn fosters creativity and a research mindset in pupils. Education is a powerful tool for raising the standards of citizenship in every country (Hammond & Snyder, 2015). People from various groups and communities are justified and given the opportunity to live moral lives, advice and lead their own communities, and uphold harmony and humanity. Precariousness among people is developed or increased by education, which aids in the creation of nations as well as educational development (Ross, 1979).

It is clear from the literature (Levin, 1993; Darra, 2006), committees and commissions (Shankdher, 1967; Mathew, 2016; Biswas, 2021), policies (Bajwa, 2003; Bassi, 2011; Rao & Siva, 2016; Sarkar & Mohapatra, 2017; Mahashveta, 2017), interventions (UNESCO, 2005, 2009, 2011), frameworks, and education-related schemes that numerous ideas have been developed and revised The average education level of the workforce is correlated with increases in student productivity, and higher education research and development are important sources of innovation. Evaluating efficacy and efficiency is necessary for increasing educational productivity. Productivity can be boosted at the source if the workplace fosters creativity and innovation.

1. Changing the Education Landscape through policies

When India unveiled its Fourth Five-Year Plan in 1972, it recognized the value of technology (1969-74). India implemented the Educational Technology Scheme under this plan, which provided the States with 100% help in purchasing resources like colour television, radios, cassette players, etc. the conclusions reached after analysing policy papers and committee/commission reports about the integration of ICT in the teaching-learning process. The Kothari Commission's recommendations, which set the stage for science and knowledge's crucial role, may be traced back to the beginning of the period. The Kothari Commission established the guidelines in an effort to enhance the role of educators. The objectives of the first national policy on education were incorporated into the second policy, which was created in 1986. Additionally, electronic tools and audio-visual aids were added to the teacher-learning process, and ICT integration has become more prevalent. By offering training programmes with a technical focus to teacher educators in pre-service and in-service, the other succeeding policy of 1992 improves other policies. The ICT orientation meant that these teachers were no longer just teachers; rather, their position was redefined as a result of this training. During that time, there was only a slight improvement. ICT utilisation in the teaching-learning process was wisely boosted throughout 2004-2005 as the journey towards ICT integration grew and improved. International interventions are important for integrating ICT into the teaching-learning process. In this case, UNESCO played a significant role in advancing the notion of

ICT-based education because many nations are active members of these organisations, and UNESCO is a key tool for advancing the principles of ICT-oriented education in Third-World nations as well. The UNESCO framework thus proved to be important and beneficial.

India participates actively in the UN, and UNESCO has incorporated the concepts, tenets, agreements, conferences, etc. in additional policies like the NCFTE 2009-2010. The overall professional development of both in-service and pre-service teachers was emphasized in this particular policy. The specific policy addressed the technological requirements in the teacher education programme. UNESCO attempted to analyse the subsequent implementation of ICT-based learning policies and laws by looking at both their national and international components. ICT is crucial to the teaching-learning process because it results in high-quality instruction, high-quality student learning, and overall learner professional development, according to UNESCO 2010-2011 is endorsed by member states as foreign interventions and programmes. In order to do this, the Indian Government created NCFTE 2014 and NCTE 2014-2015 to accelerate the quality and efficacy of teacher education programme. But in a teacher education programme, a paper on ICT and education is taught. ICT has been gradually incorporated into the curriculum and syllabi of several Indian colleges and universities. The most recent policy developed by the Indian Government, known as NEP 2020, is a representation of the progressive implementation of those earlier policies. NEP 2020 not only focuses on additional fields and disciplines, but also on the full integration of ICT tools into the teaching-learning process. This policy's suggested online course demonstrates how the use of ICT in the teaching-learning process, including teacher preparation, has increased.

2. Paradigm shift

The method and content of mass education have undergone a paradigm shift. The Gurukul method, along with the residential and classroom approaches, can be used to chart the transition from older to more modern post-modern eras. ICTs are replacing traditional methods in many important areas of life. The use of ICT in the teaching-learning process has changed how teachers teach. The practices and procedures of practically all commercial and governmental endeavours have undergone a fundamental transformation as a result of ICT. Education is a very social activity, and good teachers who spend a lot of time getting to know their students personally have historically been connected with effective education. ICT use in schools encourages more student-centred learning environments. However, as the globe quickly transitions to digital media and information, the role of ICT becomes meaningful (Amin, 2013).

Information and communication technology (ICT) development that is assertive has refuted long-standing claims about the traditional teaching paradigm by fostering new thinking, transforming the world of education. According to academic opinion, alternative teaching methods are more effective and quicker than conventional teaching methods. These days, ICT uses in teaching and learning are welcomed and promoted by both parents and teachers (Schwerdt & Wuppermann, 2011). Researchers have discovered via their studies that using ICT in the teaching-learning process is more agreeable than the most common teaching method (Mooji, 2007). The role of the teacher in an environment where technology is dominant has been redefined, and the teaching-learning process now places a strong emphasis on a student-centric approach. Importantly, the use of ICT must be integrated for effective learning (Birch & Irvine 2009; Honan 2008).

Objective of this study

1. To describe the transformation in the Indian education system.
2. To study the paradigm shift from the traditional method to ICT oriented model.

3. To examine the perception of pre-service teachers regarding ICT-oriented teaching.

Research procedure

This is an empirical study based on a field survey that was conducted in Jamia Millia Islamia, New Delhi through random sampling. The total respondents' were 100 and all of them are pre-service teachers who are associated with Teacher Training and Non-formal Education (IASE). It is important to note that during fieldwork, the data was collected through a closed-ended questionnaire. Importantly, this study is divided into two parts, the first deals with the theoretical knowledge which is based on secondary sources including policies on education and scholarly works, the second part is accomplished through primary data which is empirical in nature; this research is exploratory and explanatory in nature.

A self-developed five-point Likert scale questionnaire was used to know subjects' perception towards the possible scope from traditional method to ICT mode usage in the classroom. The questionnaire on the Perspective of Pre-service Teachers Regarding the Possible Scope of ICT usage in Classroom consisted of four sub-dimensions, i.e., ICT oriented pedagogical skills, Strengthening students learning in Techno-oriented classroom, Techno-oriented lecture strengthening students creativity and involvement in the classroom, and Techno-friendly mode of innovative communication. The Cronbach's alpha reliability of the questionnaire is 0.85. The obtained data was analysed by using descriptive statistics through SPSS v.23 such as Mean and Standard Deviation. The Mean score was calculated to know the level of perception of pre-service teachers regarding possible scope from traditional method to ICT mode usage in classroom. Standard Deviation was calculated to know the degree of heterogeneity in the responses of pre-service teachers. Frequency and percentage analysis were also calculated to determine pre-service teachers' perception level. In the following table results of the study are presented.

Results and Findings

The results of the statistical analysis are presented in Table 8.1.

Table 8.1: Mean, Standard Deviation (SD) of pre-service teachers' perception towards possible scope from traditional method to ICT mode usage in the classroom

S. No	Sub-Dimensions	N	Max. Possible Score	Mean	SD
1	ICT oriented pedagogical skills	100	20	16.85	1.978
II	Strengthening students learning in Techno-oriented 21st classroom	100	20	15.92	1.895
III	Techno-oriented lecture strengthening students, creativity and participating involvement in classroom	100	20	15.96	1.974
IV	Techno-friendly mode of innovative communication	200	20	15.89	1.622

The mean score of sub-dimension I, i.e., 'ICT oriented pedagogical skills' was 16.85 and the value of SD 1.978 respectively. The mean value indicated an above average whereas the percentile value indicated a nearly high level of perception of pre-service teachers with regard to this sub-dimension of the study. It is thus safely concluded that the pre-service teachers perceived that ICT is moderately useful to enhance teachers' pedagogical skills.

The mean score of sub-dimension II, i.e., 'Strengthening students learning in Techno-oriented 21st classroom' was 15.92 and the value of SD was 1.895. The mean value indicated an average whereas indicated an above average level of perception of pre-service teachers with regard to this sub-dimension of the study. This finding reveals that the pre-service teachers perceived that ICT is moderately useful in strengthening students, learning in Techno-oriented 21st classroom.

The mean score of sub-dimension III, i.e., 'Techno-oriented lecture strengthening students' creativity and participating involvement in classroom' mean value was 15.96 and the value of SD was 1.974. These two values indicated an above average level of perception of pre-service teachers with regard to this sub-dimension of the study. Hence, it can be safely concluded that the pre-service teachers perceived that ICT is moderately useful in techno-oriented lecture strengthening students, creativity and participating involvement in classroom.

The mean score of sub-dimension IV, i.e., 'Techno-friendly mode of innovative communication', the mean value was 15.89 and the value of SD was 1.622. These two values indicated an above average level of perception of pre-service teachers with regard to this sub-dimension of the study. This leads to conclude that the pre-service teachers perceived that ICT is moderately useful to enhance techno-friendly mode of innovative communication in teaching-learning process.

Table 8.2: Responses of Pre-service teachers (N=100) on the Possibilities and Scope from Traditional to ICT mode in classroom usage

Sl. No.	Items	Responses in %				
		SA	A	UD	DA	SD
1	ICT is one of the effective sources of the teaching-learning process	50%	40%	10%	0%	0%
2	The use of ICT creates effective teaching skill	30%	55%	10%	5%	0%
3	ICT-integrated lectures have the scope to cover the content in best possible manner	28%	50%	20%	2%	0%
4	ICT enhances the active involvement of learners	40%	50%	10%	0%	0%
5	Use of ICT promotes creativity among learners	33%	45%	15%	7%	0%
6	ICT is a constructive tool for teaching-learning	40%	45%	10%	5%	0%

Sl. No.	Items	Responses in %				
		SA	A	UD	DA	SD
7	Communication becomes effective by using ICT in the classroom	38%	54%	8%	0%	0%
8	Transfer of knowledge could be more effective by using ICT	27%	60%	13%	0%	0%
9	ICT makes complex and difficult lessons easy to understand	34%	55%	8%	3%	0%
10	ICT enables students to express their ideas and thoughts in a better way	47%	51%	2%	0%	0%
11	Students pay more attention in class when the teacher teach the lesson through ICT	25%	63%	10%	2%	0%
12	ICT can help in making effective lesson plans	38%	53%	9%	0%	0%
13	Evaluation can be done effectively by using ICT	30%	50%	12%	8%	0%
14	ICT facilitates collaborative work among students and teachers	35%	55%	10%	0%	0%
15	ICT enhances teaching-learning in a dynamic way by expanding the body of knowledge and covering new domains of quality education	38%	58%	4%	0%	0%
16	ICT provides the facility to conduct learning sessions with a large number of students	28%	55%	12%	5%	0%

Legend: SA-Strongly Agree; A-Agree; UD-Undecided; D-Disagree; SD-Strongly Disagree.

Table 8.1, shows that nearly 90% (50%, SA, 40% A) of pre-service teachers agreed, that ICT is one of the effective sources of the teaching-learning process. Whereas 10% were undecided and none of the selected subjects were found to disagree with it.

On the examination of the responses of Item 2, i.e., 'Use of ICT creates effective teaching skills', it found that nearly 85% (30% SA, 55% A) pre-service teachers agreed that the use of technologies brings changes in their teaching-learning strategies, whereas 10% were undecided and 5% disagree about this statements.

The analysis of the responses to Item 3, i.e., 'ICT integrated lecture have that scope to cover the content in the best possible manner' revealed that nearly 78% (28% SA, 50% A) of pre-service teachers agreed with it, whereas, 20% were undecided, and 2% of them found disagreeing regarding this item.

On observing the responses to Item 4, i.e., 'ICT enhances active involvement of learners', it was found that nearly 90% (40% SA, 50% A) agreed with it, whereas, 10% were undecided, and none disagreed with the statement.

The responses to Item 5, i.e., 'Use of ICT promotes creativity among learners' showed that nearly 78% (33%SA, 45%A) of pre-service teachers agreed with it, whereas, 15% were undecided, and 7% disagreed with it.

Analyzing the responses to Item 6, i.e., 'ICT is a constructive tool for teaching-learning', it was found that nearly 85% (40% SA, 45% A) agreed with it, whereas 10% were undecided, and 5% disagreed with it.

As far as Item 7 is concerned which reads as 'Communication becomes effective by using ICT in the classroom', the responses indicate that nearly 92% (38% SA, 54% A) agreed with it, 8% were undecided, and 6.5% disagreed with it.

The responses to Item 8, i.e., 'Transfer of knowledge could be more effective by using ICT' showed that nearly 87% (27% SA, 60% A) agreed with it, whereas, 13% were undecided.

The analysis of the responses to Item 9, i.e., 'ICT makes complex and difficult lessons easy to understand' indicated that nearly 89% (34% SA, 55% A) agreed with it, whereas 8% were undecided and rest of them 3% disagree with that statement.

On observing the responses to item no. 10, i.e., 'ICT enables students to express their ideas and thoughts in a better way, it was found that nearly 98% (47% SA, 51% A) agreed with it, whereas 2% undecided.

The analysis of responses to Item 11 which was 'Students pay more attention in class when teachers teach a lesson through ICT' revealed that nearly 88% (25%SA, 63% A) agreed with it, whereas, 10% were undecided, and 2% disagreed with it.

On examining the responses of Item 12, i.e., 'ICT can help in making effective lesson plans, the responses indicate that nearly 91% (38%SA 53% A) agreed with it, whereas 9% were undecided and 0% disagreed with the statement.

The observation of responses to Item 13, i.e., 'Evaluation can be done effectively by using ICT' showed that nearly 80% (30% SA, 50% A) agreed with it, whereas 12% were undecided and 8% disagreed with it.

The responses to Item 14, i.e., 'ICT facilitates collaborative work among students and teachers, indicated that nearly 90% (35% SA, 55% A) agreed with it, whereas 10% were undecided.

Analysis of responses to Item 15 which stated, 'ICT dynamically enhances teaching-learning by expanding the body of knowledge and covering new domains of quality education' revealed that nearly 96% (38% SA, 58% A) agree with it, whereas,4% were undecided about it. None of the respondents found disagreed with it.

By examining the responses of respondent Item 16 which was, 'ICT provides facility to conduct learning sessions with a large number of students', it was found that nearly 83% (28% SA, 55% A) agree that the ICT provides facility to inculcate learning with a large number of students in the classroom, while 12 % were undecided and 5% disagree on the statement.

Major Findings with Discussion

The research shows that the educational landscape of the country is getting murkier through the ICT interventions; the syllabus, curriculum and policies are monitored by ICT. This study indicated that the pre-service teachers are effectively adopting ICT skills in their learning-process which enhances the quality of education and makes a degree efficient. The traditional modes of teaching are now upgraded through innovative skills; the teacher education programmes placed a pivotal role in providing efficient teachers to the educational institutions so, the teachers should be techno-friendly and techno-orientated. Therefore, ICT orientation makes pre-service teachers effective and qualitative. Researchers have shown that ICT can enhance students' content knowledge, involve them in creating their knowledge, and support the development of complex thinking skills when it is successfully incorporated into a high-quality learning environment (Kozma, 2005; Kulik, 2003; Webb & Cox, 2004).

ICT pedagogical skills place significant role in shaping the further agenda which enhances the quality based education, smart work, effective time management and participatory involvement of teachers and students. Henceforth, the finding shows that the effective roles of ICT pedagogical skills are vital in teacher education programme and also create possibilities of accessible education. In today's technological environment, traditional teaching methods are dwindling. The traditional and less creative teaching methods have declined as a result of ICT. Although the operation of ICT is hegemonic in today's technologically oriented societies and academic spaces, students and parents prefer ICT-oriented learning and teaching. Due to the rise of innovative teaching methods that offer more opportunities and comfortable learning environments, chalk and blackboard instruction is now more prevalent (Siddiqui *et al.*, 2021).

Conclusion

ICT is now recognized as a ground-breaking tool that has significantly influenced nation-building. People can now access ICT not only in first- and second-world countries, but also in third-world countries where it is ingrained in the culture. ICT resources must now be used effectively and efficiently if a teaching-learning process is to be effective in instilling 21st century skills. ICT use in pre-service teacher education is progressive and improves the quality of the teaching-learning process, according to this study's indication that the empirical findings are substantiated by secondary sources. An empirical finding suggests that pre-service teachers are at ease in environments focused on ICT and it is imperative to note that ICT based learning enhances pedagogical skills, quality improvement, constructive learning, creativity, digital education etc. Future teachers are moving with techno-fashioned leanings so they can easily implement in future teaching-learning process. It is crucial to remember that there are a number of drawbacks to ICT-based learning, which must be compassionately addressed by key stakeholders.

References

20th Annual Report. (2014-2015). National Council of Educational Research and Training. Retrieved form. https://ncte.gov.in/website/PDF/AnnualReport/2014-15.pdf

Ahmad, J., (2018). Teacher education in India: A critical analysis. *Voices of Teachers and Teacher Educators, 6* (1).

Amutha, D. (2020). The role and impact of ICT in improving the quality of education. *EngRN: Electronic. Available at SSRN 3585228.*

Bassi, R. (2011). ICTs in education (ICT4E) policies and plans worldwide. *Global e-School and Communities Initiative (GeSCI).*

Balanskat, A. (2008). *National policies and case studies on the use of portfolios in teacher training.* Online available https://en.unesco.org/icted/content/icts-education-policies-and-plans-worldwide

Bajwa, S.B. (2003). ICT Policy in India in the era of liberalisation: Its impact and consequences. *Global Business and Economic Review (GBER), 3* (2), 49-61.

Birch, A., & Irvine, V. (2009). Pre-service teachers' acceptance of ICT integration in the classroom: Applying the UTAUT model. *Educational Media International, 46*(4), 295-315.

Biswas, A. (2021). Recommendations of commissions and committees on LIS education in India: An analytical study. Project: A Critical Study on the Recommendations of Commissions and committees. DOI: 10.13140/RG.2.2.24807.16800.

Darra, M. (2006). Productivity Improvements in Education: A replay. *European Research Studies, 9*(3).

Darling-Hammond, L., & Snyder, J. (2015). Meaningful learning in a new paradigm for educational accountability: An introduction. *Education Policy Analysis Archives,* 23, 7.

Government of India. MHRD. (1968). National Policy on Education. Retrieved from https://www.education.gov.in/sites/upload_files/mhrd/files/document-reports/NPE-1968.pdf

Government of India, MHRD (1986). National Policy on Education. Retrieved from https://www.education.gov.in/sites/upload_files/mhrd/files/upload_document/npe.pdf

Government of India, MHRD (2020). National Policy Education 2020. Retrieved from https://www.education.gov.in/sites/upload_files/mhrd/files/NEP_Final_English_0.pdf

Honan, E. (2008). Barriers to teachers using digital texts in literacy classrooms. *Literacy*, *42*(1), 36-43.

Kulik, J.A. (2003). Effects of using instructional technology in elementary and secondary schools: What controlled evaluation studies say. Arlington, VA: Sri International.

Kozma, R.B. (2005). National policies that connect ICT-based education reform to economic and social development. *Human Technology: An interdisciplinary journal on humans in ICT environments.*

Levin, B. (1993). Students and educational productivity. *Education Policy Analysis Archives*, 1, 5-5.

Mahashevta (2017). Review of ICT Policies in India. *International Journal of Education & Research*, *7* (1), 1-10.

Mathew, A. (2016). Reforms in Higher Education in India: A Review of Recommendations of Commission and Committees on Education. Centre for Policy Research in Higher Education. NUEPA, New Delhi.

Ministry of Information and Broadcasting (1969-1972). Government of India, Patiala House, New Delhi.http://14.139.60.153/bitstream/123456789/11384/1/FOURTH%20FIVE%20YEAR%20PLAN%201969-74_SUMMARY_G-1183.pdf

Mooij, T. (2007). Design of educational and ICT conditions to integrate differences in learning: Contextual learning theory and a first transformation step in early education. *Computers in Human Behavior, 23*(3), 1499-1530.

National Council for Teacher Education (NCTE) (2010). National Curriculum Framework for Teacher Education. Retrieved from http://ncteindia.org/ncte_new/pdf/NCFTE_2010.pdf

Rao, J.P., & Prasad, R.S. (2016). Educational Technology Policies in India and Access. Retrieved from https://oasis.col.org/colserver/api/core/bitstreams/ddb867d5-8709-4c79-9647-8ccf7b451fcf/content

Ross, A.M. (1979). Education and National Development. *India International Centre*, *6*(4), 307-315.

Sarkar, S., Mohapatra, S., & Sundarakrishnan, J. (2017). ICT Policies for Primary Education and Different Initiatives Taken in India. In *Information and Communications Technology in Primary School Education*, pp. 163-193. Springer, Cham.

Schwerdt, G., & Wuppermann, A.C. (2011). Is traditional teaching really all that bad? A within-student between-subject approach. *Economics of Education Review*, *30*(2), 365-379.

Shankdher, S.L. (1967). Comments and reactions—a study Report of the education.

Siddiqui, S.A., Alam, M.A., Javed Azmi, M., Ahmad, O., Wiquar, R., & Aziz, A. (2021). Integration of ICT-learning Environments: A paradigm Shift from Traditional Teaching Pattern. *ICIDSSD 2020*, 275.

The Gazette of India Extraordinary Norms (2014). National Council for Teacher Education. Retrieved from. https://ncte.gov.in/WebAdminFiles/RCDownloadMaterial/NormsE-2014.pdf

UNESCO (2005). Convention on the Protection and Promotion of the Diversity of Cultural Expressions. Retrieved from https://en.unesco.org/creativity/sites/creativity/files/info-kit_brochure-final-en-web.pdf

UNESCO (2009). Competency Standards for Teachers: Policy Framework.

UNESCO (2011). ICT Competency framework. Retrieved from https://ictedupolicy.org/resource-library/resource-library/unesco-ictcompetencyframework-teachers

Webb, M., & Cox, M. (2004). A review of pedagogy related to information and communications technology. *Technology, Pedagogy and Education*, *13*(3), 235-286.

9
ICT Trends in Education

Shafeeqa Bano

Introduction

If the computer games industry can get millions of children to see themselves as player developers, how could we instill some of that culture of disciplined self-help and creativity into the education system? When children play computer games they feel part of the action; too often, at school they feel as if they are being "done to". (Leadbetter 2006).

The past three decades have seen the rapid development of new and emerging technologies revolutionizing the way we live, work and learn. Where Information and Communications Technologies are concerned, policy and practice do not appear to converge into a coherent strategy to move learning forward in an inclusive way, addressing the needs of all. As the divisions between wealth and poverty become more visible, there is recognition that individuals from some backgrounds are less likely to achieve in schools. Large numbers of young people are rejecting school and further learning. Numbers who can be categorized as "not in education, employment or training" in the 16 to 25 year old age range are increasing. This same group is overrepresented in the increasing prison population. Against this backdrop, there is an expansion of the European

Union which has lead to an unprecedented number of economic migrants to some areas increasing pressure on housing, education and infrastructure whilst language and textual literacy remains a barrier to skilled employment.

Need of ICT in Education

Significant skills are needed to use the products of a digital world, but education it seems has been left behind in this new technological age because it has not fully embraced the digital revolution for a complexity of reasons. Many schools have failed to implement ICT policy due to an embedded cultural resistance to new technologies, which have not always been viewed as valuable. Although widespread change has become more apparent, it has been largely infrastructural rather than pedagogical and the needs of learners have been marginalized. Pedagogical practice has not kept pace with an increasingly technological society and remains the root of disaffection from education by young people. Because new technologies are integrated into our lives, they represent a powerful tool for learning which is often unrecognized and undervalued. Activities which are fun and enjoyable such as the use of computer games are often considered to be leisure and not learning. Collaborative discussion online as a precursor to or even an integral part of learning is frequently not accepted as valuable. Similar activities conducted face to face, such as group work and discussion in the classroom are considered to be good practice. Virtual learning environments in schools are increasingly commonplace, but often represent content push models that reflect a culture which continues to focus substantially on teaching rather than learning and delivery rather than participation. The tendency here is often to attempt to recreate online the same fixed delivery approach of traditional pedagogies offering little more than a digital version of classroom texts with little flexibility, less portability and often at greater expense.

Text, toys and tools

Technological developments and the market penetration of digital devices have accelerated faster than any accompanying educational or pedagogical change. The concept of ICT has broadened and is now often referred to in some forums as digital technologies. The notion of the digital divide is no longer being discussed solely in terms of lack of access to technology but in terms of bandwidth. Inclusion is often considered in terms of digital inclusion. A whole new technological language has become embedded in our vocabulary, with phrases such as text speaks and digital immigrant in common use. Notably, the term digital native is reserved for those who have grown up with new technologies, unlike the current generation of educators.

The development of Wikipedia, blogs, podcasting and free online communities such as MySpace, You-Tube and even Friends Reunited are raising questions and challenges to academics about the nature of learning and how to analyze and how to draw meaningful conclusions from non-static and non-textual electronic data. Even text itself offers cultural and contextual challenges with the widespread popular use by teenage culture of patois, text speaks and African American Vernacular English popularized by rap music. A new generation of teenagers expects access to computers, mobile phones, programmable videos and CD players in their day to day life, whilst the culture in our schools continues to restrict that access, seeing them to be of limited educational value. Nevertheless, access to some of these tools demands problem solving an ability and higher level ICT skills.

The need for ICT in education is to create a learning environment that focuses on students. ICT tools address the gap between teacher and learner-centred environment. As ICT gives access to a wide range of information, all students unique educational requirements are met. Teacher can access the use of such information through quizzes and exams.

Teacher can find adequate supplementary material off the internet for students who require extra attention. Using ICT, teachers can share those materials either with entire classroom or with individual learners.

Evolution of Education (1.0-4.0)

Education 1.0

Education 1.0 reflects an authoritarian teaching setting where the student is only a passive recipient of the concepts or ideas taught by the respective teacher within a physical classroom setting. It forbids the use of any type of technological application. The teacher acts as a knowledge leader and determines the most significant topics for the student to learn without having any regard in understanding the learning interests and needs of students.

Education 2.0

The Education 2.0 reflects the growth of communication and teacher-student interactivity within the physical classroom setting. Here, the involvement of technology for sharing learning resources can be effectively observed in terms of using broadcasting mediums like television and radios for designing and communicating learning programmes. Likewise, the use of a projector in class is also observed for the rendering of learning materials via slides.

Education 3.0

The Education 3.0 is essentially student-centric where the teacher acts as a facilitator and advisor. The Education 3.0 setting involves a blend of both classroom and online-based teaching practices. This type of teaching framework is driven by factors like self-directed learning, problem-solving activities, needed creativity, and potential interactivity between the teachers and students.

Information Technology (IT) is extensively used in the teaching process for the development of approaches like blended learning, flipped classrooms, and also the development of e-learning platforms. Learning resources that can be accessed by the students based on their convenience are shared by the teachers online.

Though both blended and flipped learning approaches reflect a combination of both physical and online learning and instructional modes yet the latter involves greater interactivity between the student and teacher.

Education 4.0

Education 4.0 is regarded as the most innovative platform that is noted in terms of the Evolution of the Education. The framework of Education 4.0 is still in its developmental stage that focuses on enabling students to carry out learning irrespective of time and place. Education 4.0 encourages the carrying out of project-based and practical learning approaches wherein the students are evaluated rather than being examined as done in the traditional frameworks.

The use of social networking platforms like YouTube for the development of learning videos; use of Zoom platforms for conducting webinars involving teachers, students, and experts coming from diverse industries; use of Artificial Intelligence (AI) for generating instantaneous responses to students are some effective examples of the Education 4.0.

The appearance of new technologies in our day to day life has made it possible for the use of ICT in education to increase considerably in recent years. ICTs have gained great relevance in our environment, in various sectors such as entertainment, administration, education and all kinds of companies.

ICT Trends in Education

When we talk about ICT we are referring to information and communication technologies. ICT is "a set of techniques and devices based on new technological tools and the different supports and channels of information and communication". It help in the process of obtaining, storing, processing and transmitting information digitally. ICT is already becoming a fundamental tool for new teachers and students in the classroom.

Discussions with experts and readings of the latest researches and reports identified ten of the latest trends that will affect learning. Of these trends that were identified in the year 2000, three are directly relevant to ICT.

These are:

- **Technology-Smart Curricula:** Technology is increasingly becoming integrated into the school curriculum. The current goal is to help teachers learn how to use the computer as a tool to teach English, mathematics, science and other subjects.
- **The Digital Divide:** This refers to the chasm in technological know-how between the haves and have-not. There are many on-going efforts to bridge the chasm. These efforts range from collaborative efforts aimed at providing the massive funding required, to capability building programmes for utilizing ICT.
- **Distance Learning via Internet:** There is a clear direction towards using the Internet to open education to students everywhere. The use of the Internet ranges from making course materials available on-line, to using the Internet as the communication tool for the course.

Trends in Educational Technology.

- Computers in schools
- Networking
- Television in the school
- Smart panel
- Advocacy for educational technology
- New delivery systems for educational technology
- Technology literacy for teachers
- Educational technology and educational reform

It is worth noting that advocacy and educational reform, as they relate to technology, are among the trends. Most trends have been about the hardware, the software, and their applications. This could indicate growing awareness of the political and social environment that is needed for technology use to flourish.

Conclusion

Although education has focused on what it feels children need to be taught, it has paid scant attention to learning in its variety of forms, yet young people have used new technologies to develop how they learn using a range of ICT tools for innovation and creativity. Much of this learning has taken place at home because most schools do not recognize the value of many of these new ICT devices and web based environments. It appears that the very fabric of the education system has failed to fully recognize the value of computer technologies in learning.

ICT has revolutionized the way the education industry functions. The importance of ICT in the education sector is huge, and soon it will be an integral part of all school systems. Along with implementing the tools, it is necessary to train the educator to harness the true potential of ICT. Digital literacy among teachers and students transforms the way we use technology to learn. With ICT, we can build school systems that are more efficient, cost-effective, and inclusive of everyone.

Since our educational system has for too long been a one-size-fits-all structure, it also raises questions about the ethos of education, the structure of the curriculum, and its suitability for sustaining ourselves as a society both economically and environmentally in the 21st Century. It is difficult to predict how education will change over the next decade let alone the next century, but there will most certainly be changes in pedagogies which more readily recognize the way young people learn with new technologies. Learning outcomes and measurable outputs will need to adapt to reflect this.

Technology has disrupted all areas of our life and education is no different. Especially after the pandemic, more schools are looking towards online learning as a permanent teaching method along with traditional classroom teaching. But while most of the institutes have used some form of online teaching in the past year, they lack a systematic approach to virtual learning. ICT opens a world of possibilities for the betterment of the education sector.

References

Court of Auditors (2006). Special Report. Official Journal of the European Union, no.1/2006 Available from:http://www.eca.europa.eu/audit_reports/special_reports/docs /2006/rs01_06en.pdf

Dooley, K. (1999). Towards a Holistic Model for the Diffusion of Educational Technologies: An Integrative Review of Educational Innovation Studies.

Handy, C. (1997). Schools for life and work, in Living Education, Edited by Mortimore, P. and Little, V., 1997.

Jervis, A. and Steeg, T. (2000:1). University of Manchester Using the Internet in Schools 1997-1999.

Kitching, R. and Morgan, S. (2001). Violence, Truancy and School Exclusion in France and Britain

Leadbetter, C. (2006). Are you thinking what I'm thinking? The Times Online October 13, 2006, p.1. Available from: http://technology.timesonline.co.uk/article/0,,20411-2400772.html

Mintz, J. (1999). The Education Revolution. *Education now*, issue 27, Spring 2000.

Mori (2005). Young people and Mobile Phones.[online]. Available from: polls/2004/nestlesrp3.shtml [accessed January 2006].

National Literacy Trust (2005). citing Child Poverty Action Group Britain Divided. Available from:http://www.literacytrust.org.uk/Database/stats/poorexam.html#No%20GCSE.

Owers, S. (2001). The place and perception of technology in the curriculum. Current Developments in Technology-Assisted Education (2006) 139.

Prensky, M. (2004). Capturing the Value of "Generation Tech" Employee. [Online].Available from:http://www.strategy-business.com/media/file/enews

S. *et al.* (2006). E-learning Nordic 2006—Impact of ICT on Education.

Sidnell, J. (2006). African American Vernacular English.[online]. Available from: http://www.une.edu.au/ langnet/aave.htm.

Tan, V. (2000). Lessons from Cultural Change. Available from: http://adtimes.nstp.com.my/ jobstory/aug26a.htm.

10

Impact of COVID-19 on Students

An Analysis of Pandemic Scenario and Way Forward

Prasenjit Das and *Nakul Barman*

Introduction

The World Health Organization (WHO) announced the corona virus infection (COVID-19) a pandemic on March 11, 2020, and recommended a number of measures to lessen its impact on the population (Concepción & Romero, 2022). Eventually, this deadly virus spread around the globe and was called a pandemic. The world's factories, businesses, transit systems, agriculture activities, and educational institutions are all closed for the moment. As a consequence, lives of people all over the globe quickly changed (Das & Singha, 2022). Due to school closures, social isolation, and the transition to fully online or blended learning, it has significantly impacted students' well-being (Valladolid, 2021). They have experienced a lot of stress as a result of being quarantined at home and worrying about contracting the illness. Numerous researches have shown that the experience of studying at home has a significant impact on students' subjective well-being (Treviño *et al.*, 2021). In this area, research has suggested that the quantity and difficulty of college assignments and homework are predictors of well-being; specifically, when the work load at a college or university is high and/or difficult, it has been linked with a decrease in subjective well-being during the pandemic (Abreu *et al.*, 2021). Additionally, learning activities are related negatively with behavioral issues (such as emotional symptoms, hyperactivity/inattention, and issues with peer relationships) (Tso *et al.*, 2022). Additionally, students who report having better home learning experiences admit to having less emotional reactions as well as fewer cognitive responses (Larsen *et al.*, 2022). This significant issue with online teaching and learning draws attention to the system's inadequacies even more. Higher education students thus encountered a wide range of difficulties and troubles in the new learning environment. As a consequence, higher education students across the globe encounter major obstacles while attempting to continue their studies and research (Das & Singha, 2022). As a result, the focus of this study is on the impact of COVID-19 on subjective well-being by higher education students in the pandemic outbreak.

Review of Related Literature

In this study, the researcher examined and summarized the vast majority of relevant research papers on the impact of COVID-19 on students' subjective well-being that had been done in India and abroad.

In order to determine the impact of the COVID-19 on the subjective well-being dimension, Bonomi *et al.* (2021) conducted a study on deprivation and subjective well-being. According to the study's findings, spatial clustering of disadvantages and neighborhood inequalities has gotten worse as a result of the pandemic. A further research by Cheng and Kim (2020) found that those who reported a decrease in family income during the COVID-19 epidemic also experienced a loss in overall life satisfaction. According to Arabia *et al.* (2020), social withdrawal and self-isolation demands are stressful and harmful for many people, which has led to concerns about students' health and well-being. Positive affect may encourage people to adopt information-processing strategies during the COVID-19 outbreak, as per

Blasco-belled *et al.* (2020)'s research. On the other hand, Mayara *et al.* (2021) looked at correlations between study circumstances and depressed symptoms and discovered that generalised linear regression suggests that better student mental health was connected to stronger confidence in finishing the semester. A different study by Kimhi *et al.*, (n.d.), revealed multidimensional harm and a notable decline in the population's resilience on the individual, community, and national levels. Hu *et al.*, (n.d.) investigations into perceived lifestyle changes and their relationship to subjective well-being (SWB) revealed both positive and unfavorable effects on various aspects of lifestyle choices. Contrarily, Brindal *et al.* (2021) found that in order to promote behaviors that are protective of well-being, it will be critical to understand why and who may be differentially affected. The results of a different study by Mutz & Mutz from 2021 indicate that the COVID-19 pandemic negatively impacted the mental well-being of the populace in Germany. In their investigation into the crucial factor affecting children's subjective well-being, Treviño *et al.* (2021) discovered that parents' socio-economic status is a significant predictor of both formal and informal parental practices. Psychosocial intervention studies can improve students' subjective well-being, according to Gundogan (2021). Krautter *et al.* (2021) claim that significant life events or psychological interventions may result in changes in personality and subjective well-being (SWB). In another study by Zhou and Yu (2021), online learning self-efficacy partially mediates the beneficial effects of social support on well-being. Sood & Sharma (2021) discovered that the higher education industry has a number of practical ramifications for academics, mental health professionals, and counselling psychologists. The second wave of COVID-19 in late 2020 showed considerably decreased well-being, according to Hansen *et al.* (2022). According to Sarasjärvi *et al.* (2022), higher education institutions may be essential in ensuring students' well-being in times of anxiety.

Research Gap

Numerous studies have been conducted to identify the various factors that have an impact on the higher education students' subjective well-being during a pandemic outbreak using a variety of relevant studies from around the world. However, no study has made an attempt to look at the subjective well-being of higher education in West Bengal's Uttar Dinajpur district under a pandemic scenario. As a consequence, there is a research gap in this area. In order to identify the variables that have an impact on college students' subjective well-being, the researcher used the standardized College Student Subjective Well-being Questionnaire (CSSWQ), developed by Renshaw (2020). As a result, this study's goals, contexts, samples, and methods of implementation will not be the same to previous studies.

Objectives of the Study

The researcher has set the following objectives for the study:

- To study the mean differences between male & female students in terms of their subjective well-being.
- To study the mean differences between UG, PG level students in terms of their subjective well-being.
- To study the mean differences between rural and urban students in terms of their subjective well-being.
- To study the mean differences between nuclear and joint family students in terms of their subjective well-being.
- To study the relationship between age and subjective well-being among the higher education students.

Hypotheses of the Study

$H_0$1: There exist no significant mean differences between the male & female students in terms of their subjective well-being in COVID-19 pandemic.

$H_0$2: There exists no significant mean difference between UG & PG students in terms of their subjective well-being in COVID-19 pandemic.

$H_0$3: There exists no significant mean difference between rural and urban students in terms of their subjective well-being in COVID-19 pandemic.

$H_0$4: There exists no significant mean difference between nuclear and joint family students in terms of their subjective well-being in COVID-19 pandemic.

$H_0$5: There exists no significant relationship between age and subjective well-being among the higher education students in Uttar Dinajpur District.

Methodology of the study

Nature of the Study

The investigator used a descriptive survey method for the current study. The researcher has collected data in quantitatively and also analyzes that.

Population of the Study

For the purpose of this study, the population has been defined as all higher education students enrolled in UG and PG programmes in the Uttar Dinajpur district of West Bengal for the current academic year.

Sample of the Study

For the present study, the researcher's sample consisted only of 103 students from various higher education institutions in the Uttar Dinajpur district.

Sampling Technique

The technique of random sampling was employed for selecting the sample. The researcher initially has chosen a variety of higher education institutions in the district of Uttar Dinajpur. Then, in order to get accurate, genuine, and unbiased data, the researcher randomly choose 103 students from higher education institutions.

Tools used for the study

Renshaw created the 16-item College Student Subjective Well-being Questionnaire (CSSWQ) in 2020 as an evidence-based rating scale for evaluating the well-being of college students (Zhang & Renshaw, 2020). It consists of four sub scales: academic efficacy, school connectedness, academic satisfaction, and college gratitude. According to a seven-point Likert scale, the items are scored as follows: strongly disagree = 1, disagree = 2, slightly disagree = 3, neutral = 4, slightly agree = 5, agree = 6, and strongly agree = 7. For every item, there is no reserve scoring. The total sub scale score is divided by the number of items in each sub scale to get the score on each sub scale. If the academic satisfaction sub scale score is 8, then the average item response can be interpreted as "sometimes" experiencing academic satisfaction as follows: 8 (total sub scale score)/4 (total number of items in sub-scale) = 2. The composite score for each sub-scale, which is also derived by dividing the total score by the scale's total item count of 16, represents the subjective well-being of college students as a whole (Renshaw & Bolognino, 2016).

Findings of the Study

Presentation of Data

$H_0 1$: There exist no significant mean differences between the male & female students in terms of their subjective well-being in COVID-19 pandemic.

Table 10.1: Summary of the Mean and SD in subjective well-being of higher education students

Demographic Variables		Number (N)	Mean (M)	SD(σ)	Test Employed
Gender	Male	49	5.62	1.01	t-test
	Female	54	5.67	.87	

Demographic Variables		Number (N)	Mean (M)	SD(σ)	Test Employed
Course	UG	33	5.65	.97	t-test
	PG	70	5.64	.92	
Residence	Rural	76	5.61	.92	t-test
	Urban	27	5.76	1.00	
Family Type	Nuclear	70	5.73	.73	t-test
	Joint	33	5.46	1.26	

Table 10.2: The significant mean difference between Male and Female Students in terms of their subjective well-being in covid-19 pandemic

Sex	N	Mean	Std. Deviation	df	t-value	Significance (2-tailed)
Male	49	5.62	1.01	101	0.26	.790
Female	54	5.67	0.87			

The above Table shows that the average subjective well-being score for female students was greater than that for male students (M=5.67, SD=0.87). It also found that the calculated 't'-value is 0.26 and it is less than the critical value at 0.05 level of significance with 101 degree of freedom (df). We may thus draw the conclusion that there is no significant mean difference between male and female students considering their Subject well-being in a pandemic outbreak

$H_0 2$: There exists no significant mean difference between UG & PG level students in terms of their subjective well-being in COVID-19 pandemic.

Table 10.3: The significant mean difference between UG & PG level students in terms of their subjective well-being in covid-19 pandemic

Education Level	N	Mean	Std. Deviation	df	t-value	Significance (2-tailed)
UG	33	5.65	0.97	101	0.31	.975
PG	70	5.64	0.92			

Table 10.3 shows that undergraduate students were found to have a slightly higher subjective well-being (M=5.65, SD=.97) than postgraduate students (M=5.64, SD=.92). Additionally, it discovered that the computed "t"-value is 0.31, which is less than the critical value at 0.05 level of significance with 101 degree of freedom (df). We may thus draw the conclusion that there is no significant mean difference between UG and PG level students regarding their subject well-being in a pandemic condition.

$H_0$3: There exists no significant mean difference between rural and urban students in terms of their subjective well-being in COVID-19 pandemic.

Table 10.4: The significant mean difference between Rural and Urban students in terms of their subjective well-being in covid-19 pandemic

Residence	N	Mean	Std. Deviation	df	t-value	Significance (2-tailed)
Rural	76	5.61	0.92	101	0.70	.480
Urban	27	5.76	1.00			

Table 10.5 shows that students in urban areas scored higher on subjective well-being (M=5.76, SD=1.00) than students in rural areas (M=5.61, SD=.92). Additionally, it discovered that the computed "t"-value is 0.70, which is less than the critical value at 0.05 level of significance with 101 degree of freedom (df). We can therefore draw the conclusion that there is no significant difference between the subject well-being of rural and urban students in a pandemic situation.

$H_0$4: There exists no significant mean difference between nuclear and joint family students in terms of their subjective well-being in COVID-19 pandemic.

Table 10.5: The significant mean difference between nuclear and joint family students in terms of their subjective well-being in COVID-19 pandemic

Family Type	N	Mean	Std. Deviation	df	t-value	Significance (2-tailed)
Nuclear	70	5.73	0.73	101	1.39	.167
Joint	33	5.46	1.26			

Table 10.5 shows that students from nuclear families score slightly higher on subjective well-being (M=5.73, SD=.73) than students from joint families (M=5.46, SD=1.26). Additionally, it discovered that the computed "t"-value is 1.39, which is less than the critical value at 0.05 level of significance with 101 degree of freedom (df). We can therefore draw the conclusion that there is no significant difference between students from nuclear and joint families regarding their subject well-being in a pandemic situation.

$H_0 5$: There exists no significant relationship between age and subjective well-being among the higher education students in Uttar Dinajpur District.

Table 10.6: Showing the relationship between age and subjective well-being among the higher education students in Uttar Dinajpur District

Age & Subjective well-being	
Age	Subjective well-being score
1	.096
	.334
103	103

Table 10.6 shows that Pearson coefficient of correlation was computed between age and subjective well-being score of the students. There was a very weak negative correlation between age and subjective well-being, which indicates that as age increased, their subjective well-being slightly decreased.

Discussion

It was discovered that the subjective well-being mean score for female students was higher (M=5.67, SD=0.87) than it was for male students (M=5.62, SD=1.01). However, it was also shown that there were no significant differences between male and female students in terms of their subject's well-being during pandemic outbreak.

The researcher discovered that students of undergraduate level found to have slightly more subjective well-being (M=5.65, SD=.97) than students at postgraduate level (M=5.64, SD=.92). It also found that there is no significant difference among the UG and

PG level Students regarding their Subject well-being in pandemic situation.

The researcher found that students of urban area subjective well-being score was higher (M=5.76, SD=1.00) than the students of rural area (M=5.61, SD=.92). It also found that there is no significant difference among the Rural and Urban Students regarding their Subject well-being in pandemic situation.

In the present study, it was discovered that students from nuclear families had a slightly higher subjective well-being score (M=5.73, SD=.73) than students from joint families (M=5.46, SD=1.26). Additionally, it was shown that there is no significant difference between students from joint and nuclear families in terms of their subject well-being during a pandemic.

The results of this study revealed a very weak negative correlation between the students' subjective well-being scores and age which indicating that with increasing age, subjective well-being slightly decreased.

Future Development and Way Forward

It is necessary to create specialized online modules that are focused on clearly defined skill areas and to carefully arrange blended learning activities. The apparent gap in teaching practical expertise may be filled by gaining access to tele-health exchanges in addition to online learning courses. We need to create more innovative teaching-learning techniques based on adult learning principles rather than only attending online courses (Carracedo & Pintor, 2016). We must take advantage of this once-in-a-lifetime moment, when major abrupt changes are occurring in all spheres of life. If this rapid transition is maintained in the direction of future trends in optometry practice, it will provide advantageous results in the years to come (Rajhans *et al.*, 2020). The ideal environment for institutional change is created by COVID-19. Realizing the value of using technology in the teaching-learning process, it opens up chances for the education sector to investigate new technologies. Each institution has to build an online mode of education as a substitute mode for the teaching-learning process, together with a curriculum that is geared towards education, modern technology, designated faculty, and proactive administration. The use of technology in education involves more than just using technological tools; it also involves using resources methodically, rationally, and with the appropriate pedagogy in order to successfully convert knowledge and skills.

It is still too early to predict how a COVID-19 pandemic may affect the whole planet. Some industries, like airline, lodging, and tourists, are becoming more exposed to its impacts. The education sector is one of the most significant industries since it is linked to the birth, development, and success of hundreds of thousands of children and youth. The COVID-19 pandemic has been severely hurting people's lives and economies in practically every aspect. Recognizing the above realities, large number of research rooms are available to investigating its effects, possibilities, and risks during the pandemic period, merging productive and meaningful like interaction with peers, individual development of the students, self-control and multi-tasking skills, desire to know, student interest, willingness to take responsibility, ability to focus, ability to respond to change and mistake, instructor perceptions, instructional strategies, and so many others (Gautam & Gautam, 2021).

Being from India, we are sick of hearing how expensive great education is—we know first-hand—but because to growing e-learning trends and resources, access to an education will no longer be a barrier for those who are less privileged or from low-income families. Students may effectively and efficiently concentrate on developing skills or becoming job-ready while also identifying their own interests. The notion of e-learning is only emerging, and it has the ability to bring about the much-desired reform in India's whole educational system and provide the aspirant millennial a far better learning environment (Saha *et al.*, 2021).

References

Abreu, Pascale M.J. Engel De, *et al.* (2021). "Subjective Well-Being of Adolescents in Luxembourg, Germany, and Brazil During the COVID-19 Pandemic." *Journal of Adolescent Health*, Vol. 69, No. 2, Elsevier Inc., 2021, pp. 211-18, doi: 10.1016/j.jadohealth.2021.04.028.

Arabia, Saudi, *et al.* (2020). Mental Health and Well-Being during the COVID-19 Pandemic in Higher Education: Evidence from G20 Countries, pp. 60-68, doi:10.4081/jphr.2020.2010.

Blasco-belled, Ana, *et al.* (2020). The Costs of the COVID-19 on Subjective Well-Being: An Analysis of the Outbreak in Spain.

Bonomi, Franco, *et al.* (2021). The Combined Effect of Covid-19 and Neighbourhood Deprivation on Two Dimensions of Subjective Well-being: Empirical Evidence from England, pp. 1-19, doi:10.1371/journal.pone.0255156.

Brindal, Emily, *et al.* (2021). Individual Differences and Changes in Lifestyle Behaviours Predict Decreased Subjective Well-being during COVID-19 Restrictions in an Australian Sample, pp. 1-7, doi:10.1093/pubmed/fdab040.

Cao, Wenjun, *et al.* Since January 2020 Elsevier Has Created a COVID-19 Resource Centre with Free Information in English and Mandarin on the Novel Coronavirus COVID-19. The COVID-19 Resource Centre Is Hosted on Elsevier Connect, the Company's Public News and Information. No. January, 2020.

Concepción, José, and Gaxiola Romero (2022). Positive Family Environment, General Distress, Subjective Well-Being, and Academic Engagement among High School Students Before and During the COVID-19 Outbreak, doi:10.1177/01430343211066461.

Copeland, William E., *et al.* (2020). Impact of COVID-19 Pandemic on College Student. No. January, 2020.

Das, Prasenjit, and Raju Singha (2022). "Perception, Level of Satisfaction and Challenges Faced By Higher Education Learners of West Bengal: A Study in Covid-19 Perspective." *Towards Excellence*, Vol. 14, No. 2, pp. 1855-68, https://www.researchgate.net/publication/363295183

Eloff, Irma. (2021). "College students' well-being during the COVID-19 pandemic: An exploratory study." *Journal of Psychology in Africa*, 31.3 (2021): 254-260.

Gundogan, Selim (2022). "The relationship of covid-19 student stress with school burnout, depression and subjective well-being: Adaptation of the covid-19 student stress scale into turkish." *The Asia-Pacific Education Researcher* (2022): 1-12, doi:10.1007/s40299-021-00641-2.

Hansen, Thomas, *et al.* "Covid Fatigued/? A Longitudinal Study of Norwegian Older Adults' Psychosocial Well Being before and during Early and Later Stages of the COVID 19 Pandemic." *European Journal of Ageing*, Vol. 19, No. 3, Springer Netherlands, 2022, pp. 463-73, doi:10.1007/s10433-021-00648-0.

Hu, Zhao, *et al.* Impact of the COVID-19 Epidemic on Lifestyle Behaviors and Their Association With Subjective Well-Being Among the General Population in Mainland China: Cross-Sectional Study Corresponding Author: pp. 1-10, doi:10.2196/21176.

Huang, Liang, and Ting Zhang (2022). "Perceived Social Support, Psychological Capital, and Subjective Well-Being among College Students in the Context of Online Learning during the COVID-19 Pandemic." *The Asia-Pacific Education Researcher*, Vol. 31, No. 5, Springer Singapore, pp. 563-74, doi:10.1007/s40299-021-00608-3.

Huerta, Carolina Mayen, and Ariane Utomo (2021). "Health and Place Evaluating the Association between Urban Green Spaces and Subjective Well-Being in Mexico City during the COVID-19 Pandemic." *Health and Place*, Vol. 70, No. June, Elsevier Ltd., p. 102606, doi:10.1016/j.healthplace.2021.102606.

Kecojevic, Aleksandar, *et al.* (2020). The Impact of the COVID-19 Epidemic on Mental Health of Undergraduate Students in New Jersey, Cross-Sectional Study, pp. 1-16, doi:10.1371/journal.pone.0239696.

Kimhi, Shaul, *et al.* A Renewed Outbreak of the COVID-19 Pandemic: A Longitudinal Study of Distress, Resilience, and Subjective Well-Being.

Krautter, Kai, *et al.* No Party No Joy? — Changes in University Students' Extraversion, Neuroticism, and Subjective Well-Being during Two COVID-19 Lockdowns. no. December, 2021, pp. 1-19, doi:10.1111/aphw.12336.

Labrague, Leodoro J., and Janet Alexis A. De Los Santos. (2021). Social and Emotional Loneliness among College Students during the COVID-19 Pandemic: The Predictive Role of Coping Behaviours, Social Support, and Personal Resilience, pp. 1-16.

Larsen, Linda, *et al.* (2022). "The Impact of School Closure and Social Isolation on Children in Vulnerable Families during COVID-19: A Focus on Children's Reactions." *European Child & Adolescent Psychiatry*, Vol. 31, No. 8, Springer Berlin Heidelberg, 2022, pp. 1231-41, doi:10.1007/s00787-021-01758-x.

Marelli, Sara, *et al.* (2021). "Impact of COVID-19 Lockdown on Sleep Quality in University Students and Administration Staff." *Journal of Neurology*, Vol. 268, No. 1, Springer Berlin Heidelberg, pp. 8-15, doi:10.1007/s00415-020-10056-6.

Mayara, Paula, *et al.* (2021). Perceptions of Study Conditions and Depressive Symptoms During the COVID-19 Pandemic Among University Students in Germany: Results of the International COVID-19 Student Well-Being Study. No. June, 2021, doi:10.3389/fpubh.2021.674665.

Mutz, Michael, and Michael Mutz (2021). "Forced Adaptations of Sporting Behaviours during the Covid-19 Pandemic and Their Effects on Subjective Well-Being. Taylor & Francis, 2021, doi:10.1080/14616696.2020.1821077.

Renshaw, Tyler L., and Sarah J. Bolognino. (2016). "The College Student Subjective Well-being Questionnaire: A Brief, Multidimensional Measure of Undergraduate's Co-vitality." *Journal of Happiness Studies*, Springer Netherlands, pp. 463-84, doi:10.1007/s10902-014-9606-4.

Sarasjärvi, Kiira K., *et al.* (2022). Subjective Mental Well-Being among Higher Education Students in Finland during the First Wave of COVID-19. No. January, pp. 765-71, doi:10.1177/14034948221075433.

Sood, Sarita, and Ananya Sharma. Resilience and Psychological Well-Being of Higher Education Students During COVID-19: The Mediating Role of Perceived Distress. No. March 2020, 2021, doi:10.1177/0972063420983111.

Terence, C. Cheng, Seonghoon, Kim, Kanghyock, Koh (2020). The Impact of COVID-19 on Subjective Well-Being: Evidence from Singapore The Impact of COVID-19 on Subjective Well-being: Evidence from Singapore, No. 13702.

Treviño, Ernesto, *et al.* (2021). Socio-economic Status, Parental Involvement and Implications for Subjective Well-Being During the Global Pandemic of Covid-19. No. November, pp. 1-10, doi:10.3389/feduc.2021.762780.

Tso, Winnie W.Y., *et al.* (2022). "Vulnerability and Resilience in Children during the COVID-19 Pandemic." *European Child & Adolescent Psychiatry*, Vol. 31, No. 1, Springer Berlin Heidelberg, pp. 161-76, doi:10.1007/s00787-020-01680-8.

Valladolid, Violeta C. (2021). The Role of Coping Strategies in the Resilience and Well-Being of College Students during COVID-19 Pandemic. No. 2, pp. 30-42.

Zhang, Don, and Tyler L. Renshaw. (2019-20). Personality and College Student Subjective Well-being: A Domain-Specific Approach. No. April 2019, 2020, doi:10.1007/s10902-019-00116-8.

Zhou, Jihong, and Hongying Yu (2021). "Contribution of Social Support to Home Quarantined Chinese College Students' Well-being during the COVID-19 Pandemic: The Mediating Role of Online Learning Self Efficacy and Moderating Role of Anxiety." *Social Psychology of Education*, Vol. 24, No. 6, Springer Netherlands, pp. 1643-62, doi:10.1007/s11218-021-09665-4.

Section III
Transformation of Education in the Light of NEP 2020

11

Transforming Education Landscape through Massive Open Online Courses

Exploration through the lenses of Trainee Teachers

Sachi Jain and *Archana Anil*

Introduction

MOOC stands for Massive Open Online Course. A gigantic open online course, also known as an open online course, is an online course designed for open access and unlimited participation on the Internet. Massive Open Online Courses (MOOCs) are a modern thing in higher education that has seen significant growth and attracted a lot of interest from a variety of students, educators and teachers. The name "MOOC" was coined in 2008 by George Siemens and Stephen Downs, in part because Stanford professor Sebastian Thrum offered free courses in artificial intelligence in 2013. Over 500 people registered for this typically large MOOC (Pilli & Admiraal, 2016). Universities generally provide MOOCs in collaboration with companies like Coursera and Udacity. With more than 30 university partners, including Princeton, Brown, Columbia, Duke, Stanford, and Johns, Curser is the MOOC provider with the quickest rate of growth. It currently has 28 million students and registers 1.4 million new course registrations each month. Advocates of MOOCs believe that they can assist higher education institutions, teachers, and students in terms of education. Through a search engine like Google, Yahoo, etc., the resources are likewise freely available. The primary benefit of MOOCs is that students can use them for free.

Need of the Study

One of the pertinent areas where MOOCs are witnessing very strong integration is the area of 'Education' particularly with reference to the cognitive control and holistic sense of learning. Millions of people utilize MOOCs to learn for a variety of purposes, such as job progression, career change, college preparation, supplemental learning, lifelong learning, corporate eLearning & training, and more. MOOCs have significantly changed how people learn around the world. Researchers have also reported that mindfulness practice by school students results in engagement of learners who self-organise their participation according to learning goals, prior knowledge and skills, and common interests. Additionally, studies have shown that MOOCs significantly increase educational outcomes, which has a direct impact on higher education. Additionally, a 65% boost in educational results was attributed to MOOCs. MOOC providers offer paid certificates once you complete a MOOC, however, there are a few platforms that provide free certificates as well.

The most important goal when you are considering participation in online learning experiences through a MOOC is what you as the learner want to gain from the experience therefore one needs to make sure that they set their goals and find a method of learning that works well for them. MOOCs are one of many great learning sources and a great way to add more tools to your knowledge arsenal. Therefore, it seemed important at this juncture to conduct such a study that can explore the impact of MOOCs with reference to pre-service or trainee teachers who are the important stakeholders in the field of education.

Objectives of the study

1. To find the trainee teachers' level of awareness of the concept of MOOCs.
2. To study the experience of the trainee teachers while pursuing various MOOC courses.
3. To explore the trainee teachers' views concerning the practical aspects of MOOCs post the training programme.

Research Methodology

The present chapter is based on an explorative study which intends to find out the overall level of awareness about the concept of MOOCs among the trainee teachers both with reference to the theoretical aspects as well as applied aspects through a small survey.

Sample of the Study

For finding the awareness and usefulness of MOOCs among trainee teachers, we conducted a survey of which our participants were from first and second year of the B.Ed. programme.

Tool for Data Collection

The primary tool used for the data collection was a self-constructed questionnaire with open ended and closed ended questions. This comprehensive questionnaire was used for gathering the information regarding the awareness of MOOCs among the trainee teachers and the experience of those who have used one. Besides the basic demographic details, following were the major dimensions of the questionnaire.

- Awareness about MOOCs
- Experience while pursuing MOOCs
- Some general questions on MOOCs

Analysis and Interpretation of Data

Both closed-ended and open-ended questions were used to collect the data from the survey. Objective-wise data analysis was done for the systematic analysis of the data that was gathered from the trainee teachers. Basic statistical analysis using percentage was done for quantitative data.

Objective 1

This objective tends to find the awareness of the concept of MOOCs among the trainee teachers of 1st and 2nd year B.Ed programmes.

With reference to this objective, the trainee teachers were asked to share their understanding of the concept of MOOCs. Most of the trainee teachers were observed to be aware of MOOCs as is seen from the pie chart shown below.

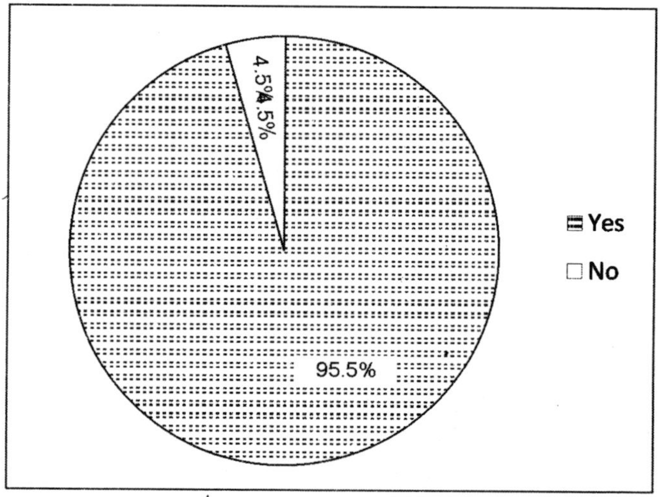

Fig. 11.1: Results of Test Item 1: Have you heard about MOOCs?

Further most of them came to know about it from the internet, however, other sources were from friends and their college. However, not everyone has enrolled in the same till now.

Here, the questionnaire was carried out using just yes/no answers that were closed-ended. The majority of respondents have not enrolled in any MOOC courses. They brought in 52.9% of those who hadn't joined any such course and 47.1% of those who had joined up for different MOOC courses.

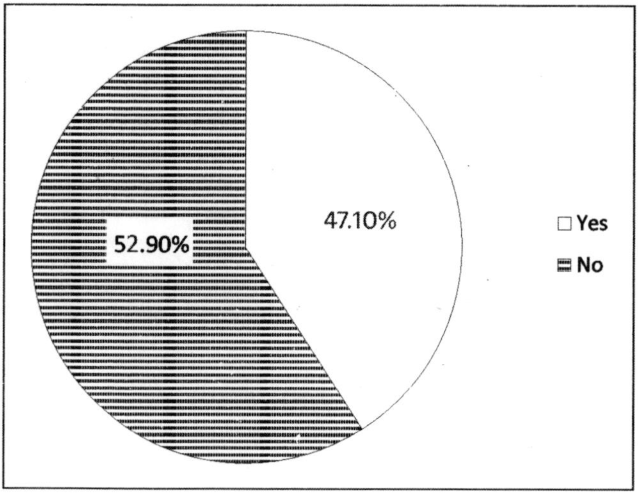

Fig. 11.2: Results of Test Item 2: Have you ever taken a MOOCs course?

It has been seen that most of them are looking forward to joining a MOOC course in future. Also many of them already have experience with this type of learning platform.

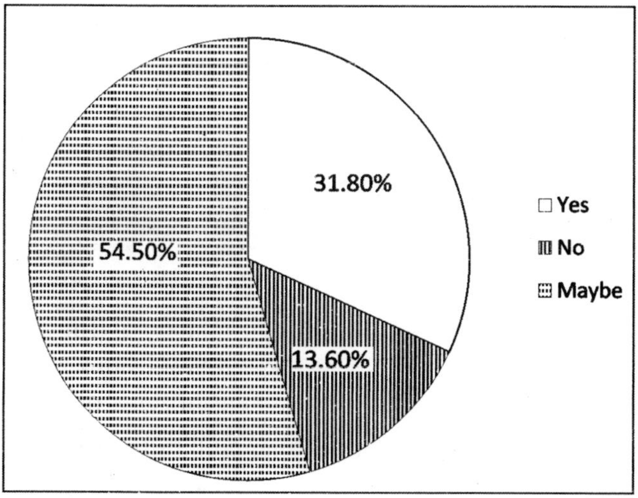

Fig. 11.3: Results of Test Item 3: Do you plan on joining any MOOCs course in future?

From the chart below, it is observed that NPTEL and Coursera are among the most known MOOC platforms among the trainee teachers whereas other known platforms are Udemy, Swayam, Future learn and others. It was a multiple select question in our survey through google form.

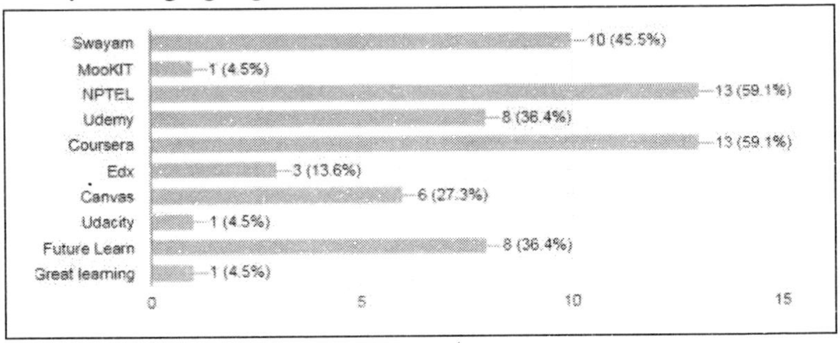

Fig. 11.4: Results of Test Item 4: Which MOOCs platforms are you aware of?

There are many trainee teachers who have done one or more such courses in the last six months. This was an open-ended question so that the responders can have some freedom to tell the number of courses they have done.

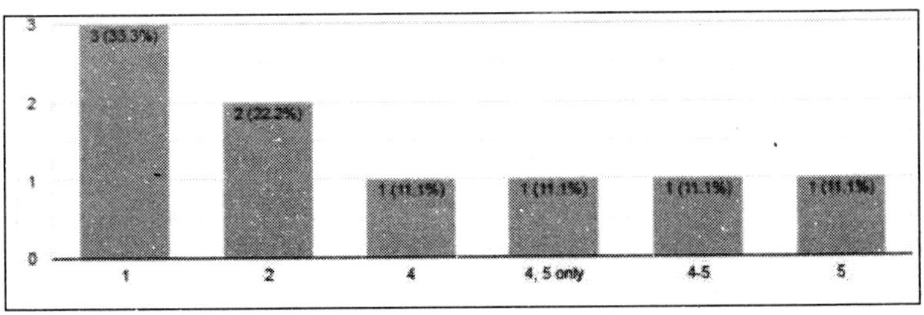

Fig. 11.5: Results of Test Item 5: Do you know about any Indian MOOCs? If yes, then mention the name.

Objective 2

This objective aims to find the experience of those trainee teachers who have enrolled in a MOOCs course at sometime in their life.

To begin with they were asked the platform/s they have enrolled for their course. It was an open-ended question giving freedom to answer the question. Following chart shows that most of them enrolled on Udemy while others have enrolled on platforms like NPTEL, Swayam and others.

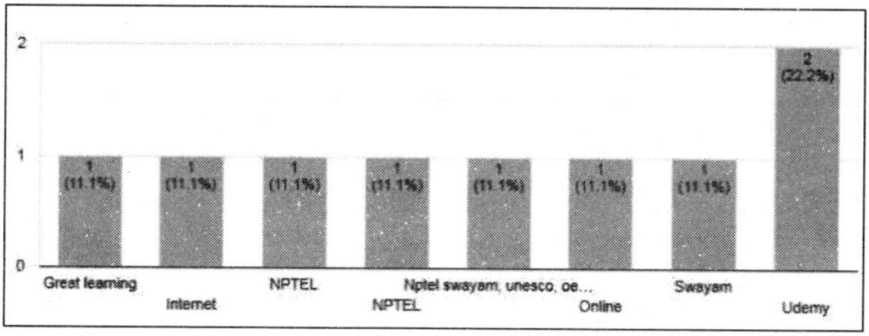

Fig. 11.6: Results of Test Item 6: On which platform did you enrol?

Further, they were asked the reason behind joining one such course. This was also an open-ended question to know the real inspiration behind joining any of the courses. The vast majority stated that their primary motivation for enrolling in a MOOC is to either acquire skills to do my job better or to satisfy personal curiosity. The vast majority of students polled said they already had a bachelor's degree, but they were still enrolling in classes for their own and their employers' personal and professional growth. Various other responses had various different reasons like for better earning, for knowledge, to crack the exam of NET, for experience, to know about the different courses like design thinking etc., for knowledge along with certificates. A very different response for this question was that many of them were doing one or the other course as a compulsion in their course for collecting credits.

They were asked about the device used by them to access the video lectures and other things to pursue the course. It was seen that most of them have used their mobiles or laptops while few of them used their mobiles and laptops both as per their convenience.

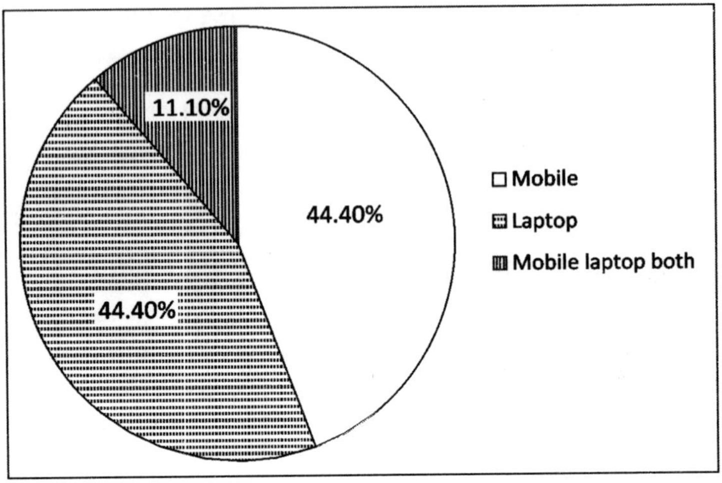

Fig. 11.7: Results of Test Item 7: On which device did you access the course?

They were also asked about the time they spent on this course per week and we found that they gave time ranging from 30 minutes till 5 days per week.

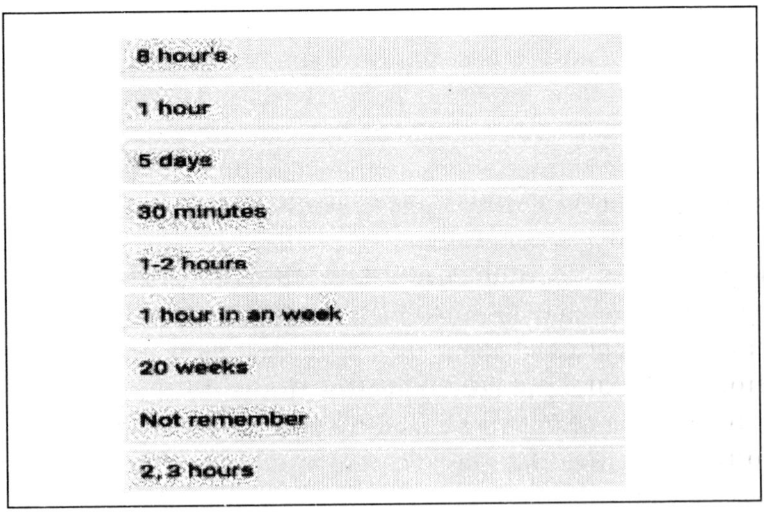

Fig. 11.8: Results of Test Item 8: How much time did you spend on it per week?

Furthermore they were asked to mention the most important element of the MOOC courses and it is found that video lectures are the most important part of the course for complete understanding.

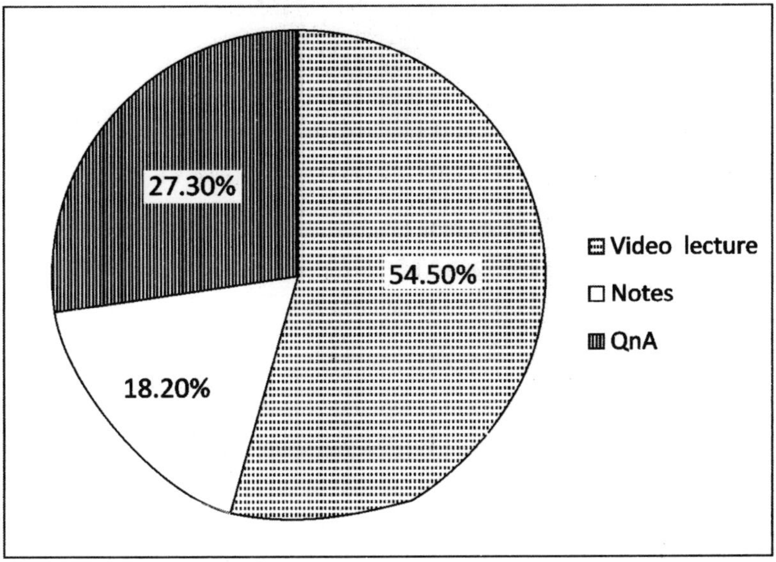

Fig. 11.9: Results of Test Item 9: Which element of MOOCs do you feel is most important?

As follow-up questions, they were also asked about the drawbacks or the problems they might have faced. Most said problems were the increased screen time and the language barrier because most courses are available in English language only.

Some of them wanted a few changes to be done in the way MOOCs run while most of them are seen to be satisfied by the process. Some of them believe that these courses must have a deadline so as to improve their concentration and avoid procrastination. One such suggestion is "Yes the change is that video lectures provided in this should also be available in offline format too."

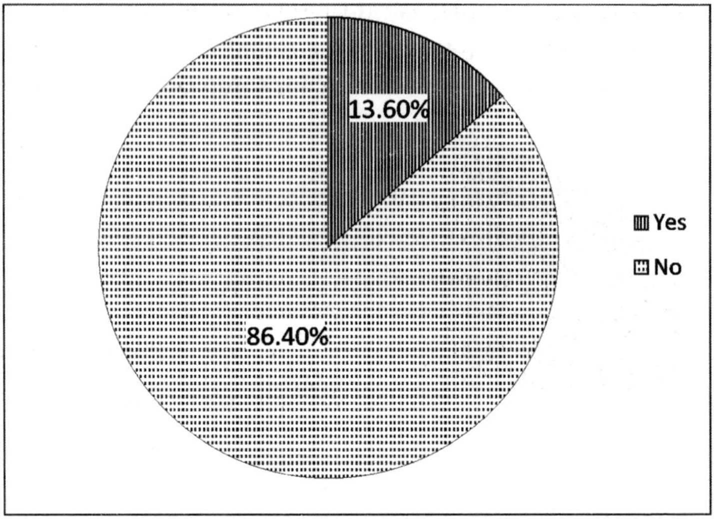

Fig. 11.10: Results of Test Item 10: Do you want any changes to the way MOOCs are run?

Objective 3

For many professions to remain licenced, such as those in law, accountancy, and real estate, continuing education credits are necessary. Teachers also benefit from MOOC courses. They keep them professionally up-to-date and provide them professional development opportunities. Massive Open Online Courses (MOOCs) can be a cost and resource effective means to complement the traditional methods of professional development of teachers. This optimism is based on the assumption that use of MOOCs will facilitate mass training of teachers as per their convenience and ease. We carried out a personal interview to determine the usefulness of these MOOCs for new teachers in terms of doing a practical task. The results of the personal interviews were summarised as:

1. gaining specific job skills
2. preparing for additional education
3. obtaining professional certification
4. positive learning and professional development experience,

pedagogical and technological knowledge to integrate Web-based tools in educational practice.

5. MOOCs promise to support teacher professional development by providing accessible, flexible and fast-track completion of certified courses.
6. MOOCs can help to develop certain teaching, digital and academic skills.
7. Teachers might enrol in courses in human or child psychology that will improve in understanding their students better.
8. One of the benefits of learning from MOOCs is the chance to become a student again and learn from the different teaching styles of other educators. This way, teachers can experience for themselves what works and what doesn't, and thus incorporate the best practices in their classrooms.
9. Teachers can recommend specific MOOCs to students who are self-motivated and really want to prepare for advanced knowledge.
10. Following were the benefits of doing MOOCs as given by the trainee teachers through the survey form we circulated among them.
11. It would enhance the skills and overall personality.
12. I can learn different subjects having some common concepts in same duration and later will be able to develop my interdisciplinary skills.
13. It provides a platform to have a global learning experience.
14. Learn about the digital form of teaching.
15. We can easily enhance our knowledge and develop different skills through MOOCs from different countries without even visiting and also boost our resume.
16. It is advantageous in the form that you can access learning at any time.

Also, the survey through google form asked them if they are planning to develop their own MOOC course in future on any of the platforms of their preference and got to know that most of them are not yet sure if they will be doing so or not. However, there are many others who are planning to do so while others are not at all thinking about the same at present. This is presented through the following pie chart.

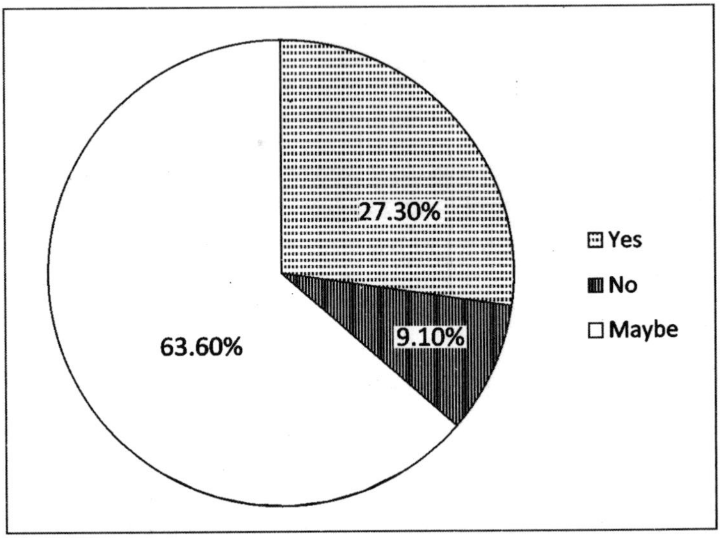

Fig. 11.11: Results of Test Item 11: As a trainee teacher do you plan to develop your own MOOCs course in future?

Discussion

This study includes both the trainee instructors' participation in MOOCs as well as the subsequent effects on their awareness of the notion of MOOCs from both a theoretical and practical standpoint. As a result of taking these courses, a sizable portion of participants indicated that their awareness and understanding of MOOCs had increased. This is pretty obvious in light of the study's findings. In fact, the participant-shared narratives provide both a confirmation of the findings and an honest statement of how trainee teachers view the advantages of MOOCs.

References

Kasih, R., Hanafi, N., & Amin, M. (2019). Education and the 21st Century Skills: A Case Study of Smartphone Use in English Classes. *Advances in Social Science, Education and Humanities Research*, *465*, 48-51.

Kesar, H., & Semerci, A. (2019). Technology trends, Education and beyond. *Contemporary Educational Researches Journal, 9* (3), 39-49.

Mathew, A. (2016). Reforms in Higher Education in India: A Review of Recommendations of Commission and Committees on Education. Centre for Policy Research in Higher Education. NUEPA, New Delhi.

Mooij, T. (2007). Design of educational and ICT conditions to integrate differences in learning: Contextual learning theory and a first transformation step in early education. *Computers in Human Behavior, 23*(3), 1499-1530.

NPTEL. n.d. https://nptel.ac.in/

Swayam. n.d. https://swayam.gov.in/

Coursera. n.d https://www.coursera.org/

edX. n.d https://www.edx.org/

About MOOCs. n.d. https://www.mooc.org/

Massive open online course. n.d.
ttps://en.wikipedia.org/wiki/Massive_open_online_course

12

Impact of N.E.P 2020 on Transforming Indian Education System

Himanshoo Kumar Sharma and *Rubina Shahnaz*

Introduction

Comprehensive educational reforms are done by about 845 universities and about 4000 Higher education Institutions affiliated by Universities. There are many small sized institutions recognized by universities. It is regret to state that about 25% colleges have annual enrolment less than 100 students. It is endeavored that India will be the third largest economy, in the world by 2030-2032 with estimated GDP of ten trillion dollars. This object will be achieved by knowledge resources and not by natural resources of the country. For the development of Education sector New Education Policy 2020 was introduced. This Policy is considered a potent means to do the fourth Industrial Revolution to bring India to new heights.

History of Evolution of Education Policy of India Since 1968

India was suffering with many drastic problems after independence like illiteracy. So Government of India started many programmes and plans to eradicate this menace. Union Govt. set up University Education Commission in 1948-1949, Secondary Education Commission in 1952-1953, Kothari Commission in 1964-1966 and University Grants Commission in 1956. Nehru Government promoted Engineering and Science.

On recommendations of Kothari Commission, the then Prime Minister Indira Gandhi in 1968 declared First National Education Policy. This policy recommended the equal opportunities to rural and Urban sectors of education to secure credible cultural and economic development and to preserve the national integration. The policy stressed the learning of the Hindi Language throughout India.

Second National Education Policy was launched in 1986 by former Prime Minister Rajeev Gandhi. In this policy special emphasis was given on elimination of inequalities and mobilizing the educational opportunities irrespective of caste, gender and economic status. This policy promoted the scholarship, subsidies and allowances. The special emphasis was given to adult education and social integration.

The Second Education Policy was revised by former Prime Minister P.V. Narsima Rao and introduced Common Entrance Examination (CEE). Former Prime Minister Manmohan Singh setup Common Minimum Programme Policy. Revised Second National Education Policy in 1994 mandated Common Entrance Examination for all India based vocational and technical training admissions.

A draft was released by Ministry of Human Resource Development (MHRD) in 2019 of NEP 2020. The objectives of this policy were to reduce the curriculum burden of the students. In this policy, the stress is given to promote holistic experiential analyzed and discussion based learning. The significant change is done in pedagogical structure from 10+2+3 system to 5+3+3+4 system.

Need for change in Pre-education Policy

1. To ensure global access in Indian Education system.
2. To enhance the quality of education.
3. Promote innovation and research based education.

4. To cater the needs of knowledge based economy in the changing global scenario. The changes were needed in current Education system.
5. To increase the enrollment ratio in higher educational institutions.
6. The National Education Policy 2020 is meant to rebuild school curricula and teaching methodology.
7. The aim of launching the National Education Policy 2022 is to remodel India's education system.
8. Under this new National Education Policy, nobody is forced to take any particular language. Now the students can choose the language according to their interest.

Salient features of National Education Policy (NEP) 2020

1. More than hundred foreign Universities will be facilitated to operate in India through new law. According to New Education Policy, Foreign universities will be given special dispensation regarding regulatory, governance and content norms on par with other institutions of India.
2. E-Courses will be available in regional languages. Technology will be part of education planning, learning, teaching, assessment, teacher, school and student training.
3. Quality technology based options for adult learning such as apps, Satellite based TV channels, on line Courses/ modules, online books and ICT-equipped Libraries and Adult Education centres etc. will be encouraged
4. NEP emphasis to establish Higher Education Commission of India which will be single regulatory body except for medical and legal education.
5. There will be multiple entry and exit options to those who wish to leave the Course in middle. Their credits will be transferred through Academic Bank of Credits.
6. National Testing Agency will conduct the Common Entrance Examination for all the higher education institutes.

Stages of New Education Policy

Foundation stage

In foundation stage of new education Policy the children from 3 to 8 years are included. This stage will be of 5 years. First three years of children shall be Preschool education in Anganwadi and class 1 to 2 shall be of school education in which language skill will be developed.

On 20 October, 2022, the National Curriculum Framework for Foundational Stage (NCF-FS) was released by India's Ministry of Education. The NCF-FS is one of the most important dimensions in the implementation of the National Education Policy (NEP) 2020, and is likely to have a deep impact on the education and overall well-being of our children.

The NEP is reconfiguring our system of schooling. It has created a 4-stage '5+3+3+4 curricular and pedagogical structure'. The '5' refers to the first five years of education from ages 3 to 8, called the Foundational Stage, and then ages 8-11 (Preparatory Stage), 11-14 (Middle Stage) and 14-18 (Secondary Stage). The importance of the Foundational Stage is driven by the deep and long-term implications of the first eight years of a child's life. Research from across the world in multiple relevant disciplines shows that these years are the most critical for lifelong well-being and overall development of individuals—physical, cognitive and socio-emotional. Brain development happens the fastest in these years. Thus, 'Early Childhood Care and Education' (ECCE), which refers to the care and education of children from birth to eight years, is of central importance to all societies. This recognition has grown steeply in the past two decades, spurring significant investments across countries. For India, the NEP is one of the most important mechanisms for delivering high quality, equitable ECCE to all our children. Children of ages 0-3 are mostly taken care of at home; institutional settings take over from age 3 onwards, so the Foundational Stage addresses ECCE for ages 3-8. This would include pre-schools, kindergartens, nursery, Aanganwadis, etc—all institutions that take care of children ages 3-6, and classes 1 and 2 across all schools.

Preparatory Stage

This is 3 years time stage when the children pass from 8 to 11 years age. This stage is up to class 5. In this stage, Science, Arts, Mathematics shall be taught knowledge numerical skill and regional language shall all be developed in children.

Creative imagination, with sound ethical moorings and values. It aims at producing engaged, productive, and contributing citizens for building an equitable, inclusive, and plural society as envisaged by our Constitution.

While the NEP 2020 is pushing for experiential learning process in the future, National Centre for Excellence does a lot to promote a hands-on learning approach within and outside their classrooms. Among many others things, these include:

- Conducting mock classroom trials and debates.
- Creating out-of-class community service opportunities for students.
- Using interactive learning apps to create an immersive and engaging environment, wherever they may be.
- Role-playing activities that replicate famous real-life events to help students memorize different people.
- Encouraging scientific experiments and open-minded questions to determine cause and effect.
- Creativity, Collaboration and Innovation in teaching and learning.

Middle Stage (Blossoming Stage)

In this stage, children from 6 to 8 grade will be included. This stage shall be of 3 years period. In this stage, vocational testing and vocational internship will be imparted to enable the children for employment. Subject based curriculum will be taught and coding will be started from grade 6.

Learning is the process whereby knowledge is created through the transformation of experience. The NEP 2020 focuses on experiential learning, equity and discovery-based teaching learning methods. We at our schools promote this with the help of peer tutoring, fun creative.

Collaborative and joyful exploratory activities in classroom for experiential learning and deeper student learning. We also focus on skill enhancement of the students.

The Middle Stage comprises of three years of education. It builds on the pedagogical and curricular style of the Preparatory Stage. It helps in preparing students across various streams. Experiential learning is explored in relations with different subjects.

- To develop scientific temper.
- To take the education journey from capacity to capability.
- To equip children with 21st century skills.
- To create a Holistic and Multidisciplinary education.

Secondary stage

The period of this stage shall be of 4 years, students from 9th grade to 12 standards are included. Liberty shall be given to the students to choose the subjects of their own choice like Science, Arts or Commerce. Intense study of subjects will be started. There shall be Board Examination in class 10th and 12th. The format of board examination will be changed reducing the burden of examination. In examination, multiple choice questions will be included. Examination will be conducted two times a year. Objective and Subjective test will be conducted once in a year.

The secondary stage will comprise of classes 9th to 12th (age group - 14 to 18 years). It will include multidisciplinary study, flexibility, greater critical thinking, and student choice of subjects.

Reduction in the curriculum was long-term due. Secondary Stage attributes the following points:

- The curriculum in all subjects to be reduced to core essentials.

- Interactive classes with reduced dependency on textbook learning. Students will be encouraged to ask questions.
- The focus will be on critical thinking, discovery, inquiry, discussion, and analysis-based teaching and learning methods of holistic education.
- Experimental learning will be encouraged through creative, fun, collaborative, and exploratory activities in the classroom for deeper student learning.

Higher Education

Under National Education Policy 2020, the gross enrolment ratio will be enhanced. More than 3.5 crores new seats will be added in higher educational institutions, there shall be Higher Education Commission of India for higher education of except legal and medical education. HEC of India will replace UGC.

There shall be 4 years multidisciplinary bachelors' degree in an undergraduate programme with multiple exit options. This will include professional and vocational training and will be conducted as follows:—

1. A certificate after completing 1-year study.
2. A diploma after completing 2-years of study.
3. A bachelor degree after completing 3-years study.
4. 4-Year multidisciplinary bachelor's degree.

Some Autonomous Education Bodies

a. **Higher Education Commission of India (HECI):** It will regulate higher education. The object of the Commission shall be to increase the gross enrolment ratio.
b. **National Higher Education Regulatory Council (NHERC):** Regulates higher education particularly of teacher's education.
c. **National Accreditation Council (NAC):** This is Meta accrediting body.
d. **Higher Education Grants Council (HEGC):** This

education body shall replace the National Council for Teacher's Education, All India Council for Technical Education and University Grant Commission.

e. **General Education Council (GEC):** This is the education body which is responsible in framing National Higher Education qualification framework. National Council for Teacher Education will come under this body.

f. **The National Testing Agency** will perform the responsibility of conducting entrance examinations for admissions to University across the country in addition to NEET and JEE main.

g. In addition to above educational bodies, Indian Council of Agricultural Research, Council of Architecture, Veterinary Council of India and National Council for Vocational Education and Training.

h. **Benefits on National Education Policy**

1. The policy proposes to internationalize education in India, now the foreign universities will set up Campus in India.
2. The Fee of public and private university will fix.
3. The policy proposes the higher education institutes like the IIT make changes with regard to diversity of learning.
4. Different types of languages added to the school curriculum so that the students have proper relationship with different languages.
5. The curriculum content will reduce in order to help the students to enhance their learning and critical thinking ability.
6. There will also experiential learning at all stages of the school and the students will empower through flexible course.
7. The volunteer events will be performed in school so that the students and teachers can rebound their relationship with each other and understand the differences between them.
8. The learning will be provided to the students with enjoyable manner, this will enable the students to develop a form of understanding.

9. Emphasis will be given to the drop-out reads and universal access to the education will be provided at school.
10. The students will have well trained social workers and counsellors on the campus.
11. The nutrition and health of the children will address including mental health of children.

Conclusion

Effective and time bound implementation is essential for the New Education Policy 2020. The NEP 2020 is potential and crucial moment for higher education. This policy is remarkable milestone in the field of Education. The constant reformation is attributed to new skill of India by this policy. The education system must be more evidence based and decision making, this basic requirement is completed by this policy. Through this policy has appreciable vision but its success absolutely depends upon this idea to what extent this integrate with other policies of India such as skill India, New Industrial policy.

India needs to remain ready for future. This policy paves the way to equip the Indian students with enthusiastic skill. The NEP 2020 develops the professional skill in Indian aspirants in the field of Agriculture and other like areas.

References

Braun, V., & Clarke, V. (2006). *Using thematic analysis in psychology. Qualitative Research in Psychology, 3*(2), 77-101.

Chima, J.S. (2020). Are participants in ethno-nationalist movements rational choosers, socially-embedded actors, or psychologically-instinctive beings?: motivations and worldviews of Sikh separatists from India. *Studies in Conflict and Terrorism, 0*(0), 1-22. https://doi.org/10.1080/1057610X.2020.17 11604.

Naidu, M. Venkaiah (8 August 2020). "The New Education Policy 2020 is set to be a landmark in India's history of education". *Times of India Blog.*

Govt. of India (1968). *National Education Policy, 1968.* https://web.archive.org/web/ 20090731002808/http://www.education.ni c.in/policy/npe-1968.pdf Govt. of India (1986).

Chopra, Ritika (2 August, 2020). "Explained: Reading the new National Education Policy 2020". *The Indian Express.*

Education Policy, 1986. https://web.archive.org/web/20090619075631/http://education.nic.in/cd50years/g/T/49/0T490401.htm Govt. of India (2020).

National Education Policy 2020. https://www.mhrd.gov.in/sites/upload_files/mhrd/files/NEP_Final_Engli sh_0.pdf.

Hindustan Times 2020.08.08; "NEP will play role in reducing gap between research and education in India'—PM Modi.

M.M. Goel (2020). A View on Higher Education in New Education Policy 2020.

Nandini, ed. (29 July, 2020). "New Education Policy 2020 Highlights: School and higher education to see major changes". *Hindustan Times.*

13

School Drop-out

A Hurdle in becoming India as a Global Education Hub

Soram Sonia

Introduction

India has made a significant and remarkable progress in almost every field after independence. Education being one of the important sectors for the progress and development of a nation has contributed in the development of a nation. Education serves as ladder through which an individual in particular and a nation in general can develop. For youth, education is a powerful instrument through which it can enable them to lift them from economically and socially marginalized conditions and move out of poverty and become a productive citizen.

Realizing the importance of education, the then government has formulated several policies and programmes for providing education to all. National Education Policy (NEP) 1986 and its programme of action (POA) 1992 have stressed on universal access and equity and has resulted to the coming up of 'Right to Free and Compulsory Elementary Education' in the year 2009. India is home to some of the best educational institutions in the world. Higher educational institutes like Takshashila and Nalanda are the glaring examples that India has a rich heritage of higher education since time immemorial. Indian universities had produced brilliant minds who have made a global impact with their work in different fields of science, arts and humanities. Studying in India is a great experience where students can explore the rich cultural heritage of the country.

The major hurdles that come up in achieving the goal of making India a global education hub is the increasing numbers of school drop-out and out of school children because in any education system grass root levels play a great role, since it is the foundation of higher level of education. Even though, we established a world class colleges and universities equipped with latest and modern facilities, if the primary and secondary stage of education in the country is in deteriorating condition, then it will directly impact on the status and position of higher educational system. In United Kingdom, which is also considered as one of the global education hub, attending primary and secondary education is mandatory, which enabled itself to keep a strong foundation of the education system.

As per the record of the Ministry of Human Resource Development (MHRD), in 2014-15, at the primary school stage, the national drop-out rate was 4.34 % and at the secondary stage, it was even higher at 17.86 %. Poverty, non-availability, and difficulty in accessibility are considered as the three main reasons of children dropping out of school. There may be many reasons, ranging from child marriage and migration of families, lack of school infrastructure such as proper shelter, toilets, drinking water etc., which may lead to a child dropping out from school.

School drop-out and out of school is a global problem. New data published by the Higher Education Statistics Agency (HESA), shows that in 2019-20, the drop-out rate for UK students was 5.3%, a fall of 1.4 percentage points on the previous year, and the lowest rate on record. The average drop-out rate at high school in the United States of America is reported as 4.7% and Japan's drop-out rate at high school is reported as low as 1.27%.

In India, students drop-out rate of school is reported as 12.6% and discontinued education rate at the secondary level as 19.8%, while at the upper primary level the rate of dropped out is reported as 17.5%, as per recent survey conducted by National Statistical Office (NSO) and defined a drop-out as an "ever-enrolled person" who does not complete the last level of education for which he/she has enrolled and is currently not attending any educational institution. It is evident that the countries having better education hub are having lower drop-out % in school stage also. In the new National Education Policy, by 2030, the target of the government is to achieve cent per cent Gross Enrolment Rate (GER) at the school level and considers school drop-out as a major deterrent factor. Presences of a large numbers of school drop-out and out of school students create an overall negative impact when we are striving to convert India into a global education Hub.

School Drop-out and Out of School Children

Dropping out of school, is defined as leaving a school without completion to a formal qualification awarded. School drop-out has a critical importance on communities and families due to its economic and social consequences. Therefore, several measures are being taken up by the policy makers to enable the school drop-out to re-enrol themselves and enable them to improve their skills and academic achievement, and also enable them to enhance their employability through work experience and training. A child 6-14 years of age will be considered 'out of school' if he/she has never been enrolled in any elementary school or if after enrolment has been absent from school without prior intimation for reasons of absence for a period of 45 days or more. 'Out of School' children fall in the most vulnerable category. Many of out of school children belong to SC, ST, street children, orphans and homeless children, migrant children etc. The survey conducted on 'out of school' children in 2009 estimated 29 lakhs children with special needs in the age group of 6-13 years, of which 34.12% were not in school. Besides the social and economic reason, the school system has perhaps been unable to connect with vulnerable children and make the education process relevant and valuable for them. School drop-out which further leads to out of school children is mainly due to lack of interest in school, negative experience in schools and a sense of underachievement.

Some of the causes which keeps the young children out of schools in South Asia are due to disaster and armed conflict, child marriage practices, child labour, gender discrimination and factors related to disability. India and Pakistan combined account for more than 80% of the total out of school children of South Asia followed by Bangladesh, Afghanistan and Nepal.

Government had launched several policies and programmes in order to revolutionise the whole education system in different levels but still large gap can be seen at secondary level particularly those belonging to social and economically marginalised section of the society. These underprivileged group are not only lagging behind economically but are also lagging far behind in the field of education. Socio-Economically Disadvantaged Groups consist of people belonging to Scheduled Castes, Scheduled Tribes, Other Backward Classes. People residing in villages, hilly areas, person with disabilities, victims of child trafficking. Socio-Economically Disadvantaged Group (SEDG) students can be broadly categorized based on geographical identities (from villages, small towns, and aspirational districts), socio-cultural identities (students belonging to Scheduled Castes, Scheduled Tribes, OBCs, and minorities), socio-economic conditions (students from migrant communities, low income households gender identities (particularly female and transgender students), disabilities (students inclusive of learning disabilities) and children in vulnerable circumstances (victims of child trafficking, orphans including child beggars in urban areas, and the urban poor). The overall admissions in schools decline gradually from Class 1 to Class 12, this decrease in admissions is significantly more distinct for many of these SEDGs, with even more decrease for female students within each of these Socio-Economically Disadvantaged Groups and often even more evident in higher education.

Causes and Measures that can be taken up to reduce the numbers of school drop-out

Poverty is one of the main causes for drop-out and out of school children in rural and slums area of the country. Many of the small children are engaged as child labour both in urban as well as rural India. Hunger made them to do any available works so that they can fill their empty stomach and also of their family. Measures the policy of earn while learning if practiced then there will be remarkable decrease in the rate of drop-out. Hands on training and skill-based education should be provided to school children in every stage of learning. National education policy 2020 strive to achieve that by 2025, 50 per cent of the school going learners will be introduced to vocational courses so that they can earn their livelihood and can stand on their own feet. Lack of access to quality school is also main reason for dropping out of students especially female students. Many a time it was reported that a girl child after reaching certain stage tend to drop-out from the school due to unhygienic sanitation. Parents are often reluctant to send their girl child to such school which doesn't have proper toilet and safe drinking water facilities. Therefore, the need of the hour is to provide the school with hygienic sanitation and safe drinking water. Children of first-generation learner are more likely to drop-out from school as they could not get the maximum support from the parents. Therefore, adult literacy programme should be encouraged for the parents of first-generation learners. Realizing the importance of adult literacy, National Education Policy-2020 is planning to develop a curriculum framework which focuses on developing foundational literacy and numeracy, life skill, vocational skills, basic education, and continuing skill. Mass awareness programmes and campaign using both print and electronic media as well as other medium can be organised to promote adult literacy programme. National Education Policy-2020 envisages ensuring equitable access to quality education to all students. According to Unified District Information System for Education Plus (UDISE) 2016-17, the percentage of students belonging to Scheduled Castes at the primary level was reported to be 19.6%, but this percentage of students of the same category falls at the higher secondary level to 17.3%. These enrolment drop-offs are more severe for Scheduled Tribes students (10.6% to 6.8%), and differently-abled children (1.1% to 0.25%). The decline in the number of students were even greater for female students within each of the categories. The decline in enrolment in higher education is even steeper. Inclusive education should be practised and encouraged to a large extent. Provision should be made either in the form of scholarship to encouraged the students from deprived section to enrol and continue their education.

The concept of school complexes or cluster which were proposed by Kothari Commission (1964-66) and recently laid stress by National Education Policy-2020, if comes into existence than can solve many problems relating to inadequate infrastructure, resources and facilities.

Another reason for a child to opt out of school is inability to cope with the academic pressure. It has been reported that children who do not read competently are four times more likely to drop-out of school. Studies also proven the fact that students who fail to perform in mathematics are 75% more probable to drop-out of high school. Schools should try to inculcate innovative teaching methods to lure students towards education and trigger interest in teaching-learning process.

Unsatisfactory health conditions of a child have a negative impact on his learning ability and performance at school. Chronic ailments that occur during childhood which continue for a long period of time may restraint a child's ability to continue school. Provision of regular medical check-up and vaccination programme should be organised in collaboration with medical department.

Early warning system for drop-out may be carefully observed at the schools to recognize students and to give more attention to these students who are at risk of dropping out of school.

Conclusion

In conclusion, we can say that India can convert its higher education into the global education hub. The foremost things to be done is to make sure that no child is left out from receiving early education as it is the foundation of higher learning. We need to improve the quality of education being provided in our schools to universities.

References

Advameg (2011). *Drop-out rate (%), Primary Education Statistics,* assessed 30 October, 2022 Available from: https://www.nationsencyclopedia.com/WorldStats/Edu-primary-drop-out-rate.html

Ahmad, M. (October 24, 2022). School drop-outs: Causes and concerns, assessed 25 October, 2022 Available from: http://risingkashmir.com/school-drop-outs-causes-and-concerns

Ministry of Human Resources Development, Govt. of India, *National Education Policy 2020* accessed on 1 November, 2022 Available from: https://www.education.gov.in/sites/upload_files/mhrd/files/NEP_Final_English_0.pdf

Prakarti Walia, *School drop-outs in India: the causes and prevention,* accessed 30 October, 2022 Available from: https://www.turnthebus.org/blog/school-drop-outs-in-india-the-cause-and

PTI (25 September, 2022). *In Several States, School Drop-out Rate At Secondary Level Higher Than National Average, Shows Study.* accessed 25 October, 2022 *Available from:*https://news.abplive.com/news/india/in-several-states-drop-out-rate-at-secondary-level-higher-than-national-average-1555295

Reducing the number of out-of-school children, accessed 2 November, 2022 Available from: https://www.unicef.org/rosa/what-we-do/out-of-school-children

Sampath, G. (December 11, 2016). *Why children drop-out from primary school* accessed 30 October, 2022 Available from: https://www.thehindu.com/news/nationaxl/Why-children-drop-out-from-primary-school/article16792949.ece

14

Making India into a Global Knowledge Hub

Role of NEP 2020

Amit Ahuja and *Rajani Upadhyay*

Introduction

The introduction of the National Education Policy 2020 in India has ushered in a new era of change in the country's educational system. The policy framework foresees an all-encompassing, experience- and discussion-based, investigation-driven, and student-centric road map from school to higher education in the twenty-first century. To foster the coherence and integrity of all knowledge, NEP 2020 envisions a holistic and multidisciplinary approach, a process of teaching, learning, and assessment that allows for multiple points of entry and exit and the elimination of artificial barriers between different fields of study. Essential aspects of the policy framework that will bring about a radical shift in the Indian education system include an emphasis on conceptual understanding, creative and critical thinking with a three-language formula, respect for local and diverse cultures, life skills, extensive use of new information and communication technologies, and the role of a teacher as a reformer. Connecting indigenous knowledge to the global education system, NEP 2020 has several requirements that can be explained as follows.

Holistic and Multidisciplinary Approach

Long-established barriers between fields of study are rendered obsolete by the concept of a holistic and multidisciplinary approach to education. Science, humanities, social sciences, languages, professional skills, soft skills, ethical and constitutional principles, and so on are integrated with other facets of students' education to foster a more holistic approach to knowledge production and dissemination. Through this method, students appreciate the value of human life and its goals from various vantage points. It's meant to be holistic, fostering growth in people's minds, hearts, bodies, and spirits as a whole, which is beneficial to oneself, one's community, one's country, and one's global community.

The National Education Policy 2020 proposes extensive interchanges to the higher education system by recommending the creation of a single sizeable multidisciplinary institution in each of the country's districts by the year 2030 and transforming existing universities into multidisciplinary institutions by the year 2040. To accomplish these aims, all existing single-stream institutions will be transformed into multidisciplinary ones or join thriving, multidisciplinary higher education institution clusters. Additional subcategories will be added, such as RCI (universities focused on research) and TCI (universities focused on education). A teacher's position as a reformer who influences the next generation is significant in this context. The policy proposes several changes to enhance the teaching profession, including better training, employment opportunities, working conditions, teacher autonomy, and job satisfaction.

Multiple-Entry Exit (MEE)

The policy outlines a system in which students may entry-exit academic programmes at various points throughout their studies, providing them with tremendous flexibility and choice. Certificates, diplomas, and degrees can be earned based on the number of credits earned by students, and the system has been set up in a tiered structure with entry and exit points at different levels (levels

5-10). It's a bold move in a country like India, where many students drop-out of college or high school for personal reasons like lack of funds, trouble keeping up with schoolwork, or illness in the family. Any student, at any point in their lives, can enrol in the appropriate academic programme at the proper level.

The All India Survey of Higher Education 2019-20 reports that the Gross Enrolment ratio (GER) in Indian higher education is 27.1%. This number is expected to rise to 50% by 2035, so the Indian higher education system can compete with other systems worldwide. The National Sample Survey Office (NSSO) found that 3.22 crore students aged 6-17 stopped attending school in 2017-18.

It is crucial to get them back into school and stop them from dropping out altogether. By 2030, NEP 2020 aims to attain full GER in preschool through 12th grade, and by 2035, it will have reached its goal of 50% GER in higher education.

Academic Bank of Credits (ABC)

Academic Bank of Credit (ABC) is one of the significant features of the policy framework, allowing students entry exit higher education many times. It's a digital database that lets students sign up for an account and save their academic credits for later use. ABC keeps track of students' credit histories and allows them to select courses of study leading to a degree, diploma, or certificate, all with flexible entry and exit options. It paves the way for lifelong education at one's own pace and in one's environment.

Multilingualism Model of Education

In the NEP 2020, this is emphasised as a critical factor. The policy framework places emphasis on the use of many languages in the classroom and across the educational system as a means of instilling in students the ability to think critically and creatively. Knowledge generation and distribution will continue to follow the three-language formula, and students will be given opportunities to study a language other than their native tongue through various ICT resources designed to make doing so fun.

In addition, high-quality textbooks, audio-video, and electronic content shall be made available in numerous languages to accommodate the needs of the people, the region, and the union. The National Programme on Technology Enhanced Learning (NPTEL) has already begun producing similar materials in several languages, including Hindi, Bengali, Gujarati, Kannada, Malayalam, Marathi, Tamil, and Telugu. The IITs and the IISc collaborate on NPTEL, which receives funding from the Indian government's Ministry of Education (MoE). This programme will strengthen national unity and integrity by fostering a feeling of community and appreciation for linguistic diversity.

Online and Digital Education

Covid-19 has had a global impact on human culture. It has, however, opened the door to the use of information and communication technology-based platforms like Zoom, Google meet, Google class, WhatsApp, and many more in the classroom as a means of delivering and assessing instruction. NETF, CIET, NIOS, IGNOU, IITs, NITs, etc., have conducted pilot studies to evaluate the benefits and drawbacks of online learning and have proposed carefully developed online courses based on their findings.

At the same time, the policy framework pushes for improving and expanding active digital platforms and educational initiatives based on ICT. As such, the Digital India campaign's goal of ensuring that every citizen of India has access to a computer, the internet, and basic computer skills is necessary.

In addition, the Ministry of Education and the Government of India will expand their e-learning platform programmes, such as SWAYAM for higher education, DIKSHA, and SWAYAMPRABHA, to incorporate a more advanced level of instruction and assessment.

These systems will build virtual labs so all students can access high-quality, hands-on learning experiences. Concurrently, a central online hub for producing and sharing educational materials for classroom activities, interactive media, virtual and augmented reality, machine learning, and other fields will be established. To achieve these aims, a separate organisation, the National Education Technology Forum (NETF), will be created to standardise online/digital teaching, learning, and assessment regarding content, technology, pedagogical planning, and administration.

National Research Foundation (NRF)

The development and maintenance of a knowledge-based society place a premium on generating and investigating new knowledge. Creating new knowledge, which will lead to more extraordinary intellectual richness, requires a thriving research ecosystem. In comparison to the United States of America (2.8%), Israel (4.3%), and South Korea (4.2%), India's investment in R&D is only 0.69 % of GDP. India will soon need to invest heavily in more output-based research across disciplines.

All institutions and all fields of study will be eligible to submit competitive, peer-reviewed grant proposals to the National Research Foundation (NRF), which will operate as a central agency to fund research and innovation in India. It will facilitate communication between researchers, governments, and businesses to ensure that analysis follows societal and national needs. In addition, NRF will honour groundbreaking studies and developments.

The arrival of Foreign Universities

NEP 2020 has emphasised the importance of facilitating the globalisation of higher education by encouraging the establishment of campuses by prestigious foreign universities in India. Accordingly, in 2020-21, the National Institute of Educational Planning and Administration, Government of India, performed a survey titled "Establishing International Branch Campuses in India." According to the results, eight universities outside the United States are considering applying to the Times Higher Education World University Ranking 2021. Out of the eight schools, five are American, and one is British, Australian, and Canadian.

Finance Minister Nirmala Sitharaman declared in the Union Budget 2022 that international colleges would be permitted to operate in the Gujarat International Finance Tec-City (GIFT) in Gandhinagar, which would be exempt from local rules. The construction of a "Global Knowledge Hub" in India depends on the presence of universities from other countries.

Regulatory Framework for Higher Education

Heavy-handed regulation of India's higher education system has been attempted repeatedly over decades, with disappointing results. The failure to coordinate among the many regulators has resulted in conflicts of interest and a lack of accountability. The National Education Policy 2020 suggests centralising four distinct institutional bodies that perform vital functions under one umbrella, namely the Higher Education Commission of India (HECI).

The first HECI-mandated entity will be the National Higher Education Regulatory Council, a "light but strict" regulator overseeing all of higher education except for professional schools like law and medicine. The second institutional structure, the National Accrediting Council (NAC), will serve as a meta-accrediting organisation whose primary function will be to create a solid framework for accreditation. To foster the orderly expansion of educational establishments, it will establish quality parameters such as minimum requirements, transparency in reporting, institutional leadership, and learning outcomes.

The Higher Education Grants Commission (HEGC) is the third type of organisation that will pay for universities. Institutional Development Plans (IDPs) that have been developed and implemented will be evaluated throughout the process using open standards. At the same time, the General Education Council (GEC) shall serve as the HECI's fourth institutional structure. It will establish benchmarks for what students enrolled in post-secondary courses should have learned. To ease the incorporation of vocational education into higher education, the process of creating a National

Higher Education Qualification Framework (NHEQF) has been launched. This framework will be lined up with the National Skills Qualifications Framework (NSQF).

Conclusion

The National Education Policy 2020 aims to make India a "Global Knowledge Hub" in the twenty-first century by introducing significant changes to the country's school and higher education systems. The success of NEP 2020, however, will rely on how it is put into action; this will be done in stages, with specific deadlines in mind, and in consultation with interested parties; additionally, it will be necessary to examine the policy framework's provisions at the local level.

References

Garhwal Post. (2022, July 13). *Making India a Knowledge Super Power: NEP-2020.* https://garhwalpost.in/making-india-a-knowledge-super-power-nep-2020/#:~:text=One%20of%20the%20remarkable%20features,their%20own%20paths%20of%20study

Kumar, R. (2022, April). National Education Policy 2020: Transforming India as a Global Knowledge Hub. *Employment News.* https://www.researchgate.net/publication/360277876_National_Education_Policy_2020_Transforming_India_as_a_Global_Knowledge_Hub

Ministry of Human Resource Development, Government of India. (n.d.). *National Education Policy.* https://www.education.gov.in/sites/upload_files/mhrd/files/NEP_Final_English_0.pdf

Press Trust of India. (2021, August 18). *New Education Policy to turn India into global knowledge hub.* https://www.business-standard.com/article/education/new-education-policy-to-turn-india-into-global-knowledge-hub-says-pradhan-121081801025_1.html

The Indian Express. (2021, July 29). *How National Education Policy 2020 is transforming the vision for education in India.* https://indianexpress.com/article/opinion/columns/national-education-policy-nep-2020-transforming-india-7429011/

Rising Kashmir. (2021, February 19). *National Education Policy (NEP) 2020: Transforming the education system.* http://risingkashmir.com/national-education-policy-nep-2020-transforming-the-education-system

Vikaspedia. (n.d.). *National Education Policy 2020.* https://vikaspedia.in/education/policies-and-schemes/national-education-policy-2020

Tribune India. (n.d.). *NEP 2020 will build India as knowledge hub.* https://www.tribuneindia.com/news/jalandhar/nep-2020-will-build-india-as-knowledge-hub-124460

15

National Education Policy (2020)

Transforming India into a Global Educational Hub

Prathistha Tandon

Introduction

Change is the law of nature. Even after going through the same routine, we still need some changes in our lives. It has been noticed that humans are always on the verge for improvements and changes, whether it has been in the realms of transportation, communication, entertainment, health or our daily necessities. However, we have ever thought consider that even the most fundamental thing, education, which gives us the means to purchase more recent products, is still the same as it was in the 1980s or even earlier? The time has finally come to make us consider whether or not our education has to be upgraded, just like our transportation and communication and other systems. It is necessary to update the blackboard chalk teaching method to the digital boards. As we know the future of the country and the fate of its citizens are both determined by education, which has a significant impact on the creation of a nation. In 20th century is known as the "computer era", and the digital age expands, we need to update with the time so that soon we can fall in the category of developed countries. NEP 2020 is a renovation of the educational system from the classic 1980s model to the 21st century to realize changes with developing technology. Although practically all areas of our lives have been improved, but the most important and fundamental area of improvement is education, which still needs major improvement. However, we ever thought that how can we expect growth and development when children of our country are fostered and nourished behind the four walls of the classroom spending five to six hours on the strict curriculum includes a set schedule, emphasis on finishing courses, a lack of innovative teaching strategies, a focus on convergent thinking that deprives students of divergent thinking, a lack of dialogue and incentive that kills creativity and innovation, etc. In actuality, it is for the reasons that students find their lessons to be boring and stifling, and the effects of this are visible in society.

If we look before two years, the overall scenario of education has made tremendous changes, i.e., during the pandemic, online education has supplemented traditional classroom instruction and broadened the learning opportunities by making a variety of disciplines and fields freely accessible. The ease of access to courses has altered the way that people study and teach, but a more sophisticated curriculum that incorporates multiple disciplines is still needed. The long-awaited transition of every aspect of life into the digital era has been made possible by the corona pandemic, which has been present since past two years.

If we remember our history it was remarkable. India's accomplishments in education will live on forever. The Gurukul system of education is something that we are all quite familiar with. As times has changed since India's independence, the educational system has undergone some changes. In 1968, the first education policy was developed, calling for "radical reorganization." After calling for "particular emphasis on the eradication of inequities and to equalize educational opportunity" later, in 1986, we have been utilizing the same educational system for the past 34 years, with just a slight modification in 1992 but now realizing the present need, the Indian government has proposed a new education strategy for the year 2020 after extensive debate over the course of

34 years. All relevant authorities have approved the application of this strategy throughout the Indian educational system. This policy was developed in response to suggestions from students, parents, educators, and several other people who are either directly or indirectly involved in the education industry. For the first time ever, such a wide-ranging consultation was held in India prior to the formulation of any policy suggestions, which shows about the strong democracy of the country.

This policy recognizes that education is crucial for realizing one's full potential, creating a just and equitable society, and advancing one's own country's growth. The Policy will make the millions of dreams of our young come true. India's youth will be essential to the realization of Industry 4.0 and the Digital India mission, which is, as we all know, necessary in the modern world.

Vision of Policy

At the University of South Africa's entrance is a representation of Nelson Mandela's renowned quote, which reads as follows: "It is not necessary to deploy atomic bombs or long-range missiles to destroy any country. It merely calls for a decline in educational standards and the acceptance of student cheating on exams." Keeping the above statement in view, the policy has been proposed to develop the educational standard of our country which was always been in the remembrance since the ancient period.

This Policy tries to make strong an education system rooted in India that supports in transforming the golden bird sustainably into global education hub by providing a versatile knowledgeable society, empowering high-quality education to all, and converting India worldwide powerful. The Policy contemplate that the schedule of our structure must develop among the students a deep sense of respect towards the Fundamental Duties and Constitutional values, bonding with one's country, and a conscious awareness of one's roles and responsibilities in a changing world. The goal of the policy is to instill in students a deep sense of national pride that manifests itself not only in words but also in deeds, spirit, and intellect. It also aims to help students acquire the knowledge, skills, values, and dispositions necessary to live responsibly in the world and to support human rights, sustainable development, and global well-being.

The focus of NEP is on five important aspects namely: Affordability, Accessibility, Quality, Equity and Accountability. It has been demonstrated that giving students and instructors international experience gives them a competitive advantage over their counterparts. NEP hopes to draw more students from around the world to India so they can pursue higher education. It includes a number of policy actions aimed at internationalizing higher education. The goal of the government is to market India as a top-tier educational location that offers reasonable tuition. Every higher education institution (HEI) that accepts foreign students is advised to establish an international student's office (ISO) through policy interventions. These ISOs would be in charge of organizing every aspect of support. High-performing Indian universities are encouraged under the strategy to open campuses abroad, and selecting group of universities (among the top 100 in the world) will be invited to open campuses in India. This will facilitate faculty and student interchange with top-tier overseas universities as well as collaborative research and teaching.

This policy focuses on internationalization of education with a clear vision of making India "global study destination" and it has charted an ambitious roadmap for making the internationalization of higher education a reality by 2030.

Over the following ten years, vocational education will gradually be included into all schools and higher education institutions. Based on a map of local opportunities and an examination of skills gaps, focus areas for vocational education will be determined.

The fundamental goal of this policy on higher education is to stop the fragmentation of this sector by making huge interdisciplinary universities, colleges, and HEI clusters/Knowledge Hubs, each of which will aspire to have 3,000 or more students, out of existing higher education institutions. This would enable students to become well-rounded across disciplines—including artistic, creative, and analytical subjects as well as sports—build vibrant communities of scholars and peers, shatter damaging silos, develop active research communities across disciplines, including cross-disciplinary research, and increase resource efficiency—both material and human—across higher education.

Implementations

The Central and State governments' and their autonomous agencies' implementation efforts have been uneven in the first full year since the introduction of the new National Education Policy (NEP) 2020 on July 29, 2020. Given that the Union Cabinet authorized this change concurrently with the policy itself, the first step in implementation—renaming the former Ministry of Human Resource Development (MHRD) as the Ministry of Education (MOE)—was quick. The development after then, though, has been erratic.

The education ministry's Department of School Education and Literacy (DoSE&L) moved swiftly to unveil a flurry of initiatives to implement NEP 2020. Along with meetings with States and Union Territories (UTs), autonomous organizations, and all other stakeholders to debate the many suggestions of NEP 2020 and its implementation methods, it organized the "Shikshak Parv" festival for teachers from September 8 to 25, 2020. The result was the announcement on 8 April, 2021 of the complete implementation plan SARTHAQ (Students' and Teachers' Holistic Advancement through Quality Education). SARTHAQ outlines the tasks connected to each NEP 2020 guideline. It outlines 297 tasks, names the organizations in charge of completing each one, and details their deadlines and desired results.

The curriculum is the result of careful planning and thorough research, and when it is implemented, it will reduce stress on young pupils, aid in lowering the number of annual school drop-outs, develops qualified workers who can support themselves, and finally result in services of higher quality. In order for schools to implement NEP 2020 successfully, two key changes must be made to the teaching-learning process and the pedagogical framework. It is a huge relief that the 10+2 board examination format has been abandoned, and the new school system will be 5+3+3+4, which would be innovative. For instance, the fundamental stage will need to be expanded to include classes 1 and 2.

Recommendations

Paying attention to foundations: Construction of the curriculum beyond the grade to help the students to make their basics more strong. The focus should be on experiential learning, creativity and critical thinking skills.

Emphasis on the value of literacy and numbers: In order for these core abilities to be taught, strengthened, and attained by Grade 3, all schools will need to remodel in these areas to bring about a revolution in the teaching methodologies.

Promoting language power and multilingualism: The local language or the student's mother tongue should be used wherever possible to teach students up to Class 5 in schools. According to numerous studies, young children comprehend concepts better in their mother tongue or native languages. Therefore, in order to get the best results, bilingualism among teachers should be encouraged.

Modifications to classroom instruction under the NEP-Shifting focus from memorization and rote study to conceptual comprehension in order to achieve higher exam scores. Schools will need to use a top-down strategy that involves moving away from finishing the syllabus and identifying learning goals, classroom instruction through cutting-edge pedagogy, and connecting assessments to these goals. To provide students with a holistic learning experience that includes the elements of digital literacy, scientific temper, and computational thinking, educators must consider combining courses, streams, and technology.

Modification of the assessment process: Two tests will be held each year, and exams will be administered according to semesters. Board exams won't be valued as highly as they have been in the past.

Exams for the boards will become "easier" since they will focus more on evaluating fundamental skills and abilities. The progress card will now be structured to reflect a student's swivelling evaluation. Self-evaluation, peer assessment, and instructor assessment will all be included on the progress card.

There are no clear boundaries between disciplines and subjects: There should be no clear divisions between the arts and sciences, curricular and extracurricular activities, academic and vocational streams, etc., and education should be multidisciplinary and holistic. By merging the subjects and learning domains, harmful hierarchies between the various learning areas can be removed.

Motivated, Energized, and Capable Faculty

The most important factor in the success of higher education institutions is the quality and engagement of its faculty. Acknowledging the criticality of faculty in achieving the goals of higher education, the policy recommends the following initiatives to achieve the best, most motivated and most capable faculty in HEIs.

Conclusion

Through the above editorial, I have analyzed the policy that is supposed to bring changes in the education system of India and will be able to make India a Global Education Hub. This policy has been formed after keeping numerous considerations for the overall development of the education of country. The success of this policy will depend on its effective implementation and then it will make a roadmap for educational improvement of the country. As we know India is the country with young and innovative brains. If we will consider all factors then definitely we will be moving towards achieving our aim of becoming Global Education Hub and will shine like sparkling star in the world.

References

Agrawal, T. (2012). Vocational education and training in India: Challenges, status and labour market outcomes. *Journal of Vocational Education &Training.*

Aithal, P. S., & Aithal, S. (2020). Analysis of the Indian National Education Policy 2020 towards achieving its objectives. *International Journal of Management, Technology, and Social Sciences* (*IJMTS*), *5*(2), 19-41.

Aithal, P.S., & Aithal, S. (2020). Implementation strategies of higher education part of national education policy 2020 of India towards achieving its objectives. *International Journal of Management, Technology, and Social Sciences* (*IJMTS*), *5*(2), 283-325.

Ansari, M.A., & Chavan, C.U., *A Comparative Study of Prospective Teachers Towards NEP 2020.*

Batra, P. (2020). *NEP 2020: Undermining the Constitutional Education Agenda?*

Govinda, R. (2020). *NEP 2020: A critical examination.*

Kumar, A. (2021). *New education policy (NEP) 2020: A roadmap for India 2.0.* University of South Florida M3 Centre Publishing, 3(2021), 36.

NEP 2020. *National Education Policy 2020; Ministry of Human Resource Development*, Government of India: New Delhi, India, 2020.

Panda, B.N.P., & Jena, L.K. (2020, September 01). National Education Policy and the state of research in India. Retrieved from https://www.newindianexpress.com/opinions/2020/sep/01/nationaleducation-policy-and-the-state-of-research-in-india-2190912.html

Pandey, S.K., & Tyagi, H.K. (2021). A Journey towards the commitments of national education policy 2020 through concept mapping. *Indian Journal of Science and Technology*, *14*(12), 984-989.

Prasad, G. (2022). Online Education in Industry 5.0. In Pedagogy, Presence, and Motivation in Online Education (pp. 22-35). IGI Global.

SAC, F. C. L. (2021). NEP 2020: Challenges before Mission of Gender and Social Equity. *Future of Media Education*, 359.

Scheme, A.B.S.C. *NEP 2020 Curriculum.*

Sharma, G.V.S.S., Vara Prasad, C.L.V.R.S., & Santa Rao, K. (2022). Post-COVID-19 era: An Enabler for the Implementation of Blended Learning in Compliance with the NEP 2020. *International Journal of Educational Reform*, 10567879221112059.

Smitha, S. (2020). National Education Policy (NEP) 2020—Opportunities and Challenges in Teacher Education. *International Journal of Management* (IJM), 11(11).

Wankhade, R.S. (2021). *Higher Education and NEP-2020.*

16
Suggestive Pedagogy of Teaching History in J&K

A Transformative Step Towards Theatre in Education

Dyutima Kesar

Introduction

The way people see theatre and drama is just confined to commercial cinema only. But it has far reached implications since theatre and drama in education is one of the most impacting factors in ushering creativity among the students.

NCF (2005) substantiated, that, the children's life at school must be linked to the life outside the school. The syllabi and textbooks developed on the basis of NCF 2005 were the endeavours to improve upon the prevalent pedagogy and take a step further towards child-centred system of education as outlined in the National Policy of Education 1986. Theatre and Drama in education seeks to inculcate a deep sense of discrimination and a sense of self-respect to be able to think critically and make rational choices. Theatre is considered to be the **'Transformative' pedagogy** that aims to combine and meld the theory of social constructivism and critical pedagogy. The theatre-based pedagogy attempts to lay stress on bringing a paradigm shift in the way teachers teach and students learn and thus, laying the foundation of a well-developed personality of a child and achieving the goal of holistic approach. **Just like social constructivism, in which, the knowledge is constructed and further modeled through social interactions, the theatre-based pedagogy also focuses on helping children derive meaning out of their experiences.**

They build their knowledge based on their experiences and understanding. It is a critical pedagogy that focuses on both content and context of a problem. The whole idea of the theatre-based pedagogy is to be able to let loose children and giving liberty to them to see the world from their lens, where they can have an entirely different viewpoints to stereotypes and cliched notions of the world. Many classrooms have deliberately dodged the innovativeness and originality of the ideas of the children in schools, resultantly, we have children who are easily susceptible to different vulnerabilities in and outside the school or maybe in their lives too. Any topic instantly becomes more fun to do and learn for the children when theatrics is involved. **The present chapter lays impetus on signification of using theatre as a tool and pedagogy for reforming the learning in students.**

Many research studies have closely inspected the effect of drama-based teaching on various subjects especially history at secondary school level. A literature sweep has been done to examine the studies related to theatre and drama-based pedagogy for teaching in the class and supportive studies have been culled out by the researcher. NCERT (2018) published a teachers' handbook JOY OF THEATRE on May 21st, it extols the capacity of theatre for pedagogical purposes. It lays stress on answering "Why Theatre is a must-have?", "How can teachers be sensitized for creating meanings in experiential terms" etc. The position paper ideates theatre and drama from two aspects: Drama as an approach and Drama as a subject. The subject viewpoint includes the skill of applied part of theatre and drama while the latter focuses on dramatic tactics for pedantic and instructive purposes. The whole paper deliberates around letting a child to go on a quest all by himself, seeking his/

her own answers to the problems of life and everyday challenges at hand, thereby multiplying and enriching his/her likelihood of self-development. Similarly, Sengul (2010) employed a new approach in teaching of history for the secondary school students. The textbooks of history were thoroughly examined and activities were created for 9th grade students. Drama method, still image technique, impromptu method, improvisations, role-playing were used to teach topics like Malazgirt Battle, Turkish and Muslim Pundits, Turkish monuments, Ancient Egypt. The researcher has adored the diversity and concluded that teachers must use drama-based techniques to transact the curriculum in the classroom. Modany (2012) coached a workshop for teachers and educators that focused on ways of employing the dramatic elements into their classrooms while teaching the subject matter. Drama games & exercises and role-playing were conducted for the teachers which made them realize that these drama games could prove fruitful for exploring the historical concepts and collaborative learning. Modany concluded that the workshop helped the teachers a lot in reflecting their own methodologies to teach the content and helped them understand their strengths and weaknesses. Cochran (2015) in his action research project analyzes many studies on the drama-based practices. The study accentuated that drama-based activities had a positive impact on the motivation of the students. Kisida, (2020); Goodwin, (2020); Bower, (2020) inquired into decreased emphasis on drama and arts instruction in schools. The findings of the study suggest that arts integrated education and theater-based activities have overall positive influence on students for learning history infused with live interactive theater performances

Theatre as a pedagogy in secondary schools

As already discussed earlier, teaching history through theatrics can increase the interest of the students by leaps and bounds. Theatre based pedagogy can prove to be a fruitful approach to teaching various subjects, especially History in secondary schools. The researcher has suggested theatre as a pedagogy to teach the children.

Acknowledging the massive changes theatre-based activities brings in a traditional classroom learning, its empirical verification stands strong. Theatre can be harnessed as a pedagogy for teaching history to the secondary school children by taking a gallimaufry of its versions that include tableaux, pantomime, impressionism, plays and other dramatic activities. By incorporating theatre for transacting the syllabi of history to secondary school students, a wide array of drama games and exercises can be introduced in the classroom such as pantomiming various historical characters and using impressionism for learning about certain historical events etc. A teacher must actively interact with the students and understand from their lens the ways in which history can be learnt and taught. Theatre based pedagogy is supposed to simplify the complexities related to chronology and timeline of significant historical events. With theatre pedagogy in action, children at secondary school level should also be exposed to participatory theatre that facilitates effective decision-making. A cross-curricular approach should be followed, amalgamating play, theatre and art-integrated education, that focuses on domains like nature of the subject, function of subject and purpose of the subject. By using theatre as a tool, various emotions and skills of secondary school students can be honed and developed. For example, a chapter that focuses on The French Revolution should be taught with a dramatizing technique by using pageantry, tableaux and mimicking. Theatre in education has been considered only as a pilot project and thus, the government and the schools have not been able to explore theatre for pedagogical purposes.

Critical analysis of back exercises of textbooks of 9th and 10th classes of subject History

The present chapter aims to magnify the capacity of theatre in education by performing an acute and imperative breakdown of back exercises of textbooks of 9th and 10th classes of subject History of both boards JKBOSE (Jammu and Kashmir State Board of School Education) and CBSE (Central Board of Secondary Education) respectively. The researcher has culled out various questions/activities that can be better answered through theatre and dramatization pedagogy. The back exercises of the books of classes 9th and 10th have served as a north-star for the present paper. The detailed analysis is based on researchers' readings related to chapter-wise culling out of questions/activities. The researcher has tried to connect the dots in the syllabi of history with that of theatre-based pedagogy and has given a point-by-point and question by question schema in a tabular form a series of questions/ activities that can be performed by theatre-based pedagogy. The elaborate list of questions/activities will provide a deeper insight of how theatre and performing arts will influence academics. Students will be benefitted significantly, not only in terms of exploring the unexplored or untapped potentials, but also by doing away with various deterrents associated with performing in front of an audience. The whole concept of using drama and theatre into the curriculum is to sensitize students about different social issues and helps them do away with their reservations. This thorough and particularized table of activities framed below will help both teachers and students to understand about their topics more clearly with the help of theatre, drama and arts in education.

Table 16.1: The unit-wise list of questions/activities of class 9th of JKBOSE for subject History

UNIT No. 1 (Events and Process)	**Activities/Questions**
Chapter-1 (The French Revolution)	**Activity no. 1**: Imagine the impact of the events in France on neighboring countries such as Prussia, Austria, Hungary or Spain, all of which were absolute monarchies. How would the kings, traders, peasants, nobles or members of clergy here have reacted to the news of what was happening in France? **Activity no. 2**: Imagine yourself to be one woman queueing up at a bakery. Formulate a response to the argument put forward by Chaumette. **Activity no. 3**: Describe the picture (The patriotic fat-reducing press) in your own words. What are the images that the artist has used to communicate the following ideas: greed, equality, justice takeover by the state of the assets of the Church? **Activity no. 4:** Explain the rise of Napoleon?

(*Contd.*)

Chapter-2 (Socialism in Europe and the Russian Revolution)	**Activity no. 1:** The year is 1916. You are the General in the Tsar's Army on the Eastern front. You are to write a report on the same. **Activity no. 2:** Imagine you are a striking worker in 1905 who is being tried in the court for your act of rebellion. Act out a speech for your class. **Activity no. 3:** Imagine that you are a middle-level wheat farmer in Russia after collectivization, what would you describe your conditions as a farmer.
Chapter-3 (Nazim and the Rise of Hitler)	**Activity no. 1**: Imagine yourself to be a Jew or a Pole in Nazi Germany. It is September 1941, and the law enforcing Jews to wear the star of David has just been declared. Enact an account of one day in your life. **Activity no. 2:** How would you have reacted to Hitler's ideas if you were: a Jewish woman, a non-Jewish German woman.
Chapter-4 (History of Jammu & Kashmir)	**Activity no. 1**: In the absence of modern means of communication, enact out the difficulties people in J&K faced.
UNIT No. 2 (Livelihoods, Economics and Societies)	**Activities/Questions**
Chapter-1 (Forest, Society and Colonialism)	**Activity no. 1**: Reaction of tribal people to the British Forest Policy.
Chapter-2 (Pastoralists in the Modern World)	**Activity no. 1**: Brief description of the living of the nomadic people. **Activity no. 2**: Imagine 1890s. You belong to a community of nomadic pastoralists and craftsmen. You learn that the Govt. has declared your community a Criminal Tribe. Describe briefly what you would've felt.
Chapter-3 (Peasants and Farmers)	**Activity no. 1:** Reluctance of Indian farmers to grow opium.

(*Contd.*)

UNIT No. 3 (Everyday life, Culture and Politics)	**Activities/Questions**
Chapter-1 (History and Sport: the story of Cricket)	**Activity no. 1:** Enact out condemnation of the Pentangular tournament.
Chapter-2 (Clothing: A Social History)	**Activity no. 1:** Explain the dress transformation in the Colonial India. **Activity no. 2:** Swadeshi Movement in Bengal. **Activity no. 3:** Discuss the reaction of the Indians to the introduction of Western dress style.

Table 16.2: The unit-wise list of questions/activities of class 9th of CBSE for subject History

UNIT No. 1 (Events and Processes)	**Activities/Questions**
Chapter-1 (The French Revolution)	**Activity no. 1:** Compare and contrast the views of Desmoulins and Robespierre.
Chapter-2 (Socialism in Europe and the Russian Revolution)	**Activity no. 1**: Imagine that a meeting has been called in your area to discuss the socialist idea of doing away with private property and introducing collective ownership.
Chapter-3 (Nazism and the Rise of Hitler)	**Activity no. 1**: If you were a student sitting in one of these classes, how would you have felt towards Jews?
UNIT No. 2 (Livelihoods, Economics and Societies)	**Activities/Questions**
Chapter-1 (Forest, Society and Colonialism)	**Activity no. 1:** Dialogue between a colonial forester and an Adivasi.

(*Contd.*)

Chapter-2 (Pastoralists in the Modern World)	**Activity no. 1:** Imagine that it is 1950 and you are a 60-year-old Raika herder living in the post-independence India. You are telling your grand-daughter about the changes which have taken place in your lifestyle after independence.
UNIT No. 3 (Everyday life, culture and politics)	**Activities/Questions**
Chapter-2 (Clothing: A Social History)	**Activity no. 1:** Society and Culture in France at the time of revolution. **Activity no. 2:** If you were a poor peasant, would you have willingly taken to giving up mill-made cloth.

Table 16.3: The unit-wise list of questions/activities of class 10th of JKBOSE for subject History

UNIT No. 1 (Events and Procession I)	**Activities/Questions**
Chapter-1 (The rise of nationalism in Europe)	**Activity no. 1:** Imagine you are a weaver who saw the events as they unfolded. **Activity no. 2:** Imagine you were a citizen of Frankfurt in March 1848 and were present during the proceedings of the parliament.
Chapter-2 (Nationalism in Europe)	**Activity no. 1:** Enact the idea of Satyagraha. **Activity no. 2:** The year is 1921 and you are a student in a government-controlled school. Enact out a skit, urging students to answer Gandhiji's call to join the Non-Cooperation Movement. **Activity no. 3:** Discuss the Salt March to make clear why it was an effective symbol of resistance against colonialism.
UNIT No. 2 (Livelihoods, Economics and Societies)	**Activities/Questions**
Chapter-1 (The making of a Global World)	**Activity no. 1:** Imagine that you are an agricultural worker who has arrived in America from Ireland. Enact out about earning your living. **Activity no. 2:** Imagine yourself as an indented Indian laborer in Caribbean.

(*Contd.*)

Chapter-2 (The age of Industrialization)	**Activity no. 1:** Imagine that you are a merchant writing back to a salesman who has been trying to persuade you to buy a new machine.
UNIT No. 3 (Everyday life, Culture and Politics)	**Activities/Questions**
Chapter-1	**Activity no. 1:** Imagine that you are Marco Polo. Write a letter from China to describe the world of print which you have seen there.
UNIT No. 4 (Modernization of Erstwhile J&K State)	**Activities/Questions**
Chapter-1	**Activity no. 1**: Enact out Jashn-i-Kashmir. **Activity no. 2:** Kashmir Chalo Campaign and impact of land reforms on rural society.

Table 16.4: The unit-wise list of questions/activities of class 10th of CBSE for subject History

UNIT No. 1 (Events and Processes)	**Activities/Questions**
Chapter-1 (The rise of Nationalism in Europe)	**Activity no. 1**: Role of women in Nationalist struggles. **Activity no. 2**: Siberian weavers uprising.
Chapter-2 (The nationalist movement in Indo-China)	**Activity no. 1:** Imagine a conversation between a French Colonizer and a Vietnamese laborer in the canal project. **Activity no. 2:** Imagine you are a student in the Tonkin Free School in 1910.
Chapter-3 (Nationalism in India)	**Activity no. 1:** Quit India Movement. **Activity no. 2:** Satyagraha as an active resistance. **Activity no. 3:** Imagine you are a woman participating in the Civil Disobedience Movement.

UNIT No. 2 (Livelihoods, Economics and Societies)	**Activities/Questions**
Chapter-1 (The making of a Global World)	**Activity no. 1:** The Great Depression. **Activity no. 2:** Indentured Indian laborer in Caribbean.
Chapter-2 (The age of Industrialization)	**Activity no. 1:** The way in which historians focus on industrialization rather than on small workshops is a good example of how what we believe today about the past is influenced by what historians choose to notice and what they ignore.
Chapter-3 (Work, Life and Leisure)	**Activity no. 1:** Enact out a London Slum in 1889. **Activity no. 2:** Imagine you are investigating the conditions in which the London poor lived. **Activity no. 3:** Imagine you are a young person living in a chawl. Describe one day of your life.
UNIT No. 3 (Everyday life, culture and politics)	**Activities/Questions**
Chapter-1 (Print culture and the modern world)	**Activity no. 1:** Enacting out changes taking place to provoke the print culture. **Activity no. 2:** Development of print leading to dissenting ideas.
Chapter-2 (Novels, Society and History)	**Activity no. 1:** Imagine that you are a historian in 3035 A.D. You have just located 2 novels which were written in the twentieth century. **Activity no. 2:** Read 'GODAAN' and depict the life of peasants in the novel.

Suggestive pedagogy and conclusions on the basis of activities suggested for classes 9th and 10th (both JKBOSE and CBSE) in the History subject in UT of J&K shown above in the tabular form

For the present chapter, the researcher has chosen and selected a few activities from the History textbooks of class 9th and 10th of both JKBOSE and CBSE, that can be performed with the help of theatre and drama. And on the basis of this arduous task, the researcher has endeavored to put forth a few suggestions and inferences that will prove helpful for both learners as well as teachers to improve the teaching learning process. **A teacher must employ theatre-based pedagogy to instill in a learner the seeds of imagination, creativity and knowledge**. Following are the suggestions that may be of help to the educators:

- New Education Policy is seen as continuum in incorporating theatre-based pedagogy in the classrooms, therefore, a formal structure of Theatre in Education and Drama in Education should be **introduced at the school level at an early stage**.
- **Participatory Theatre** should be introduced for the children to improve their decision-making skills and thereby, **creating individuals who simply do not jump the bandwagon blindly**.
- **Drama games and exercises** should be used to create a frame of reference for formulation of theatre-based pedagogy
- Creating institutions that can actually translate theatre into classrooms and make it a reality, and this is possible only when the stakeholders understand that theatre in education is a mission.
- Training and trainers in theatre-based pedagogy is a dream, that can only be fulfilled when there are institutions that train teachers for the same.
- National School of Drama (NSD) can play a big role in this direction by advocating, for theatre-based pedagogy, **working for the standardization and scaling up game of theatre in education**.
- The curriculum should be flexible enough **to infuse 'Chaunsath Kalayein' as it forms the ground for the overall cultured development of a person**, and thus, such curriculum will help students to become better versions of themselves.
- More departments in the colleges and the universities should also be created for the students who are willing to make a future in theatre and drama in education.

- The **inconsistencies and mismatch between accreditations and qualifications of being a trained theatre teacher should be considered**. Proper training should be provided to the teachers for applying these skills in a classroom.
- After performing the activities in the class, **the children should write in a diary about their success as a performer such as 'I spoke loudly during the performance, I spoke very meekly, my voice matched my characters' feelings and emotions, my costume and body language conveyed the character that I was playing etc.'** This will develop a sense of belongingness in a child towards his class and his/her mates.
- **Show and don't tell! This is the underlying mantra** for imbibing Theatrics in a classroom. **Pantomiming is a classic example** of this.
- By smartly using theatrics, creative dramatization in the classroom to teach the children can help teachers learn so much about children **as each child is a gifted child. They unwrap their packages as and when they like!**
- Theatre and Drama in Education will help the children in **infusing local cultural values, help them understand the value of their local flavor, heritage, costumes, music, dance forms, art forms.**
- **By using theatrics in the classroom, students will better understand about their state heroes like Raja Hari Singh, Maharaja Ranjit Singh etc.**
- This suggestive pedagogy can prove to be a **game-changer on the part of 'CULTURE HEROES', i.e., parents, Teachers, Grandparents, Community members etc.**

Conclusion

It can thus be concluded that, theatre-based pedagogy, as a suggestive pedagogy **celebrates perspectives of various kinds,** helps children learn about making good judgements about relationships, helps children realize that there can be more than one solution to the problems etc. Theatre Pedagogy aims at **giving voice to those who are silent** and lets them learn what otherwise cannot be said. It broadens the horizons of the learners to express their ideas and emotions. This suggestive pedagogy should be explored for pedagogical purposes, not based on a rigid syllabus but, with flexibilities and a room for providing children with a worthwhile creative experience. **Theatre as a recreation activity and as a pedagogy is still at the embryonic stage in India as there are few trained and adept masters in this field. Consequently, creative designs and plans should be chalked out to introduce the theatre-based curriculum and theatre as a pedagogy in schools of India to make our schools, our learners and our teachers recognizable at the global level.**

References

Baldwin, P. (2021). Drama strategy: Teaching history through drama. *Drama and Theatre.* Retrieved from https://www.dramaandtheatre.co.uk on April 11, 2022.

Barlow, D., & Isenberg, D. (1967). The Use of Drama in History Teaching. *Plowden, (1),* Part V (620). Retrieved from https://www.jstor.org/stable/43252718 on April 11, 2022.

Central Board of Secondary Education. (2006). India and the contemporary world-I. CBSE.

Central Board of Secondary Education. (2007). India and the contemporary world-II. CBSE.

Cochran, D.J. (2015). Drama and History: teaching historical thinking through role-play. Retrieved from https://minds.wisconsin.edu/handle/1793/74518 on April 11, 2022.

Contractor, M.R. (1984). *Creative Drama and Puppetry in Education.*

Henry, O. (2012). How has drama or theater techniques been used for research purposes? *International Journal of Education and The Arts.* Retrieved from https://www.academia.edu/4153115/The_use_of_Drama_and_or_Theatrer_Techniques_in_Research on April 11, 2022 https://americanhistory.si.edu/blog/2012/02/teaching-with-drama.html on April 11, 2022.

Jammu and Kashmir Board of School Education. (2019). India and the contemporary world-I. JKBOSE.

Jammu and Kashmir Board of School Education. (2019). India and the contemporary world-II. JKBOSE.

Janak, H. (2021). Teaching history through theater positively impacts student learning outcomes. *Communications Education and Human Development (CEHD).* Retrieved from https://education.tamu.edu/teaching-history-through-theater-positively-impacts-student-learning-outcomes on April 11, 2022.

Karabag, G., & Aydogan, O. (2021). The Effect of History Teaching Supported by Dramatization Technique on Students Achievement and Permanence Level. *Asian Journal of Education and Training, 7*(No.1), 36-45. DOI: 10.20448/journal.522.2021.71.36.45. Retrieved from https://files.eric.ed.gov/fulltext/EJ1287582.pdf on April 11, 2022.

Kisda, B., Goodwin, L., & Bower, D.H. (2020). Teaching History Through Theater: The Affects of Arts Integration on Student's Knowledge and Attitudes. *SAGE Journals.* Retrieved from https://journals.sagepub.com/doi/full/10.1177/2332858420902717 on April 11, 2022.

Litz, R. (2020). How to Use Art To Teach History. *George Lucas Educational Foundation.* Retrieved from https://www.edutopia.org/org/artide/how-use-art-teach-history? On April 11, 2022.

Martin, C. (2020). Teaching history through theatre. *THE GLASGOW GUARDIAN.* Retrieved from https://glasgowguardian.co.uk/2020/10/26/teaching-history-through-theatre/ on April 11, 2022.

Modany, A. (2012). Teaching with Drama. *National Museum of American History.*

National Council for Education, Research and Training (NCERT). (2018). *Joy of Theatre Teacher's Handbook.* Retrieved from https://www.google.com/search?q=joy+of+theatre++&aqs+chrome on April 20, 2022.

National Curriculum Framework (NCF). (2005). Retrieved from https://ncert.nic.in/pdf/nc-framework/nf2005-english.pdf on April 20, 2022.

Sengul, T. (2010). Activity models about using drama method in history lessons. *Procedia-Social and Behavioral Sciences, 2*(2): 3155-3159, Doi: 10.1016/j.sbspro:2010.03.481. Retrieved from https://www.researchgate.net/publication/248606841-Activity_models_about_using_drama_method_history_lessons on April 11, 2022.

Ustuk, O., & Inan, Dilek. (2017). A comparative literature review of the studies on Drama in English language teaching in Turkey. *Novitas – ROYAL (Research on Youth and Language), 11*(1), 27-41. Retrieved from https://files.eric.ed.gov/fulltext/EJ1167241.pdf on April 11, 2022.

Websites accessed

www.pinterest.com

www.jkrishnamurti.org

17
NEP 2020
Vision and Mission to Transform India into a Global Leader

Umme Kulsoom Zaidi

Introduction

NEP-2020 is a paradigm shift from traditional teaching and learning approaches to student-centric, multidisciplinary, and holistic education. NEP-2020 prepares the student for the future and present, providing equal opportunities to all sans discrimination. It aims for educational reform, improves educational institutes' functioning, and increases private institutes' accountability. The salient points of NEP-2020 are presented in Fig. 17.1.

The NEP-2020 is essential in the backdrop of specific issues which, if left unattended, un-rectified, or unanswered, will affect the growth of India by impacting the socio-cultural and economic growth and gender inclusivity. As per data:

a. The gap between male and female literacy in India is expected to be 21.6% at the National Level. Alarmingly, one in every five girls enrolled for education drops out after class eight. Enrolment in higher secondary is roughly 32% (Chase K., 2022).

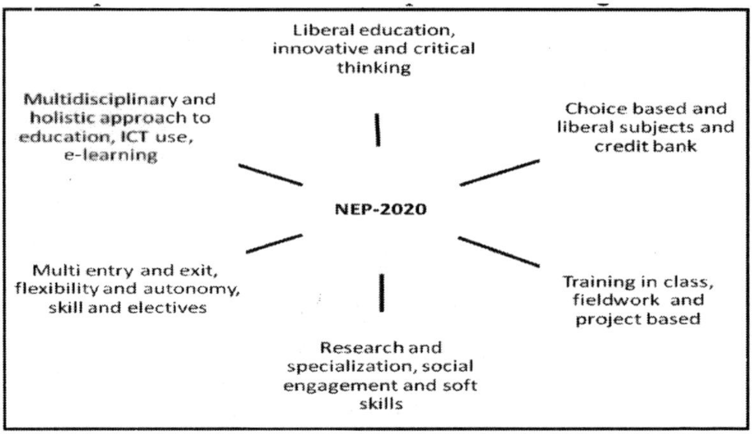

Fig. 17.1: NEP-2020 at a glance.

b. By 2026 there is expected to be an 11% increase in the "**non-traditional learners**" in the age bracket 24-35 years who enroll themselves in colleges (www. ficci-hes.com, 2021).

c. Evaluation of any system in place is important. It identifies the merits and demerits of the system and paves the way for the reforms. As per a report, 30 % of the unemployed in the country are holders of degrees (Kishore, K. *et al.*, 2021).

d. Data is suggestive that 64% of children in rural India require educational support. The drop-out is 17% at the secondary level, and 30% fail to reach senior secondary levels (Chhikara, P. *et al.*, 2022).

e. 68% of India resides in rural areas, and 25 % of the population will be in the working age group by 2025. Literature suggests a correlation between skills, level of education, and employability. Unfortunately, huge gaps exist in the criterion mentioned above in rural India, female gender, underrepresented and underprivileged classes (Karthikeyan, P. *et al.*, 2020).

f. Recently, a 7.4% increment in enrolment of students in higher education has been reported (2020-2021). Out of 4.13 crores of students who enrolled, 35.8% (growth of 31.67 %) belong to the backward class, 5.8% to ST (growth of 47%), and 14.2% (growth of 27.96%) to SC. Although there is an improvement compared to 2019-2020, much still needs to be done. The enrolment in Government universities and colleges was 73.1% and 34.5%, respectively; for private universities, it was 26.3%. Private aided and unaided colleges accounted for 21.1% and 44.4 % of enrolments. The enrolment in STEM was only 22.89%. For every 100 male teachers, there are only 75 female teachers, and the Pupil-Teacher Ratio in universities and its constituents colleges in regular mode is 19 (aishe.gov.in). The above data suggests an increase in the enrolment of students. However, inequalities still exist, especially for weaker and marginalized sections of society and the representation of females in policymakers and participation in educational activities. The gap is identified in the participation of private institutions in quality education.

g. The AI market in India is expected to reach US$7.8 billion by 2025 at the rate of 20.2% compound annual growth (www.idc.com). Data is suggestive that not more than 9% of females and 17% of males in rural India use the internet. A rural-urban divide also exists regarding access and availability of computers at home (Singh, N. *et al.*, 2022). Thus, there is an urgent need for integration of AI in technical education, optimal use to impart quality and skill-based education, and at the same time, evaluation of AI for its advantages and long-term consequences.

Ojective of the Research

The present chapter reviews the NEP-2020 as a vision and mission statement to transform India into a global education hub and also identifies the limitation and suggests recommendations.

Research Methodology

The present review was performed on the google scholar database and Government websites, newspaper reports, and other relevant

Table 17.1: Summary of the few selected and reviewed papers

Author & publication year	Type of the study	Theme	Findings	Gaps identified and challenges
Singh, N. *et al.*, 2022	Review article	Digitization of Education in light of NEP-2020 and roadblocks to online education.	Focus on print, broadcast, and electronic media for learning. E-learning tools to promote education as emphasized by NEP-2020.	Quality of education, gender disparity, digital literacy, and infrastructure.
Nandi, A. *et al.*, 2022	Qualitative analysis	Critical analysis of NEP's role in transforming teacher education and functions of a teacher.	NEP aims to improve the quality of teachers and promote public-private coordination. It aims at preparing well-trained teachers for the future and present.	The focus of infrastructure, resources, a well-defined curriculum, digital literacy, and divide.
Devi, K. *et al.*, 2022	Qualitative analysis of secondary data	Role of NEP in providing inclusive and equitable education.	Focus and emphasis on Sustainable Development Goals 4.0 by 2030. Equal learning opportunities without discrimination and bias and create a pool of well-qualified teachers. Outreach programs and delivering education in Indian Languages will pave the way for inclusive education.	Enrolment gradually decreases in higher levels, i.e., from primary to higher secondary levels, and the situation is much worse in OBC and minorities.
Bania, S., 2021	Review article	Autonomy of Educational Institutions	Autonomy provides more significant opportunities and flexibility for teaching and research innovation and paves the way for reforms.	Categorization into research and academic institutes, issues related to affiliation and giving autonomy to affiliated colleges/institutes, and providing multidisciplinary status.

(Contd.)

Author & publication year	Type of the study	Theme	Findings	Gaps identified and challenges
Chikkara, P. *et al.*, 2022	Analytical study	Focus on determinants of school drop-outs and analyze the effect, of interventions to tackle the issue.	Right to education till fifth grade, as advocated by NEP-2020, and medium of instruction in the local language will reduce the drop-outs and bridge the learning gaps. The uniformity of the educational system across the country is also expected to address the concerns of disparity and discrimination. Drop-out was correlated with the family's socio-economic status and academic levels of parents, occupation, and migration. Institutional factors which contribute to drop-outs were mainly discrimination and disparity, pupil-teacher ratio, infrastructure, and peer factors like competition.	Tackle the issue of the trend of drop-outs as early as elementary levels. A holistic approach to address the problem is required. Underprivileged and economically backward strata need attention. Uniformity of the education system in a diverse country like India needs to be implemented with proper planning.
Sarna, K.K. *et al.*, 2021	Critical review	Critical analysis of NEP-2020 to reform education in India.	Concerns related to the instruction of medium till class fifth in local language and three language formula need to be addressed and resolved. Possibility of discrimination, unequal opportunities, and drop-outs based on language in the future. Financial constraints on Institutions due to vocational/skill and choice-based learning modules.	Imposition of the language across states, autonomy to states to decide indigenous language, and parents' concerns with transferrable jobs. Allocation of finances by the Government to meet the GDP increment from 1 to 6%.

(*Contd.*)

Author & publication year	Type of the study	Theme	Findings	Gaps identified and challenges
			Clarity on the right to education to address gender disparity in school drop-outs. Updated curriculum to be rolled out promptly without any delay and foster research aptitude and opportunities to attract international students.	
Singh, A. *et al.*, 2020	Review article	Role of NEP in education of the children with special needs	75 % of children with disabilities of 5 years of age (25% of them in age group 5-19 years) do not attend any educational institute. NEP intends to increase enrolment in schools, provide financial support, and ensure the learning of local sign language. Revamp and provision infrastructure to suit the needs of children with special needs. It also aims to create a home-based educational system, train the teachers and support an open school system.	Critical to achieve SDGs by 2030 and revamp education system by 2040 and thus needs proper implementation.
Santosha, C. *et al.*, 2022	Analytical study	Impact of NEP on the education system and issues and challenges. The study was conducted in Karnataka, the first State to implement NEP-2020.	The analysis of results showed that Government needs to implement and roll out NEP with due planning and preparedness. The initial data indicates that there was uncertainty in the minds of learners concerning the framework of NEP-2020.	The students are well versed with the prevailing educational system, and thus NEP will take time to impact the mindsets of the masses. Accordingly, guidance, training, and systematic implementation assume greater significance.

(*Contd.*)

Author & publication year	Type of the study	Theme	Findings	Gaps identified and challenges
			The analysis highlights the need for NEP-relevant course books and study/reference materials. Results showed a need for more clarity and clarity while opting for skill and elective courses. Rural-Urban divide and lack of proper infrastructure were other salient findings.	
Bellary, A.S., 2022	Review article	Role of information, Communication, and technology in teaching and learning processes.	ICT use provides an excellent platform for quality and up-to-date teaching and learning. The ease of access to information and availability of study material anywhere/ anytime is an added advantage. It also aids in the delivery of content.	Lack of infrastructure, technical support, digital literacy, and unequal availability of ICT resources and access at home are significant challenges. Cybercrime and surety about the authenticity of the information available are essential issues. Since readymade details and material are available online thus, sometimes there may be a tendency to download the data and use it elsewhere.
Kurien, A. *et al.*, 2020	Descriptive study	Impact of NEP-2020 on higher education system	Flexibility in allowing foreign Universities to open campuses in India will provide opportunities for students to have exposure to International quality education. Multidisciplinary institutes will offer a holistic approach to learning. To tackle the	Issues related to designing postgraduate courses of one and two years for students who have completed four and three years of undergraduation.

(Contd.)

Author & publication year	Type of the study	Theme	Findings	Gaps identified and challenges
			issue of academic and exam stress, the NEP advocates single entrance tests and academic credit banks for students wherein the students can use the credits to get admission to existing or switch over to a new college. In case of drop-outs, the credits will remain intact for future use if the student wants to continue the education. There are provisions for multiple entries and exits.	
Bhatnagar, A.K. *et al.*, 2021	Literature review	Role of Artificial Intelligence to enhance digital learning as envisioned by NEP-2020 and associated challenges.	AI has helped in speeding up the paradigm shift of the traditional educational system to the learner, knowledge, skill, and competency centric. Digital literacy and computer-friendly skills are essential for students and teachers. AI can be used effectively for administrative, academic, teaching, assessment, and evaluation purposes. It is an essential means to promote digital entrepreneurship and quality education.	Issues related to accessibility to smartphones, computers, and the internet must be addressed to ensure uniformity of AI use in education.
Kumar, A., 2021	Review article	Analysis of the policy document of NEP-2020 as a road map for educational reforms in India.	By 2030 HEIs will be transformed into multidisciplinary institutes, and by 2040, the strength of students in them will be increased to three thousand. Establishment of counselling centres to ensure the mental well-being of students.	Issues related to profit-making by the private institution and ever-increasing capitation fees need to be checked. There is an urgent need to ensure that the Internationalization of Education is not merely reduced to a

(Contd.)

Author & publication year	Type of the study	Theme	Findings	Gaps identified and challenges
			Providing flexibility to learners to study abroad and complete the courses in India. Weightage to foreign degrees in India. Granting graded autonomy based on teaching-learning, innovation, and research to non-public Universities. Autonomy in granting and awarding degrees, but such process will be accreditated and ranked by various agencies. Promote online distance education, collaboration, and research to ensure equal learning opportunities for all, especially the weaker and marginalized sections of society. There is the provision of the National Research Foundation to achieve the same.	profit-making business. The stakeholders need to provide education delivery to meet the goals set by NEP-2020.
Kasinathan, G., 2021	Review article	Role of NEP-2020 to achieve transformative education in context to content, teachers, curriculum, participation at the community level, and infrastructure reforms.	Content: promote Indian languages, formative assessment, problem-solving attitude, reasoning and assertion, and digital learning—open access to learning resources. Teachers: need to instruct in vernacular language, create e-content, update their knowledge through online platforms.	Digital privacy, dangers of students bypassing teachers and accessing freely available content without mentoring and guidance, AI-enabled assessment raises issues of the need for more conceptualization and comprehensive understanding. Issues related to internet addiction and screen time need to be addressed.

(Contd.)

Author & publication year	Type of the study	Theme	Findings	Gaps identified and challenges
Chase, K, 2022	Review article	Analysis of NEP-2020 role in the education of women.	NEP aims to empower women's education. It advocates participation and collaboration at the state and local levels and creates a Gender Inclusion Fund. It seeks to develop fear-free campuses and an environment for greater participation of females in education. Educational institutes create awareness regarding various female welfare and protection schemes related to harassment, maternity benefits, and child marriages—motivation and opportunities in the form of scholarships and fellowships to girls and free boardings. Policymakers to implement and advocate a gender-neutral education system with equal employment opportunities for all. Promote vocational skills, encourage education completion, and provide counselling to shape their careers.	Identification of the unique needs of the girl child and determinants of gender inequality will pave the way for more inclusive education. Ways to use the Gender Inclusion Funds need elaboration—issues related to menstrual hygiene in schools.
Phulari, S. *et al.*, 2022	Literature review	Pros and cons of the Academic Bank of Credits in NEP-2020.	It is a welcome step as it ensures a multidisciplinary approach to teaching and learning, provides flexibility to a student to choose and shape a career, and tackles the issue of dropping out to a certain extent.	Issues related to the uniformity of the curriculum and content in case of transfer and choosing a different college by student. Concerns related to it diluting the degrees and quality of education across various colleges and universities in the absence of uniformity.

materials using "NEP-2020" OR "National Education Policy" AND "Vision and Mission" AND "Challenges" "India" OR "Global Leader" OR "Education Hub" AND "Solutions" OR "Road Ahead" AND "STATISTICS". Articles not in English, those without access to full text, unconfirmed reports, or references were excluded from the search. After the exclusion criterion and removal of duplicates, twenty-five articles were selected and reviewed. The search outline is provided in Fig 17.2.

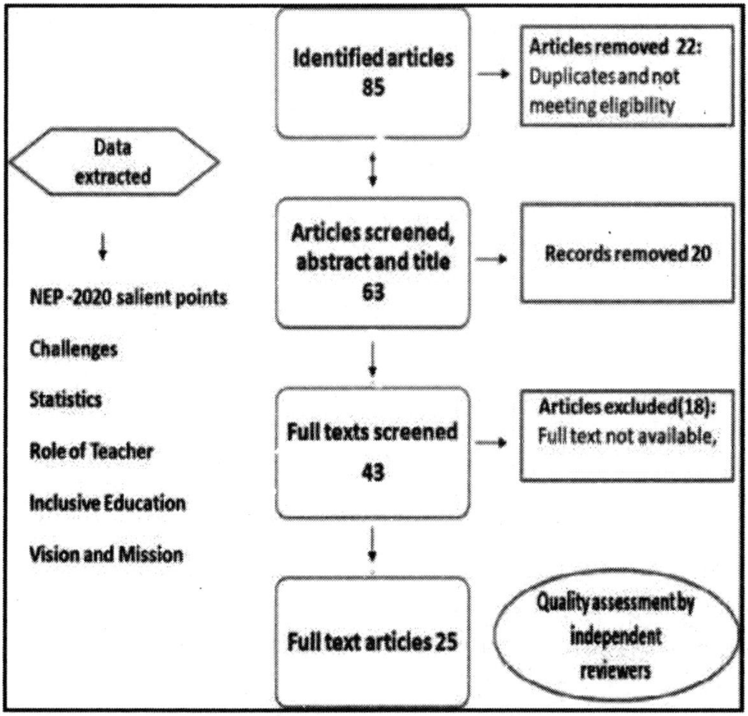

Fig. 17.2: Selection of the articles for review.

The summary of few selected articles is presented in the Table 17.1.

Discussion

Addresses issues of drop-outs: Drop-out is a significant problem challenging the future of India. According to reports, 30% of children drop-out of school after matriculation. Another issue is the need for more trained professionals to take up school teachers' jobs. The report is suggestive that 13% of the teachers need to be qualified. Improvement in class environments by making them learning-friendly, safe, and hygienic and also improving teacher: student ratio to 1:20 will ensure active and participatory learning and improve the quality of teaching. Platforms like SWAYAM and DIKHSA will ensure mentoring and provide opportunities for continuing education and career advancement for teachers. Outcome-based learning must be evaluated and monitored for better policy and decision-making by a comprehensive "Performance Assessment Review and Analysis of Knowledge for Holistic Development" (PARAKH). By 2025, rationalization of the schools to promote innovation, scientific and research temperament in students from the beginning. Setting up special economic zones to provide equal opportunities to weaker sections is another revolutionary vision of NEP-2020. Focus on extracurricular and soft skill development. A shift from institutes of academic excellence imparting quality and world-class training in a single discipline (Like IITs and AIIMS) to Multidisciplinary Education and Research Institutes (MERUs). 50% of students in schools and HEIs to have vocational training by 2025 (home. KPMG/in). NEP-2020 aims at equal learning opportunities for children with special needs and considers their learning abilities and needs. Thus, it talks about the flexibility of the curriculum and assessment programmes. Another important provision is the orientation programmes for parents and guardians of children with special needs. It thus aims at inclusive quality education without discrimination on any grounds (Ranjan, R., 2022).

Various initiatives like Sarva Shiksha Abhiyan, the Right to Education Act, 2009, and the mid-day meal programme yielded benefits in ensuring primary education in the age group 6-14 years. Government and Higher Education Institutions must ensure higher participation and create opportunities for Socio-Economically Disadvantaged Groups (SEDGs) (Devi, K., 2020).

NEP-2020 aims to remove gender disparity and provide equal opportunities: The efforts of outreach to females have yielded positive results, and there has been an increase in enrolment of women across educational institutes across India, but as per the Ministry of Human Resource Development, 2019 in STEM (Science, Technology, Engineering, and Maths) the percentage of females is still not at par with males. The representation of females in higher educational institutions and institutes of National importance is less (genderedjourneys.com/). NEP aims to bridge gender inequality by ensuring 100% and 50% enrolment of girls in schools and higher education by 2030 and 2035, respectively. It also focuses on a healthy and fear-free environment for females. It also fosters leadership roles in females to ensure greater participation and involves local players like Anganwadi workers to address the problem of drop-outs. It emphasizes counselling to change mindsets regarding female education (www.apsrtc.ap.gov.in) positively. The salient points are represented in Fig. 17.3.

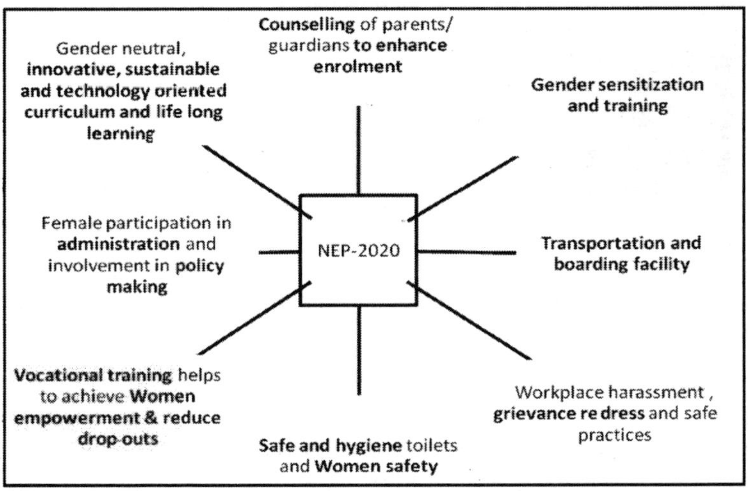

Fig. 17.3: NEP 2020 for inclusive education and gender equality.

Autonomy as a tool to reform education: One of the significant roadblocks to education reforms and hindrances to autonomy is the rigid policies and interferences in academics, appointments, and decision-making affairs of educational institutes. Another issue is related to expenditure and funds provided to HEIs. These, in turn, affect the overall teaching and learning environment and negatively impacts innovation and research. NEP-2020 aims to reform the governance of the academic bodies and also increase the GDP allocated to education expenditures. Also, there are provisions for scholarships to meritorious students without bias or discrimination. This will motivate them to excel in academics and get equal opportunities (Aithal, P.S. *et al.*, 2020). Graded autonomy to Institutes and colleges is expected to foster a sense of healthy competition and contribute to academic enrichment (Shisira, B., 2021).

NEP-2020 to realize Sustainable Development Goals: India will be a significant player in achieving sustainable development goals (SGDs) by 2030. The role of higher educational institutes assumes centre stage in the backdrop of SGDs. Teaching, research, and a multidisciplinary approach towards SGDs will ensure equity, quality education, and sustainability. Another essential aspect of NEP is to infuse qualities in learners to transform them into sound and responsible citizens. It aims to infuse a sense of social responsibility and engagement at local and community levels. Imparting quality and practical education cultivates problem-solving attitudes and a sense of mutual peaceful co-existence. NEP 2020 aims to empower marginalized, underprivileged, and underrepresented strata of society. It caters to the needs and aspirations of society and thus is futuristic and advocates the introduction of new courses (www.ugc.ac.in).

NEP-2020 to Internationalize Education: NEP also aims to increase the enrolment of international students in India. It provides an excellent medium for intercultural exchange. NEP also values the indigenous education system and incorporates India's rich cultural diversity, but at the same time, prepares the learner to compete globally. NEP considers socio-cultural integration and foreign policy alignment to meet the socio-cultural and economic needs and aspirations at the National and International levels. Thus, it talks about collaborative education (Khushnam, P.N., 2022).

Use of Technology: AI requires training, internet access, infrastructure, and gadgets. Stakeholders, i.e., learners and teachers, must be trained to use the technology effectively and efficiently. The availability of easily accessible tools like TV channels delivering educational content and free online resources in multiple languages will ensure better utilization of resources. Hands-on training and regular workshops to impart quality training will create a pool of trained learners, teachers, and users (Bhatnagar, A.K. *et al.*, 2021).

Holistic approach and focus on skills: NEP focuses on the holistic and multidisciplinary development of teachers who are well-versed with technology, passionate and dedicated to teaching, and have an aptitude for research and innovations in the field of education (Nandi, A. *et al.*, 2022). Socio-cultural, political, and economic situations are vital to the outcomes of the NEP-2020. Skills-based training, lifelong learning, and a multidisciplinary approach are expected to reduce significant economic disparity, improve the quality of life, and create equal job opportunities (Muralidharan, K. *et al.*, 2022). Educational Institutions need to focus on blended and digital learning, provide a holistic environment to learners, focus on their personality development, and equip them with skills (Sarna, K.K. *et al.*, 2021). **The salient points are presented in Table 17.2.**

Table 17.2: NEP-2020 Holistic approach and advocates soft skill development

Holistic Approach	Focus on Soft Skills
Innovation, active participation, Collaborative, Exchange of ideas, Self-paced learning	Communication skills (verbal and non-verbal)
Goal-oriented, creates job-ready learners, Caters to student diversity, and encourages communication	Professional outlook and problem-solving attitude
Incorporates research, Self-quest, the interest of the learner, and self-realization (vocational/career)	Team and managerial skills and leadership qualities

(*Contd.*)

Holistic Approach	Focus on Soft Skills
The focus is on the design and course plan, teaching and learning methodology, and assessment of achievements made by the learner	Imbibe ethical socio-cultural skills for overall personality, professional growth, and qualities essential for start-up and self-employability

Challenges identified

- Lack of trained facilitators and soft skill educators.
- Interdisciplinary training of the faculty.
- Lack of infrastructure.
- Need more resources for imparting vocational training.
- The language barrier, rural-urban divide, and e-learning and learning resources accessibility.
- School drop-outs and attendance in schools.
- The socio-economic, rural-urban, gender divide in access to education and ICT.
- Learning and assessment modules with emphasis on the ethos of NEP-2020.

Recommendations

- **Training of teacher** as facilitator.
- **Infrastructure development** to impart vocational training and soft skills.
- Minimizing school drop-outs and engaging them in vocational training.
- **Textbooks, teaching and learning resources, modules** at low cost or free of cost.
- **Private players, NGOs and media houses** should contribute to the vision and mission of NEP-2020.
- Public-private partnership.
- Regular **feedback from the stakeholders** is essential. Monitoring and evaluation of the strengths and weaknesses.
- **The traditional system of education** must be **integrated with modern scientific** and **futuristic education.**

- National Surveys are required to **identify the changing or emerging areas of importance** as feedback to educational bodies to implement/modify the curriculum.

Conclusion

NEP-2020 is a powerful tool to address the needs of the learner and prepares the present generation to cater to needs and challenges in the future. The Holistic, inter- and multi-disciplinary approach of the NEP-2020 has the ability to produce skill-oriented, problem-solving professionals with leadership qualities & lifelong learners. However, the challenges related to implementation, training, and infrastructure need to be addressed and resolved. NEP-2020 aims to transform India into a global educational hub and **Vishwaguru**.

References

Aithal, P.S., Aithal, S. (2020). Analysis of the Indian National Education Policy 2020 towards Achieving its Objectives. MRA, Available online at Online at https://mpra.ub.uni-muenchen.de/102549/.

Analysis of factors impacting gender parity in higher education in the state of Andhra Pradesh, India. Available online at https://www.apsrtc.ap.gov.in/coverage.php.

Bellary, A.S. (2022). NEP 2020 and Innovative Technology in Teaching Learning Process. National Conference on NEP-2020: Innovations in Teaching-Learning and Evaluation Process and the Role of IQAC. *Aayushi International Interdisciplinary Research Journal*, 113: 55-58.

Bhatnagar, A.K., Khanna, U., Rana, A. (2021). Digital Learning Ecosystem at Indian Higher Education System, *Journal of Contemporary Issues in Business and Government*, 7: 4360-4375.

Chase, K. (2022). *NEP and Women Education. Global Journal of Applied Engineering in Computer Science and Mathematics*. Special Edition, 1: 33-34.

Chhikara, P., Chakravorty, K. (2022). Drop-outs in Secondary and Senior Secondary Education: Understanding the Problem and Discussing its Solution. *Journal of Positive School Psychology*, *6*(11): 1090-1116.

Devi, K. (2022). Equitable and Inclusive Education with special reference to National Educational Policy (NEP) 2020. *Specialusis Ugdymas/Special Education*, *1*(43): 7017-7023.

Fostering Social Responsibility & Community Engagement in Higher Education Institutions in India 2. Available online at www.ugc.ac.in.

Gender, Higher Education and STEM in India. University of Glasgow: Economic and Social Council Research. Available online at https://genderedjourneys.com/.

Higher Education in India: Vision 2040. 2021. Available online at https://www.ficci-hes.com/pdf/2021/eyreport.pdf

https://aishe.gov.in/aishe/BlankDCF/AISHE%20Final%20Report%20 2020-21.pdf

https://www.idc.com/getdoc.jsp?containerId=prAP48288921

Impact of National Education Policy 2020 and opportunities for stakeholders. 2020. Available online at home. kpmg/in.

Karthikeyan, P., Dheepa, T., Anndal, T., Prakash, N. (2020). Employability Skills of Rural SC, ST. Youth in India: A Literature Review. *Gedrag & Organisatie Review*. *33*(2):2582-2591.

Kasinathan, G. (2021). National Education Policy 2020—Imagining Digital Technologies as a Resource to Achieve Educational Aims. *Voices of Teachers and Teacher Educators*, X(II): ISSN 2455-1376.

Khushnam, P.N. (2022). National Education Policy 2020: A Prudent Vision of India's Soft Power in the Emerging World Order. *India Quarterly*. *78*(2): 318-333.

Kishore, K., Prakash, A., Singh, K. (2021). How National Education Policy 2020 can be a lodestar to transform future generation in India. *J Public Affairs*. 21:e2500.

Kumar, A. (2021). New education policy (NEP) 2020: A roadmap for India 2.0. In W.B. James, C. Cobanoglu, & M. Cavusoglu (Eds.), *Advances in Global Education and Research*, *4*: 1-8.

Kumar, M. (2021). Inclusive Education and National Education Policy 2020: A Review. *International Journal of Creative Research Thoughts*, *9*(9): 23-29.

Kurien, A., Chandramana, S.B. (2020). Impact of New Education Policy 2020 on Higher Education. *Conference Paper*, November. DOI: 10.6084/m9.figshare.13332413.v1.

Muralidharan, K., Shanmugan, K., Klochkov, Y. The New Education Policy 2020, Digitalization and Quality of Life in India: Some Reflections. *Educ. Sci*. 2022, 12, 75.

Nandi, A., Das, T., Halder, T. (2022). A Critical Analysis of Recommendations of NEP 2020 to Reform Teacher Education in India. *AGPE The Royal Gondwana Research Journal*, *3*(5): 6-14.

Phulari, S., Pawar, A., Desai, S., Lokhande, S. (2022). National Education Po.icy-20's Academic Bank of Credits-Meaning, Process, Merits-

Demerits. *International Journal of Advanced Research in Science, Communication, and Technology*, *2*(5). DOI: 10.48175/IJARSCT-3551.

Ranjan, R. (2022). A Roadmap to Inclusive Education in NEP 2020. *Scholarly Research Journal for Interdisciplinary Studies. 10*(72): 17405-17413.

Santosha, C., Kadapatti, R.G. (2022). Uses and Consequences of NEP and Its Impact on Education System—An Analysis. National Conference on NEP-2020: Innovations in Teaching-Learning and Evaluation Process and the Role of IQAC. *Aayushi International Interdisciplinary Research Journal, 113*: 42-46.

Sarna, K.K., Puri, S., Kochar, K.S. (2021). National Education Policy-2020: A Critical Review. *Hans Shodh Sudha*, *1*(3): 8-14.

Shisira, Bania.(2021). National Education Policy-2020 & Institutional Autonomy in Indian Higher Education System: Issues and Challenges in Implementation, *East African Scholars J Edu Humanit Lit.*, *4*(6): 260-264.

Singh, A., Sharma, R.K. (2020). Role of NEP-2020 in the Education of Children with Special Needs. *Pankhuri*, *6*(2): 9-11.

Singh, N., Srivastava, N. (2022). Encumbrances in Digitization of Education: A Schema of NEP. *Management Journal for Advanced Research*, *2*(3): 5-9.

18

Educational Policy in India with Special Reference to National Education Policy 2020

Asma Ishaque

Introduction

The New Education Policy was released under the Government of India's Ministry of Human Resource Development (MHRD) ON 30 July, 2020, with the motto of Educate Encourage Enlighten; this is the first education policy to be released in the last 34 years in India. The aim of this policy is to prepare the children of India with 21th century skills. The New Education Policy is based on some important pillars of research, Innovation Quality, with the objective of developing India into a knowledge super power, Equity, and Accountability to ensure continual learning.

As per the vision of new education policy 2020, the Government of India has approved the New Indian Literacy Programme (NILP) aiming to providing Education for ALL, covering all aspects of education for non-literates of 15 years above. Finally, Indian education will have a uniqueness of its own . The NEP 2020 envision an Indian centred education system that directly contributes to the evolution of our nation enduring into an equitable and vibrant knowledge society by giving them a top-class quality of education.

India, today, is considered as a talent pool of the world, having qualified and education human resources in abundance. This has been one of the primary reasons for transformation of India into one of the fastest growing economics in the world in recent past. The number of institutions serving the sector and student enrolments in India have also expanded very rapidly.

Historical Perspective of Right to Education in India

The first National Education Policy was introduced in 1968 by the government of Indira Gandhi and it was based on Kothari Commission. This policy was famous of two things:

- Radical reconstructivity
- Equal Educational opportunity.

The second National Educational Policy which was modification of NEP 1968, so second national education policy was introduced in 1986 by the government of Rajiv Gandhi and this policy has focus on:

- Removal of disparities
- To provide education opportunities especially women of backward and minority class.

The third National Educational Policy was introduced in 1992 by the government of P.V. Narsimha Roa which is based on Ram Murthi Commission led by chairperson Shri Janardhan Reddy. The new national education policy 2020 was approved on 29th July, 2020 by the government of Narendra Modi and it is replaced by National Education Policy of 1986 after 34 years. It is the first Education Policy which is introduced by BJP government.

Ancient India had a tradition of rich culture and education since ancient times. People from different countries came to India for different purposes and got their permanent shelter here thereby merged themselves into Indian culture. This was possible for the tolerant attitude of the country for ages together and this tolerance was the outcome of the great Indian culture of non-violence. Indian education was based upon this religion of non-violence. There was a "common code of conduct" that prevailed in the society despite the amalgamation of the culture of different races that merged into Indian culture and this was due to the tolerant attitude of Indian education.

The education system in ancient India focused on the holistic development of individuals. It put emphasis on values like humility, discipline, truthfulness, self-reliance and respect for all creations. During the ancient period, two system of education were developed—Vedic, and Buddhist. Ancient Indian Education is also to be understood as being ultimately the outcome of the Indian theory of knowledge as a part of the corresponding scheme of life and values.

New Education Policy 2020 and its Challenges

The new education policy is a positive re-imagination of India's existing education regime. It has some very impressive and appreciable propositions. The policy envisions a model of holistic learning that is integrated, engaging and immersive. The New Education Policy 2020 calls for key reforms in both school and higher education that prepare the next generation to throve and compete in the new digital age. We are going to see a new era of educational learning and implementation of some new ideas. There are some important points of New Education Policy 2020:

1. National Education Policy 2020 is known as 5+3+3+4 system and new exam pattern were introduced. For the first time, the government has acknowledged the importance of pre-primary education, until now only the private schools were imparting pre-primary education.
2. The medium of Education: It has become a fashionable status symbol in India to send kids to English medium schools since childhood. This has promoted "ratta mar" education system. Kids can't even read their fancy books and all the focus is on preparing notebooks and remembering the questions and answers at the end of the chapter. Hence, it is welcome move

to make mother tongue/regional language as a compulsory medium of instruction till class 5

3. The Ministry of Education in November 2021 constituted a high-power committee, the Bharatiya Bhasha Samiti, for the promotion of Indian languages, led by the Rashtriya Swayamsevak Sangh (RSS) affiliated Sanskrit proponent and Padma Shri awardee Chamu Krishna Shastry. The committee is tasked with preparing an action plan for the growth of Indian languages as prescribed under the National Education Policy (NEP), 2020. This requires the mother tougue to be medium of instruction in schools and higher education institutions.[1] This is one of the most controversial issues that are what will be the medium of education in our schools under the new education policy. An interesting point in this regard is that the RSS affiliates that were giving their inputs in the new education policy, and were in talks with the government had demanded that Hindi should taught compulsorily from class 6 onwards in all the schools irrespective of whether it is a Hindi speaking state or a non-Hindi speaking one. When the southern states objected to the imposition of Hindi on them, the middle ground was adopted in this new education policy where it was said that the medium of education in all schools will not be Hindi but it shall be the local language or the mother tongue. So, this means that if this policy is changed into rules, then English also medium of teaching will go out of schools. There will be no teaching in English but on the other hand, all the different types of people in the country had a common base of the English language. For instance—A south Indian is working in north India or Tamilian is married to a Bengali and he is residing in Delhi, then what would be the mother tongue of their child and what would be the medium of instruction in schools? So this will be most critical issue, it must be concerned and the schools will be able to choose their medium.

4. New Education Policy: No more UGC, AICTE, and NCTE, to be replaced by single education regulator. The next important controversial issue of the new education policy 2020 is Centralization and privatization. The NEP 2020 is that it is promoting a centralization of our education system. There was a time when the founder father had kept education as a state subject. It was put in the concurrent list in 1976. Now, a lots of people are saying that NEP is trying to make education a central subject because all the other education bodies are being removed and a higher education body is being attempted to be made, in which the centre will decide what is to be done in the field of education in the entire country.
5. Equal promotion of arts, science, physical education and other extra-curricular activities so that learners can pick whatever piques their interests.
6. Multidisciplinary Education: There is some absurd propaganda that only useful subject are maths & science and we need to study other subjects to just get a degree. To hell with political correctness, this has created a whole dumped-down generation. Multidisciplinary approach (across the science, social science, arts, humanities and sports); emphasis on conceptual learning rather than rote learning: creativity and critical thinking.
7. Vocational education from class 6: This is an excellent move. The old education system was designed for a socialist India. The world has changed and the country has changed.
8. Internship: Internship will give students good insights into how different organizations and the world in general operate.
9. The New Education Policy 2020 also covers the basic points of the Right to Education Act 2009. The present investigation research has tried to explore the status of the implementation, awareness and understanding of the provisions of RTE among teachers, parents and children. Everyone has a right to education. Education shall be free at

least in the elementary and fundamental stages. Elementary education shall be compulsory (Article 26 of the 1948 Universal Declaration of the Human Rights). This UN recommendation has been reinforced in the provision of the rights of children to free and compulsory act (RTE) Act 2009 come into the effect in India on 1 April, 2010, enshrining in law for the first time the right of all Indian children age between 6-40 years to provide free and compulsory education regardless of caste, class, gender etc.

Implementation of National Education Policy 2020

On April 8, 2021, Union Education Minister Ramesh Pokhriyal Nishank launched a National Education Policy (NEP) Implementation Plan for school education called Student and Teachers Holistic Advancement through Quality Education (SARTHAQ). It will help in achieving goals and objectives of the National Education Policy (NEP) 2020:

(a) SARTHAQ has been developed by the Department of School Education & Literacy, Minister of Education. It has been released as part of celebration leading to Amrit Mahotsav on 75 years of Indian Independence. It is the plan of Action of NEP 2020 and outlines as implementation plan for the next 10 years.

(b) Ramesh Pokhriyal also chaired a high level meeting on the implementation of NEP 2020 in New Delhi.

(c) It has been developed after a wide and intensive consultative process with states and UTs.

(d) A Teacher's fest 'Shikshak Parv' was organized in September 2020 for discussing recommendation of NEP 2020.

(e) SARTHAQ will focus on outlining goals, outcomes and times frames, i.e., links recommendation of NEP with 297 Tasks along with responsible agencies, timelines and 304 outputs of these tasks.

Constitutional perspective of right to education and the Constitution of India

The Indian Constitution is a social document and the supreme law of the land. The founding fathers of the Constitution have incorporated a well-designed constitutional manifesto under Part-IV of the Constitution to achieve socio-economic justice. The Directive Principles of State Policy is not a catalogue but principles of good governance. It imposes certain obligations on the State to take affirmative action to establish a welfare State. These principles give directions to the functionaries of the State, the manner in which the Constitutional vision has to be achieved. One of the important directives is the duty of the State to provide free and compulsory education for all children until they complete the age of 14 years.

In 2009, the RTE Act declared basic education as the fundamental human right for all Indian children when the history of Indian's educational policies is examined, however, it is noted that the right to education has been prevalent throughout Indian's history, particularly since India's Independence (1947) and the creation of the constitution in 1950, the question remains as to why the Government of India choose to develop RTE as a new educational policy that present education as a human right when it has been so since the constitution? The RTE Act aims to provide primary education to all children age 6-14 years. It also provides for non-admitted child to be admitted to an appropriate class.

The recommendation of Sachar Committee Report is not implementing properly by the ruling government both Central and State. The Sachar Committee shows the following:

1. 25 per cent of Muslim children in the 6-14 year age group have either never attended school or have dropped out.
2. Drop-outs rates among Muslim are higher at the level of primary, middle and higher secondary.

3. The Committee observed that since artisanship is a dominant activity among Muslim technical training should be provided to even those who may not have completed schooling.
4. In premier colleges only one out of 25 undergraduate students and one out of 50 post graduate students is Muslim.
5. Access to government schools for Muslim children is limited.
6. There is non-availability of schools with easy reach for girls at lower levels.
7. Absence of girl's hostels and female teachers are also impeding factors.

There is some constitutional background of RTE Act 2009. Originally Part IV of the Indian Constitution Article 45 and Article 39(F) of Directive Principle of state policy had a provision for the state funded as well as equitable and accessible education.

The right which is given under Part IV of the constitution is not enforceable. For the first time in the history of India we have made this right enforceable by putting in the Part III of the constitution as Article 21. This entitle children have the right to education as a fundamental right. The first official documents on the right to education were Ramamurthy Committee report in 1990. **Ms Mohini Jain vs. State of Karnataka**[2] (2 judge's bench) this case is related to the right to education. In this case, the state of Karnataka published a notification that permitted the private medical colleges in the state of Karnataka to change exorbitant tuition fees from the students admitted other than the government seats quote. Miss Mohini Jain a medical aspirant student filed a petition in Supreme Court challengeing this notification. This apex court rose as important question that whether right to education is guaranteed to the Indian citizen under the Constitution of India.

The Supreme Court of India observed that mention of "the life and personal liberty" in Article 21 of the constitution automatically implies some other rights; those neither are necessary for the full development of the personality, though they are nor enumerated in Part III of the constitution. Education is one such factor responsible for overall development of an individual and therefore, right to education is integrated in Article 21 of the Constitution and in case finally the Supreme Court held that these part of the notification which allows the education institution to charge high fees of 25 crore to 60 crore in case of outsiders so these were held to be unconstitutional and void. The honorable Supreme Court also observed in this case that the dignity of a person is inviolable and if the person is not well educated than that person will not avail his fundamental right. So it is the duty of the state to provide education and it is declared that the right to education is the part of article 21 of the Constitution of India.

In 1993, the Supreme Court gave landmark judgment in **Unnikrishan J.P vs. State of Andhra Pradesh and others.**[3] In this case, the Supreme Court held that the right to basic education is implied by the fundamental right to life (article 21) when read in conjunction with the directive principle on education (article 14), the court held that the parameters of the right must be understood in the context of the directive principle of state policy, including article 45 of the Constitution which provide that the state is the endeavour to provide, within a period of 10 years from the commencement of the Constitution, for free and compulsor education for a child under the age of 14 years. **Tapas Majumdar Committee (1999)** was set which encompassed insert on of article 21 (A) of the Constitution. The 86th Amendment to the Constitution of India 2002 provides RTE as fundamental rights in Part III of the Constitution. The same amendment inserted article 21(A) which is provided that Act 2009 as a fundamental right for children between 6-14 years.

Conclusion

The New Education Policy 2020 empowered student to pick and choose their academic journey rather than conforming to the set standards and norms. It also moves towards international standards with a focus on digital and research based learning. The New Education Policy 2020 represents aspiration to become a knowledge powerhouse of the world inculcating the best of the global education experiments. The global education development agenda reflected in the goal 4 (SDG4) OF THE 2030. Agenda for sustainable development adopted by India in 2015 seeks to ensure inclusive and equitable education and promote lifelong learning opportunities for all by 2030.

The New Education Policy 2020 calls for Key reforms in both school and higher education that prepare the next generation to throve and compete in the new digital age. The education sector significantly affects the economic, political and social development of the nation.

The National Educational Policy empowers students to pick and choose their academic journey rather than conforming to the set standards and norms. It also moves towards international standards. Education is the fundamental for achieving full human potential, developing an equitable and just society and promoting nation development. The pursuit of Knowledge (jnan) wisdom (pragya) and truth (satya) was always considered in Indian thought and philosophy as the highest human goal.

Notes

1. *The Hindu* (newspaper) October 3, 2022.
2. A.I.R 1992 SC 1858.
3. A.I.R 1993 SC 217.

References

Basu, Das Durga. *Introduction to the Constitution of India.* 19th Ed. Agra: Wadha & Company Law Publishers, 2004.

Bakshi, P.M. *The Constitution of India with selective comments.* 5th Ed. Delhi: Universal Law Publishing Co. Pvt., 2003.

Jain, C. *The Constitution of India: Select Issues and Perceptions.* New Delhi: Taxman Publication Pvt. Ltd., 2000.

Pandey, J.N. *Constitutional Law of India.* 46th Ed. Allahabad: Central Law Agency, 2009.

Seervai, H.M. *Constitutional Law of India* (Vol. 2). 4th Ed. Delhi: Universal Law Publishing Co. Pvt. Ltd., 1991.

Journal

Prof Aklaque Ahmed, "Safeguard to minority educational institution: Judicial Attitude and administrative process", *Aligarh Law Journal*, Vol. XVI & XV, year 1999-2000, pp. 90-98.

Aligarh Law Journal, Vol. XVI & XVII Year 2000 & 2002.

Draft National Education Policy on Education 1986.

Case Laws

Miss Mohini Jain vs. State of Karnataka, A.I.R.1992 SC 1858.

Unnikrishan, J.P vs. State of Andhra Pradesh, A.I.R 1993 SC 217.

Newspaper

The Hindu, October 3, 2022.

Websites

www.researchgate.net

www.acadenia.edu

www.education.gov.in

Section IV
Ensuring Sustainable Development to All

19

Inclusive Education in Achieving SDG in India

Shagufta and *Afshan Anees*

Introduction

Inclusive education has been defined at various ways that addresses the learning needs of the differently abled children. Over past fifty years, the Indian government has been working to provide a broad array of services aimed at assisting children with special needs in their educational experiences. In order to give disabled children in general education equal opportunities and to promote their preservation, the centrally sponsored Integrated Education for Disabled Children (IEDC) scheme was introduced in 1974. The National Educational Policy of 1986, which recommended as a goal "to integrate the handicapped with the general community at all levels as equal partners, to prepare them for normal growth, and to enable them to face the real world with confidence and courage", is where the government's initiatives in the area of inclusive education have their roots.

The World Declaration on Education for All adopted in 1990 gave further boost to the various processes already set in the country. The Rehabilitation Council of India Act 1992 initiated a training programme for the development of professionals to respond to the needs of students with disabilities.

In 1990, approval of the Global Declaration on Education for All of us gave the nation's various initiatives a further push. A training programme for professionals to create was started by the Rehabilitation Council of India Act of 1992 to address the requirements of students with disabilities.

The National Policy for Persons with Disability, 2006, which attempts to clarify the framework under which the state, civil society and private sector must operate in order to ensure dignified life for persons with disability and support for their caretakers. Most recent advancement is the Right of Children for Free and Compulsory Education (2009) which guarantees right to free and compulsory education to all children between ages six to fourteen. For education for a child with disability, the Act has to be read in conjunction with Chapter V of the Persons with Disability Act, 1995. Chapter V of the PWD Act ensures that every child with disability is entitled to a free education up to the age of 18 years.

To meet the goal of Education for All (EFA) by 2010, the Indian government launched the new inclusive education programme. Inclusion is an endeavour to make sure that varied learner-individuals with disabilities, various languages and cultures, different homes and family lives, different interests and ways of learning.

According to inclusive education, all children will participate in the mainstream of instruction, regardless of their talents and shortcomings. It is evident that inclusive education in ordinary schools has become a top policy goal in India, where attention has increasingly shifted more towards children and adults with special needs. One of the most important concerns in education has arisen as inclusive education in practically every nation. With the publishing of the Salamanca Declaration in 1994 (UNESCO), a large number of developing nations started reformulating their policies to promote the inclusion of children with disabilities into regular schools.

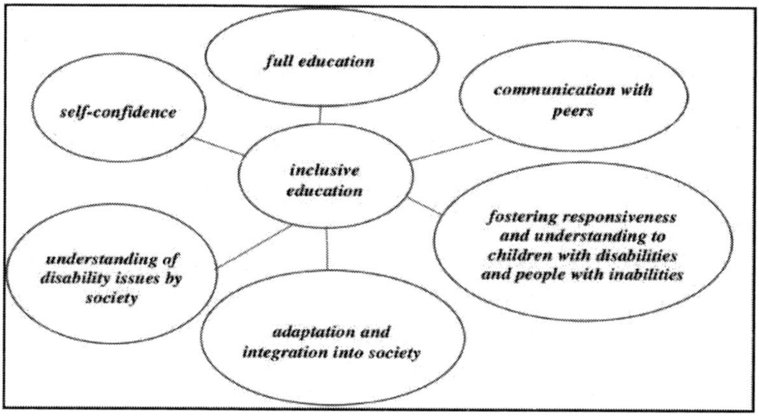

Source: Fedulovav.Ivanova and V.Nosov (2019) Inclusive Education as a basis for Sustainable Development of society.

Emergence of the concept of inclusive Education in India

One of the earliest formal initiatives undertaken by the GoI was the Integrated Education for Disabled Children (IEDC) scheme of 1974.

The Kothari Commission (1966) which highlighted the importance of educating children with disabilities during the post-independence period. In 1980s, the Ministry of Welfare, Govt. of India, realized the crucial need of an institution to monitor and regulate the HRD programmes in the field of disability rehabilitation. Till 1990s, ninety per cent of India's estimated 40 million children in the age group four-sixteen years with physical and mental disabilities are being excluded from mainstream education. The National Policy on Education, 1986 (NPE, 1986), and the Programme of Action (1992) stresses the need for integrating children with special needs with other groups. The Government of India implemented the District Primary Education Project (DPEP) in 1994-95. In late 90s (i.e. in 1997), the philosophy of inclusive education is added in District Primary Education Programme (DPEP).

Sarva Shiksha Abhiyan (SSA) was launched to achieve the goal of Universalisation of Elementary Education in 2001, is one such initiative

A zero rejection policy has been adopted under SSA, which ensures that every Child with Special Needs (CWSN), irrespective of the kind, category and degree of disability, is provided meaningful and quality education.

In 2005, the Ministry of Human Resource Development implemented a National Action Plan for the inclusion in education of children and youth with disabilities.

Inclusive Education as defined by SDG 8

Inclusive education is the most effective way to **give all children a fair chance to go to school, learn and develop the skills they need to thrive**. Inclusive education means all children in the same classrooms, in the same schools.

Inclusive Education denotes that all children irrespective of their strengths and weaknesses will be part of the mainstream education.

All students in the same classrooms, in the same schools, are what are meant by inclusive education. It entails genuine educational possibilities for formerly marginalised populations, including minority language speakers as well as children with disabilities. Inclusive education is also highlighted in SDG 4 and SDG 8

- Goal 4 is also very important for persons with disabilities. **Goal 4** on inclusive and equitable quality education and promotion of life-long learning opportunities for all focuses on eliminating gender disparities in education and ensuring equal access to all levels of education and vocational training for the vulnerable, including persons with disabilities. In addition, the proposal calls for building and upgrading education facilities that are child, disability and gender sensitive and also provide safe, non-violent, inclusive and effective learning environments for all.

- In **Goal 8**: to promote sustained, inclusive and sustainable economic growth, full and productive employment and decent work for all, the international community aims to achieve full and productive employment and decent work for all women and men, including for persons with disabilities, and equal pay for work of equal value.

Economic growth that is sustained and inclusive can advance society, produce good jobs for all, and raise standards of living. Sustainable Development Goal 8 (SDG 8 or Global Goal 8) is one of the 17 Sustainable Development Goals that the United Nations General Assembly adopted in 2015. It is focused on "decent work and economic growth" and is one of the 17 SDGs. To "Support sustained, inclusive and sustainable economic growth, full and productive employment, and decent work for all", is the official title of the initiative.

The main goal of SDG 8: **Decent work and economic growth-** The Global Goals. Promote sustained, inclusive and sustainable economic growth, full and productive employment and decent work for all.

SDG 8 has many targets but the two targets are for the inclusive education and education for differently abled children. It is clearly mentioned in target 8.5 and 8.6 that

- By 2030, achieve full and productive employment and decent work for all women and men, including for young people and persons with disabilities, and equal pay for work of equal value
- By 2020, substantially reduce the proportion of youth not in employment, education or training.

  The SDGs **provide worldwide guidance for addressing the global challenges facing the international community**. It is about better protecting the natural foundations of life and our planet everywhere and for everyone, and preserving people's opportunities to live in dignity and prosperity across generations.

It can implemented in our country through education by ***Republic Act (RA) 11650,*** inked by Duterte on March 11, provides that no learner shall be denied admission based on their disability. The new law provides that all schools, whether public or private, shall ensure equitable access to quality education to every learner with disability.

The formal sector and steps need to be taken to do the same in informal sector as well. Make trade certification compulsory. Provide finance for skill training in the informal sector. Employment exchanges and skill up-gradation and knowledge sharing for employment.

Inclusive Education at different levels

Technical and Vocational Education and Training aims to reduce the number of unemployed youth, disabled children by increasing access to training opportunities. Quality education also raises awareness about forced and child labour and helps prevent and eradicate them in all their existing forms.

Education for Early Childhood Care

- At this level, children learn to help at home and school, and to live together without any discrimination. By organizing visits to sites in their immediate vicinity, such as farms, buildings sites, police or fire stations, health centres or post office, and through role play, they learn to relate to the work of people in their local community.

Education for Primary level

- Learners at this stage develop their understanding of why people work, and the meaning of social enterprises. They learn to understand the relevance of equal access and opportunities to employment for all, while appreciating the value of different forms of work, such as paid work, unpaid care work, work for differently able children, voluntary work and creative expression.

Education for Secondary Education

- The concepts of enterprise, cooperatives, workers' rights, social justice and fair trade are introduced at this stage. Learners develop skills for problem solving, critical thinking and devising of innovative approaches in the world of work. They enhance their appreciation for fairness in trade and for the principles of shared ownership for the mutual benefit of their own communities.

Inclusive education values diversity and the unique contributions each student brings to the classroom. In a truly inclusive setting, every child feels safe and has a sense of belonging. Students and their parents participate in setting learning goals and take part in decisions that affect them. And school staff has the training, support, flexibility, and resources to nurture, encourage, and respond to the needs of all students.

Goal 8: **Promote inclusive and sustainable economic growth, employment and decent work for all**. Sustained and inclusive economic growth can drive progress, create decent jobs for all and improve living standards. COVID-19 has disrupted billions of lives and endangered the global economy.

Investing in SDG 8 means investing in a number of SDGs

- Poverty reduction (SDG1)
- Education (SDG4)
- Health (SDG3)
- Industrialization (SDG9)
- Equality (SDG5 &10)
- Sustainable Consumption & Production (SDG12)
- SDG 8 will create new & cross-cutting demands: need to enhance collaborative capacity & overcome silos Normative should guide the operational; already existing tools, mechanisms and platforms can be adapted.

Designing of Curriculum for Inclusive Education

In recent years, the concept of inclusive education has been broadened to encompass not only students with disabilities, but also all students who may be disadvantaged. This broader understanding of curriculum has paved the way for developing the National Curriculum Framework (NCF-2005) that reiterates the importance of including and retaining all children in school through a programme that reaffirms the value of each child and enables all children to experience dignity and the confidence to learn Inclusive curriculum design involves consideration of the overall course structure - including both content and delivery - **to ensure that all students are provided with an equitable and supportive learning experience that offers them the opportunity to succeed whatever their background.**

Measures for implementation of Inclusive Education in India

These are the few measures taken by Indian Government:

1. The Right to Education (RTE) must apply to all citizens of India. State and Central Governments as well as all the other social actors should recognize the importance of a broadened concept of inclusive education that addresses the diverse needs of all learners.
2. A policy of inclusion needs to be implemented in all schools and throughout Indian education system (NCF, 2005). Schools need to become centres that prepare children for life and ensure that all children, especially the differently abled children from marginalized sections, and children in difficult circumstances get the maximum benefit of this critical area of education.
3. The preparation of teachers for rural special education programmes should be planned differently, as the aim of these programmes would be to integrate disabled persons in their own environment and community.

4. As a system, inclusive education should be flexible. Its flexibility must be reflected in the methods and materials used to give these children the widest possible access to the regular curriculum.
5. A school-based support team should develop strategies for the whole school to meet the needs of learners with special educational needs.
6. The school has the primary responsibility for helping children learn alongside their typically developing peers. An inclusive school must enable education structures, systems and methodologies to meet the needs of all children, particularly those who face the greatest barriers to achieving their right to education.
7. Parents have a right to be involved in all decision-making concerning their child. They should be seen as partners in the education process.
8. Bringing special children into mainstream requires adjustments that schools need to make in advance. Transport facilities should be altered, so that these children can move around with relative ease. Architecturally, there should be ramps and wheelchair access constructed in service areas such as toilets.
9. Student-oriented components, such as medical and educational assessment, books and stationery, uniforms, transport allowance, boarding the lodging facility and stipend for girls, etc. should provide according to need of the students.
10. Differently abled children should be treated equally as the normal children and instead of looking them in sympathy their talents and abilities should be recognized for their self-respect and welfare of the society.
11. Necessary school supplies such as audio learning or textbooks in Braille should be made available. Suitable modification to examination system may be required.

12. Families with children without disabilities should develop relationships with families with children with disabilities and be able to make a contribution.
13. In-service training programmes of two to three weeks' duration for general educators and special educators in all the disabilities and in specific areas of disability should arrange to effectively teach children with disabilities.
14. Those schools that are committed to taking in children with special needs, then teachers must attend workshops in order to be adjusted to the child's needs.
15. Periodic evaluation of the training programmes should be part of the planning of teacher preparation.
16. Inclusion should not be the sole responsibility of the specific class teacher. Everybody should be involved and take responsibility.
17. The reform of the curriculum should be made in parallel with a proper training for teachers regarding their knowledge of inclusion and its principles.

Conclusion

Inclusive education has occupied its own place in the whole process of teaching and learning. Through inclusive education normal students as well as students with special needs learn and sharing all facilities and social interaction equally. It means all children enjoy learning experience of same classroom with same school. It aims at strengthening the Indian Education System so that it reaches every child and provides them opportunities for academic and social achievement.

There are 17 Sustainable Development Goals (SDGs), which are *an urgent call for action by all countries - developed and developing. SDG 4 and SDG 8 also highlighted the inclusive education.* The Sustainable Development Goals (SDGs) aim to transform our world. They are a call to action to end poverty and inequality, protect the planet, and ensure that all people enjoy health, justice and prosperity. Government has taken different measures at different level of education to achieve the goal of SDG through Inclusive education. By this effort of the government, a day will come when we completely achieve the goal of SDGs.

References

Dash, A. (1997). Impact of Adapted Physical Education on the Physical Fitness of Mentally Retarded Children. *Disabilities and Disabilities*, *11*(1): 9-15.

Jha, M.M. (2002). *School without Walls: Inclusive Education for All.* Oxford: Heinemann.

Lele, V. and A. Khaledkar (1994). A Study to Identify the Learning Problems of Hearing Impaired Children in Language Textbook (Marathi) of Primary Level and Development of Supplementary Explanatory (Instructional) Material to Improve their Uses of Language. *Independent Study*. Nasik: Shrimathi Mai Lele Shravan Vikas Vidyalaya.

Mohit, A. (2003). "Human Rights Model and Access", *International Journal of Human Rights*.

Quinn, S. and K. Ryba (2000). "Linking Inclusive Policies with Best Teaching Practices", in D. Fraser, R. Moltzen, and K. Ryba (eds), *Learners with Special Needs in Aotearoa*, New Zealand. Dunmore Press.

Rioux, M.H. and Mohit, A. (2005). Human Rights Disability and Law: National Human Rights Commission, New Delhi.

Taneja, N. (2001). "The 93rd Amendment Bill: A Fraud in the Name of Rights to Education". Communist People 's *Democracy*, *15*(47 and 25)-16.

Umadevi, M.R. (1997). Effectiveness of a Remedial Programme on Improving Read in Comprehension Skills among Dyslexic Children. Ph.D. Thesis. Kuvempu University.

UNESCO (1994). *The Salamanca Statement and Framework for Action on Special Needs Education*. Paris: UNESCO.

UNESCO (1997). *International Standard Classification of Education*. Paris: UNESCO.

https://inclusiveeducation.ca/about/what-is-ie/

20

Economic Empowerment of Elderly Women for Sustainable Development

Sana Hashmi and *Mohd. Nadeem Khan*

Introduction

It is a fact that population of elderly is increasing rapidly. The population of elderly people in India is increasing very fast and has reached approx. 104 million of which around 53 million are females and 51 million are males in 2011. With this graying population, dependency ratio among the elderly is growing. There are various reasons of it such as lack of social security in old age, average life expectancy and many more things. In many countries, like India, majority of elderly people suffer from fiscal adversities in old age because many of them are not capable of doing any type of productive labour for their livelihood. Even if the elderly people have some savings, that is not enough even for their fundamental needs how they can go for proper medical treatment in old age. Due to poverty, it is very difficult for them to meet their financial needs in old age especially for those who have no social security at this age.

Education and employment are the two major factors that may lead towards a change in the social as well as economic status of any individual. Women empowerment is placing a focal point in this era. It is the greatest required tool for inclusive growth and development of a nation. When the attention is given on labour class, those who belong to lower social strata and marginalized section of the society, i.e., slums, it is found that the level of illiteracy is very high. So, residents of these areas are mostly found working in unorganized sectors.

In old age, elderly women have lesser opportunities towards productive work. That is why they face gender inequalities at workplaces. After the onset of globalization and privatization, elderly persons of rural areas have been systematically marginalized due to the lack of modern skills. It is being analyzed that elderly people have limited knowledge about new technology so they are not suitable for various types of jobs. It is often observed that elderly people are engaged in agricultural activities. Both elderly women and men are found to be involved in this occupation. But within this occupation we find the participation of elderly females is lesser as compared to elderly males. Because, the works done by elderly females are invisible such as transplanting, weeding, sowing, etc. It is seen that most of the elderly people are self-employed in old age. They are not economically dependent on others even at this stage of life which demands care and attention. They earn by themselves and fulfil their daily needs by their own earnings. On the other side, it is also being observed that their participation in economic activities is unaccountable.

Review of Literature

Singh (2013) analyzed in the article 'Ageing Population in India: Select Economic Issues' that it is considered that older people are less productive as against younger generation. In this age older people are dependent on others. Workforce participation rate is very low among oldest old people but it relatively high among older males as against older females while the dependency ratio among elderly female is higher than the elderly males. Even in this age people engage in some type of productive work in order to fulfil their basic needs, not by their own choice.

Gopal (2006) discussed in the article 'Ageing and Social

Security' that in Indian society the work of domestic labour and family tasks are always associated with unpaid work that is why majority of women in productive labour in unorganized sector, get hardly any protection. Author said that elderly people continue to work till they are totally unable to do so. Their work, usually lasting from morning to till evening is not considered worth a paid.

Dhar (2014) focused in the article 'Workforce Participation among the Elderly in India' that the increasing number of elderly population enacts the load on social security, housing planning, health services etc. The ratio of dependency is directly proportional to the greying population. Workforce participation rate among elderly people is declining from 1983 to 2004-05. The reason is that elderly people are increasing in higher age-cohort and this age group is less capable to participate in productive labour. Education affects elderly people for getting any employment. That is why they are mostly found in informal sector.

Selvaraj and others (2014) mentioned in their Article 'Elderly Workforce Participation, Wage Differentials and Contribution to Household Income' that less earning in the young age and limited savings in old age compel elderly people to engage in productive activity. After globalization and liberation jobs require skill persons. They prefer young generation so old age people have to engage in self-employment after retirement while they have no social security. Authors also mentioned that rural elderly female are found more in casual labour while in urban areas elderly female are engaged in informal sectors. Elderly people suffer wage differences as against their young generations. Still they have to opt such kind of works due to lack of money, limited job opportunities, distance problems etc. It was observed that these elderly people earn limited amount of money still they contribute in household income.

Objectives of the Study

1. To recognize the economic participation of elderly women of slum areas of Aligarh City.
2. To analyze the role of elderly women in different kinds of

productive works leading towards empowerment.

Research Methodology

Universe and Sample

All the elderly women residing in slum areas of Aligarh City constituted in the universe of study. All the respondents for this study were selected by systematic random sampling.

Research Design

The research design was descriptive as well as explanatory.

Sources of Data

Both primary as well as secondary data were used for data collection.

Methods for Data Collection

Primary data was collected from face to face interview schedule having open-ended questionnaire while secondary data was collected from articles, journals, books, census handbook, newspapers, reports and magazines.

Significance of the Study

It is a fact that slums are marginalized sections of the society. As elderly people are considered to be a burden on their families, the condition is even worse in this marginalized section of the society owing to limited resources. The situation of elderly women residing in these areas is getting worst day by day because of triple jeopardy, i.e., being old, being poor and being women. It is widely acclaimed that Indian society is patriarchal one so women of this country have to face gender discrimination throughout their lives. It is seen that elderly women of these areas work all the day to accomplish their daily livelihood but it is not considered as productive work, and their work is always neglected. Through the literature review, it was noticed that much of the research targeted elderly people in general, not much work has been done in the field of gerontology with special attention to elderly women as they are always considered as a burden on their family. The findings of the present study thus provided a new dimension to the existing literature in this area. Research of this nature is significant because it discusses the empowerment of elderly women by engaging in different kind of productive works and also to know the economic participation of elderly women of slum areas of Aligarh City. So, this study was done having an aim to bring in light the problems faced by the elderly people particularly the elderly women of the slums areas to fulfil their daily requirements. This research places itself into the field of feminist studies, which provide space for multidisciplinary intellect to engage with each other. Here, problems of elderly women are studied from a feminist perspective, placing elderly women at the centre of analysis, which enhances the significance of the present research.

Delimitations of the Study

The study was limited to only 60 elderly women in slums areas of Aligarh city.

The study was limited only on one aspect, i.e., elderly women's empowerment through employment.

Results and Discussion

This chapter primarily deals with the issues related to the elderly women who are residing in slum areas of Aligarh city and as this segment of society is considered to be the marginalized community. Elderly women have to live in these areas as they have no other option of residence. They find themselves in rough situations, where they maintain certain quality of lives. The condition of the elderly women is miserable beyond imagination in these corner cases (slums) of our society. They do not have access to the most fundamental requirements like food, shelter, clothing and even basic demands like sanitation, hygiene, access to potable water, etc. Elderly women of these areas depend on others for their above-mentioned needs as slums are deprived of them. Even their children do not take care of them and treat them as an extra member or as a burden on the family. That is why they have to be engaged in some types of productive works for their daily requirements while they are not physically and mentally capable of performing it.

On the contrary, this result gives an interesting outside about elderly women of slum areas of Aligarh City. All these elderly women of this study are self-employed. They fulfil their daily needs by themselves. They are not economically dependent on others for their daily livelihoods. They feel empowered in their own way.

Table 20.1: Self-employed Women

Occupation	No. of Respondents	% of Respondents
Business	19	31.6
Animal Husbandry	14	23.3
Labours	27	45.0
Total	**60**	**100%**

This Table 20.1 depicts that all these women are self-employed and earning for spending their lives without being economically dependent on other at this stage of life which demands support of their children and others. The perception of these elderly women who reside in slum areas is that to be economically dependent on those persons who already suffer financial problems would add burden on them. So, these women started to earn money by engaging in different kinds of productive works. Out of this sample size, 31.6 per cent respondents run their own business. This particular category includes two kinds of activities where one category comprises of those who own a small shop having 'gutka', 'supari', 'namkeen', biscuits, baked corn etc. while the other category includes those elderly women who make papad at their own homes and sell it door to door. To start their own business in this male dominated society is too much problematic for these elderly women. Still they started and now they are enjoying their lives involving in this activity. 23.3 per cent elderly women rear the domestic animals. They take care of their animals all the day and spend all their energy in hope of earning something. Domestic animals are one and only source of income for them.While remaining of the respondents, i.e., 45 per cent work as labourers. They work 3-4 hours per day. They mentioned that it is very difficult to work at this age but they are compelled to do so as they have no other means of income. All these respondents remarked that in this way they utilize their time and earn money to fulfil their daily livelihoods. All these elderly women of this sample not only fulfil their own needs but also some of them are participating to rise their family earning by which their family members may fulfil their desires easily. These women mentioned that they are illiterate that is the reason why they are unable to search other kind of productive works.

It was found an interesting case during this research. The case is that one respondent who has her own shop explained her story, i.e., X is a 69 years old woman. She lives separately. She has 3 daughter and 2 sons out of which 2 daughters and 1 son are married. She basically belongs to Mugalsarai, a district of Uttar Pradesh. She moved here approx. 25 years ago when her husband abandoned her and her children refused to take care of her. So, she has to move here in search of livelihood. At her native place, it was very difficult for her to engage in any kind of productive work because of societal taboos. She mentioned that her husband used to assault her physically, without any reason. Her husband was drunkard. She suffered a lot of domestic violence by her husband's hands. Her husband did not take any responsibility of his wife and his children. X suffered lots of difficulties to fulfil her children's fundamental needs. It became worse when her health started to decline and her children refused to take her responsibility. To overcome these difficulties, she migrated and started begging to arrange for herself. She felt ashamed of herself for doing so. At that point of time she lived at a bus station because she had no space for living. After some time, she started to run her own small shop in the form of 'khokha'. Now she carries push-cart as a kind of 'khokha' containing 'gutka', 'supari', 'cigarette', etc. This push-cart carries all in it. She has one gas burner chulha in which she cooks food for herself. This push-cart is the only property that she own. Now X is spending her life happily. We can say that this is real example of empowerment. You can do anything which you want without any fear of societal taboos and anything else.

Conclusion

The study shows that the occupation of the elderly women, residing in slum areas are based on their educational level, family background, employment facilities in their vicinity and skills. The reality is that these elderly women are not burden on their family even they also participate in family earnings by engaging in different productive works. These elderly women had to face a lot of difficulties in search of employment due to less knowledge and less skills. The income of every elderly woman of these areas varies on the basis of their choice of occupation. Despite significant problems in this male dominated society, these elderly women of this marginalized section of the society found their way out for growth and empowerment without any help.

References

Beechey, V. (1987). *Unequal Work*, London:Verso, p. 126.

Chakraborti, R.D. (2004). *The Greying of India: Popultaion Ageing in the Context of Asia*, Sage Publication, p. 66.

Dhar, A. (2014). "Workforce Participation among the Elderly in India: Struggling for Economic Security". In *Indian Journal of Labour Economics*, Vol. 57, No. 3.

Agewell Foundation (2011). "Financial Status of Older People in India: An Assessment". In *Special Consultative Status with the ECOSOC at UN since 2011*. Agewell: Research and Advocay Centre.

Dubey. A. (2014). "A Study on Slum Tourism". *Int. J. Ad. Social Sciences*, Vol. 2, Issue-1, January-March, pp. 08-11.

Gopal, M. (2006). "Ageing and Social Security". In *Economic and Political Weekly*, Vol. 41, No. 42, October 21-27.

Hashmi, S. (2017). "Status of Elderly Women in India". In *Indian Journal of Human Relations*, Vol. 51, Issue-2, July-December, ISSN: 0974-1089.

Hashmi, S. (2018). "Government Policies and Programmes for Elderly Women Living in Slum Areas of Aligarh". In *Indian Journal of Gerontology*,

Vol. 32, Issue-4, pp. 460- 468, ISSN: 0971-4189, UGC No. 20786.

Hashmi, S. (2019). "Elderly Women's Work: Neglected or Noticeable (A Case Study of Slum Areas of Aligarh City)". In *Indian Journal of Social Research*, Vol. 60, Issue-3, May-June, 2019.

Hashmi, S. (2021). "Elderly Women of Marginalized Section of Aligarh City: Problems and Challenges". *International Journal of Physical and Social Research*. Vol. 11, Issue-4, pp 22-31, ISSN: 2249- 5894.

Hashmi. S., Nausheen, H., Shumaila, P. and Mohd. N.K. (2022). "Perception of Young Generation towards Elderly Women". *International Journal of Trend in Research and Development*, Vol. 9, Issue-3, pp. 148-151, ISSN: 2394-9333.

Joseph, L.P. (2017). "Problems of Elderly Women in Kerela: A Social Work Concern". In *The Journal of Development Practice*, Vol. 3 (Annual), ISSN 2394-0476.

Kumar, Y. & Bhargava, A. (2014). "Elder Abuse in Indian Families: Problems and Preventive Action". In *International Journal of Scientific and Research Publication*, Vol. 4, Issue-10, October.

Selvaraj, S., *et al.* (2014). "Elderly Workforce Participation: Wage, Differentials and Contribution to Household Income". In G. Giridhar, K.M. Sathyanarayana, S. Kumar, K.S. James & M. Alam (eds.), *Population Ageing in India*, Delhi: Cambridge University Press.

Singh, C. (2013). "Ageing Population in India: Select Economic Issues". In Indian Institute of Management Bangalore, *Working Paper No. 442.*

Rajan S.I. & Mathew, E.T. (2008). "Living Arrangements among the Elderly". In S.I. Rajan (ed.), *Social Security for the Elderly: Experiences from South Asia*, London, New York and New Delhi: Routledge (Taylor and Francis Group).

Tondon, SnehLata (2001). *Senior Citizens: Perspective for the New Millennium*, New Delhi: Reliance Publishing.

United Nations Population Fund (2012). *Report on the Status of Elderly in Selected States of India.*

Vincent, John. (2003). *Old Age*, London: Routledge.

21

Sustainable Development Goals

The Role of Libraries

Mohd. Mubashshir Ali

Introduction

The United Nations Member States adopted the 2030 Agenda for Sustainable Development in 2015, an integrated framework of 17 Sustainable Development Goals (SDGs) with a total of 169 Targets addressing economic, environmental, and social development. The UN 2030 Agenda will help all Member States concentrate their efforts on the eradication of poverty and other deplorable conditiond in order to ensure that "no one is left behind" and that peace and prosperity are achieved by 2030. The Sustainable Development Goals (SDGs) are set of 17 objectives that must be achieved in order to combat climate change and protect the environment. Some of the Goals are listed below:

1. **No Poverty:** People can enhance their lives by using libraries, which also support informed decision-making. In rural and remote communities, mobile libraries make books, services and internet accessible, giving opportunities to people who might otherwise be alone.

2. **Zero Hunger:** Public and community libraries also promote literacy, offer ICT training, provide access to information in local languages and act as a gateway to government services and funding for rural communities as well as fostering partnerships to support local development. Agriculture libraries provide access to research and data on crops, market information, and farming methods that help to develop resilient sustainable produce.
3. **Good Health and Well-being:** Public access to health information in all libraries helps people to make better lifestyle and stay healthy. Public libraries have a key role in providing health information to vulnerable groups like new immigrants and people experiencing homelessness. Services include accessing trustworthy health information, developing healthy lifestyle habits and finding reliable sources of information.
4. **Quality Education:** Education is the key to prosperity and opens world opportunities, making it possible for each of us to contribute for a progressive healthy society. Learning benefits every human being and should be accessible to all. It liberates the intellect, unlocks the imagination and is fundamental for self-respect. Ensure inclusive, equitable, high-quality education and promote changes for all people to learn throughout their lives.
5. **Gender Equality:** Programmes are available in libraries to help women and girls access information about their rights and physical health. Along with offering coding clubs and entrepreneurship training, they also offer ICT and literacy courses. Libraries provide a secure environment to read, learn, use computers, access the internet, learn technology, and interact with other women.
6. **Affordable and Clean Energy:** Libraries, and library-like rural information centres, can offer public access computers, sometimes powered by solar panels or generators, allowing users to conduct meetings, charge devices, and access the

Internet at night. Many public and community libraries around the world represent the only place where people can get consistently access light and energy to read, learn and apply for job. Make sure that everyone has access to modern, affordable, reliable, and sustainable energy.

7. **Reduced Inequalities:** Individuals' independence depends on having equitable access to information, freedom of association, freedom of expression, assembly, and privacy. In both urban and rural areas around the world, libraries provide safe, public spaces that are accessible to all, thereby assisting in the reduction of inequality.
8. **Peace, Justice and Strong Institutions:** Every democratic society needs compassion and a strong moral compass, but abuse, injustice, and persecution continue to be pervasive and are tearing at the very foundation of civilization.

In this scenario, libraries play an important role in helping to addressing the issues "from promoting literacy, to providing free access to information; libraries are welcoming safe environment in the communities. They support digital inclusion via access to ICT, an internet connection and skills. They promote innovation, creativity and access to the world's information for future generations" (https://www.ifla.org/publications/libraries-and-the-sustainable-development-goals—a-storytelling-manual). As given that access to information is key enabling right for governments to provide their citizens with high quality, inclusive services (Ashwill and Norton, 2015).

Literature Review

Since the 1990s, there has been an increase in the amount of library literature on sustainability and environmental issues, with the majority of this literature focusing on four categories: sustainability of scholarship and collections, Green library operations and practices, Green library buildings, and measuring and improving sustainability (Jankowska and Marcum, 2010). Following more than three years of negotiations and active participation from numerous stakeholders, including the IFLA, the 2030 Agenda for Sustainable Development, the post-2015 development agenda that will replace the Millennium Development Goals, was adopted by the Member States of the UN in September 2015.

According to the 2013 IFLA statement, "Information access is a fundamental requirement for personal and social development" (IFLA, 2014), "Access to information fosters development by empowering people, especially marginalized people and those living in poverty, to exercise their rights, be economically active, learn new skills, enrich their cultural identity, and participate in decision-making."

Roles of Libraries in supporting SDGs

The Lyon Declaration of the IFLA states that "public access to information helps people to make informed decisions that can enhance their lives". Communities that have timely and relevant information available to all have an advantage in being able to eradicate poverty and inequality, advance agriculture, provide high-quality education, and promote people's health, culture, research, and innovation. The UN 2030 Agenda initiative made it possible to test whether ideas on paper were effective (Bradley, F., 2016). IFLA ALP (Action for Development through Library Programme), the committee that oversaw IFLA's work on the UN 2030 Agenda, offers capacity building on advocacy to library associations, libraries, and people all over the world through the Building Strong Library Associations programme and the International Advocacy programme. As a result, Goal 16's Objective 16.10, "Ensure public access to information and protect fundamental freedoms, in accordance with national legislation and international agreements", which is a subgoal of the goal of **"Peace, Justice, and Strong Institutions"**, reflects the results of testing whether ideas on paper were effective (Bradley, F., 2016).

The project Public Libraries and Sustainability: Gathering Evidences of Contribution to SDGs (Projects PLS), launched in November 2016, is focused on fostering public libraries' sustainability. To evaluate public libraries' contributions to the SDGs, a framework will be created. Pinto and Ochôa (2017) discussed the role of impact evaluation practices and competencies in the evidence gathering and advocacy process of libraries' contributions to the UN 2030 Agenda. A framework will be developed and then tailored for Portuguese public libraries in order to support contribution to the SDGs.

Pinto and Ochôa (2017) discussed about the role of impact evaluation practices and competencies in evidence gathering and advocacy process of libraries' contributions to the UN 2030 Agenda. Initiated in November 2016, the project Public Libraries and Sustainability: Gathering Evidences of Contribution to SDGs (Projects PLS) is focused on fostering public libraries' sustainability. In order to evaluate public libraries' contributions to the SDGs, a framework will be created and then customised for Portuguese public libraries. The National Swiss Library Association, or "Bibliosuisse", has established the "Biblio2030" working group, which educates, teaches, and coaches libraries on their role in the SDG work. As a part of it, they hold workshops for library personnel, provide examples of best practices in SDGs work, network with people in society and policy, and build various working tools. They hope to raise awareness of how libraries may contribute to the SDGs through their work (Siegrist, 2019). Singh, Brahma, and Vaiphei (2019) evaluated the national information and library policies and their contents that were formulated in India to understand whether they have supportive perspectives to UN SDGs. In the event that such policies are updated and recast in the future in the country, they have suggested including provisions for the same. They stated that it is necessary to include clauses for them to carry out their duties in order to further the objectives. The study also chalked out the possibilities of comprehends of provisions in the policy documents to achieve SDGs to India.

Australian Library and Information Association (2018) created a framework for academic libraries (school, college, and university libraries), national and state libraries, and Australian Public Library Alliance to participate in and support the SDGs.

According to Ali & Bhatti (n.d.), the Higher Education Commission Digital Library (HEC DL) plays an important role for the SDG 4 goal of spreading information and high quality in higher education of Pakistan. This is Pakistan's largest network for resources sharing among higher educational institutions.

Some of the steps taken by the Government of India for the promotion of education and research, SDG 4: "Ensure inclusive and equitable quality education and promote lifelong learning opportunities for all", according to Garcia-Febo, *et al.* (2017), "requires relationship among government, private sector, educational institutions, and civil society."

The following steps has taken by the Indian government to advance education and research:

- **NITI Aayog** (https://www.niti.gov.in/): With its government big approach, NITI Aayog has undertaken a "mapping of schemes" of the SDGs and their targets, working with the lead and supporting ministries for each target. This emphasizes the interconnected nature of the SDGs with regard to the economic, social, and environmental pillars.
- **e-shodhSindhu** (https://ess.inflibnet.ac.in/): The e-shodhSindhu member institutions have access to more than 15,000 core and peer-reviewed journals as well as a number of bibliographic, citation, and factual databases in various disciplines from a huge number of publishers and aggregators.
- **Shodhganga** (https://shodhganga.inflibnet.ac.in/): A reservoir of Indian thesis. Theses and dissertations are renowned for being a comprehensive and unique source of information, frequently the only place of research work that doesn't find its way in different publication channels. The fact that theses and dissertations are still an underutilised resource, which causes duplication and repetition is the exact opposite of what research is supposed to do.

The online accessibility of electronic theses through centrally-maintained digital repositories would ensure easy access and archiving of Indian doctoral theses as well as contribute to raising the standard of research, resolving the major problem of research duplication and low quality brought on by "poor visibility" and "unseen" factors in research output. The Indian Electronic Theses and Dissertations digital repository, known as "Shodhganga", is to be hosted, maintained, and made available to all institutions and universities in accordance with the Regulation by the INFLIBNET Centre.

- **ShodhGangotri** (http://shodhgangotri.inflibnet.ac.in/): The repository will show the patterns and directions of the research being done in Indian universities; on the other hand, it would avoid duplication of research. Shodhgangotri is a new initiative that complements "Shodhganga" and contains synopsis of research topics that are submitted to the universities in India by the research scholars who are registering for the Ph.D. programme.
- **e-PG Pathshala** (http://epgp.inflibnet.ac.in): e-PG Pathshala is a project of the Ministry of Human Resource Development, carried out by the University Grants Commission, as part of its national mission on ICT-enabled education. This platform provides high-quality, curriculum-based, interactive e-content with 23,000 modules (e-text and video) in 77 post-graduate disciplines of social science, fine arts, arts and humanities, as well as natural and mathematical sciences.
- **The Swayam Prabha** (https://www.swayamprabha.gov.in/): The Swayam Prabha is a collection of 22 DTH channels that uses the GSAT-15 satellite to broadcast of high-quality educational programmes on 24×7. The students can choose when they want new content every day for at least four hours, which will then be repeated five more times during the day. The channels are uplinked from BISAG-N, Gandhinagar. NPTEL, IITs, UGC, CEC, and IGNOU are responsible

for providing the contents. The web portal is maintained by INFLIBNET Centre.

- **VIDWAN** (https://vidwan.inflibnet.ac.in/): The most comprehensive database of profiles of scientists, researchers, and other faculty members employed by academic institutions, top universities and other R & D organizations engaged in both teaching and research in India, it provides important details about the expert, contact information, experience, publication, qualifications, and accomplishments, among other things. The Information and Library Network Centre (INFLIBNET) develops and maintains the database (NME-ICT) with funding from the National Mission on Education through ICT. The database will be useful in selecting expert panels for committees and task forces that have been established by government agencies and ministries for monitoring and assessment purposes.
- **NPTEL** (http://nptel.ac.in/): National Programme on Technology Enhanced Learning (NPTEL) is a collaborative project of the IITs and IISc, funded by the Ministry of Education (MoE), Government of India, was created in 2003. NPTEL was first founded as a mission to bring high-quality education to all areas of the nation, and it presently provides around 600+ courses for certification every semester in about 22 disciplines.
- **NDLI** (http://ndl.iitkgp.ac.in): The National Mission on Education through Information and Communication Technology (NMEICT) has supported the National Digital Library of India (NDLI) project and arranged funding through the Ministry of Education to make community learning resources accessible to students through a single-window.
- **SWAYAM** Online Course (http://storage.googleapis.com/uniquecourses/online.html): SWAYAM is a programme started by the Government of India with the aims of achieving the three principles of education policy: access,

equity, and excellence. This platform is available to all learners without any charge or registration.

- **eGyanKosh** (https://egyankosh.ac.in/) : Materials in eGyanKosh are copyright protected, with all rights maintained by IGNOU. It serves as a national digital repository to store, index, preserve, distribute, and share the digital learning resources created by the Open and Distance Learning Institutions in the country.
- **The Social Science Cyber Library** (https://socsccybraryamu.ac.in/): The Social Science Cyber Library brings all open access e-resources in the disciplines of social sciences, including e-books, e-journals, video lectures, subject gateways, databases, and useful websites, for the benefit of students, researchers, and faculty from various disciplines around the world.
- **The Gazette of India**: The Gazette of India is a public journal and an authorised legal documents published weekly by the Department of publication, Ministry of Housing and Urban Affairs, Government of India. The Gazette publishes official announcements through the https://egazette.nic.in/(S(5jk4mso02wygbhi5dioxxpjs))/default.aspx#
- **India Code** (https://www.indiacode.nic.in/): Information about the India Code From 1836 onward, the system contains all central Acts of parliament. Every Act comprises a brief title, enactment date, sections, schedule, and footnotes. The text of the Constitution of India and its amendments are listed in full alphabetical and chronological order in the India Code.
- **Lok Sabha Debates** (http://164.100.47.194/Loksabha/Debates/Debatetextsearch16.aspx): There are three different versions of the Lok Sabha Debates, including an original version, an English version, and a Hindi version. English and Hindi translations of these are printed and disseminated to the members and others. The original copy is retained in the Parliamentary Library and is suitably bound for record-keeping and reference only.

- **Rajya Sabha Debates** (https://rsdebate.nic.in/): The full verbatim report of the proceedings of the House on any particular day is contained in Rajya Sabha debates, also known as "Official Reports", which are published in accordance with Rule 260 of the Rules of Procedure and Conduct of Business in the Council of States (Rajya Sabha). The digitized debates are kept in the official debates repository in pdf format (text and image files).
- **The Consortium for Educational Communication (CEC) YouTube Channel** (https://www.youtube.com/user/cecedusat): The Consortium for Educational Communication (CEC), one of the University Grants Commission of India's Inter University Centres, was founded with the aim of addressing the needs of Higher Education by making effective use of the potent medium of Television with the appropriate application of emerging Information Communication Technology (ICT).

In addition to the Government of India initiatives, there are many other initiatives by NGOs corporate and researchers working to achieve different SDGs.

In addition to contributing to the SDGs, higher education institutions are also making an impact on global rankings. Examples include the Kalinga Institute of Information Technology, Bhubaneswar (KIIT), one of the few Indian institutions to reach the Times Higher Education (THE) in the World University Impact Ranking. KIIT has received good ratings for sustainable development parameters like Reduced Inequalities (SDG 10), Peace, Justice, and Strong Institutions (SDG 16), Partnership for Goals (SDG 17), and Quality Education (SDG 4). According to Sircar (n.d.), the M.A. Developmental Programme at Azim Premji University provides a broad grasp of the interconnected nature of development difficulties as well as critical abilities to engage with these challenges at the level of theory, policy, programme, and social activities.

After analysing the above-mentioned literature, the author decided it's important to share about the SDGs work that is taking place at the institute.

Conclusion

India has always struggled with issues like eradicating poverty, providing food, health and cleanliness, quality education, clean water and sanitation etc. In addition, the UN has issued a universal call to work jointly to achieve the SDGs that will make it possible to improve living conditions for future generations in a sustainable manner. The world aims to secure a healthy planet with humanity free from poverty by adopting the 2030 agenda for SDGs, which also aspires to eliminate gender inequality and develop peaceful, inclusive societies for future generations. The UN mentioned 17 SDGs in which designers can actively participate alongside other professionals to work with various communities. While working to achieve the SDGs, social innovations that meet the social needs of various components, such as education, health, community development, etc., are urgently needed. It is common knowledge that social innovations are an effort of mental creativity involving the fluency and flexibility of many different professions. The Al-Barkaat Educational Institutions (ABEIs) in Aligarh is mindful of social needs and wants to make a difference by utilising its outstanding design-oriented think tank to foster social innovations that will have a positive impact on society. The ABEIs will support the activities by creating, disseminating, and preserving knowledge for future generations.

References

IFLA. Libraries and the Implementation of the 2030 Agenda. (n.d.). Retrieved from https://www.ifla.org/wp-content/uploads/2019/05/assets/hq/topics/libraries-development/documents/libraries-un-2030-agenda-toolkit.pdf

Ali, M.H., & Bhatti, R. (n.d.). HEC Digital Library Pakistan: An Integrated Information Source for University Students in Pakistan. Retrieved from http://library.ifla.org/2626/1/180-ali-en_poster.pdf/

Cornish, L. (2018). Do libraries have the key to the framework for implementing the SDGs? Retrieved October 12, 2019, from Devex website: https://www.devex.com/news/do-libraries-have-the-key-to-the-framework-for-implementing-the-sdgs-92375

The SDG Library. (2016). Retrieved October 12, 2019, from Sustainable Development Goals Fund website: https://www.sdgfund.org/library

Singh, C.I., Brahma, S., & Vaiphei, L. (2019). National Information and Library Policies in Support of the UN Sustainable Development Goals: Perspectives in India. Libraries: Dialogue for Change. Presented at the IFLAWLIC, Athens. Retrieved from http://library.ifla.org/2471/1/264-singh-en.pdf/

Pinto, L.G., & Ochôa, P. (2017). Public libraries' contribution to Sustainable Development Goals: Gathering evidences and evaluating practices. Libraries. Solidarity. Society. Presented at the IFLAWLIC, Poland. Retrieved from https://library.ifla.org/id/eprint/1946/1/190-pinto-en.pdf

Bradley, F. (2016)."A world with universal literacy: The role of libraries and access to information in the UN 2030 Agenda." *IFLA Journal, 42*(2), 118-125. https://doi.org/10.1177/0340035216647393

Garcia-Febo, L., Kim, J.H., Lallaisangzuali, Jain, V., & Tugwell, Y. (2017). "Advancing the United Nations Sustainable Development Goals." *College & Research Libraries, 78*(9), pp. 516-520.

22

Training and Development Practices in Indian Hotel Industry

A Critical Study

Atin Das and *Umesh Sharma*

Introduction

In all businesses, training and development should be a carefully planned and implemented process. The expansion and success of a hotel depend heavily on training and development. One of the crucial roles of the human resources (HR) department is training and development. Because the hotel business has a high rate of staff turnover, this role is now steadily becoming more crucial. Specific training must be given in accordance with the needs of the hotel. The quality of hospitality education in India has substantially increased as a result of the opening of numerous new colleges, and graduates are now more proficient and well-prepared to operate in this glamorous and quickly expanding sector.

Along with other human resources operations including recruiting, selection, performance evaluation, and pay, training is a component of human resource development. The purpose of the human resources department is to increase organizational effectiveness by equipping employees with the knowledge, abilities, and attitudes necessary to perform better on the job now and in the future. The training specialist should be knowledgeable of the benefits and drawbacks as well as the efficiency of each training approach in order to apply the best training strategies. Additionally, measurement should be carried out in accordance with the models in order to assess the efficiency of training. Training is a methodical approach to learning and development intended to increase the effectiveness of individuals, teams, and organizations (Goldstein & Ford, 2002). As an alternative, development describes actions that result in the acquisition of new information or abilities for the purpose of personal development.

Training and development (T&D) is essential for improving employee performance and productivity, which boosts the efficiency of the firm. The expense, time, and effort associated with training and development initiatives should be viewed by organizations as an investment rather than a cost.

With a skilled team, a company performs better and more effectively. As a result, businesses prioritize and spend money on good training and development initiatives (Mayfield, 2011). The efficient design and delivery of training activities as well as the methodologies used for training and development determine how effective training and development is (Khan *et al.*, 2011). Performance evaluation, business goal/needs, self-assessment and personal regard, questionnaire survey, competency matrix, client/customer satisfaction index, client/project requirement, employee rate and gap analysis, personal interviews, direct observation, peer feedback, work sample, floor work, and personal interviews are the methods to analyze or assess the need for training in an organization a dash board and error chart, 360-degree feedback on evaluations, the team's necessary knowledge and abilities (Singh & Dangwal, 2017). This allows for the practical decision-making of strategy, delivery approaches, structure, duration, evaluation, and feedback (Quigley, Eoghan, 2019). Although many businesses employ a variety of delivery or training methods, according to Clark (2019), there is no one ideal approach for producing good training. Learning is conducted using a combination of delivery channels, or blended learning. Different training techniques are employed depending on the situation and the necessity. Going with entirely computer-based or instructor-led training will not be beneficial. When students become psychologically invested in the training sessions, learning occurs (Clark, 2019). It is a learning process that includes information acquisition, skill improvement, idea clarification, rule clarification, or attitude and behaviour modification to improve employee performance. Employees receive ongoing training to help them gain expertise and learn how to contribute effectively to the firm. Staff training is a crucial and vital component of human resource management, and its significance and worth have long been acknowledged. Give a person a fish, and you feed him for a day, said Confucius. A person can be fed for life if they learn to fish. This proverb has succinctly stated how crucial it is to invest in an employee's training rather than simply providing them with a source of money. The demand for training is more than ever when considering the current economic environment, the exponential rise of technology, and how these factors affect both the economy and society.

Rationale of the Study

In the tourist and hospitality industries, staff training is a crucial and vital component of human resource management. The need for training is greater than ever, especially in the tourist and hospitality industries, given the current business environment and the exponential rise of technology and how it affects the economy and society. The successful hotels always include employee training as a key component of their development strategies, thus this research paper examines the training system as well as the significance of training and development in the hotel and tourism business. Even if we are a competent employee today, we could be out of line some other day if we do not keep studying because of how quickly technologies are developing and how competitive the corporate world is. A business needs structured staff training if it wishes to compete with others.

Statement of the Problem

Training should be viewed as an investment rather than an expense. In the hospitality sector, training is crucial. Training is a crucial HRD activity that supports an organization's human resource planning. Training improves job-related abilities and makes it easier to acquire new skills needed to prevent skills obsolescence in an organization, which is part of the need for internal staffing. Programmes for employee training boost satisfaction. The growth and success of a hotel are correlated with training and development. Without training, an employee won't be able to assist a customer in the proper manner, the customer won't be satisfied with the hotel's service, and eventually the employee will grow weary of the business management and his or her quality of service will decline.

The most important and significant factor for the hotel and tourism industry's success is training and development because it directs staff members in their efforts to achieve customer satisfaction and, ultimately, business success. This is because a strong service-based philosophy is consistently demonstrated by service providers. The goal of the current study is to examine the importance and advantages of training and development in the hotel and tourism sectors in a hilly region of India where tourism is the main industry.

Review of Literature

According to Ramli *et al.* (2018), focusing just on increasing Knowledge, Skills, and Abilities (KSAs) may not result in an employee that is dedicated to their profession. Innovative behaviours must be cultivated in the workforce through training and development.

According to Falola, Osibanjo *et al.* (2014), training is crucial for both the survival of any firm and the efficient functioning of its staff. Increase in knowledge to help employees enhance their ability to think creatively and solve problems. Improvement in employees' capacity to adapt to the tough and ever-changing corporate environment and technology for greater performance.

According to Mapelu and Jumah (2013), a good training programme is one organizational strategy that can increase employee commitment and create a more stable workforce because most employees think that going through training increases their chances of getting promoted.

According to Biswas (2012), training is crucial to an organization since it helps it stay current in the ever-changing business world. Training enables the current personnel to pick up new skills, stay relevant in the company, and increase the degree of comprehension that promotes an organization's expansion.

According to Bharwani & Butt (2012), training is a crucial step in the hospitality sector. It helps the staff members grow their knowledge and abilities so they may be used in the hotel operations. In addition to improving work productivity, the training given to hospitality staff in many departments and sectors also makes the employees happy with their positions. The personnel receives extensive training in a variety of areas, including food safety, modernization of room amenities, and financial transactions. After receiving training and putting it into practice, the personnel feel at ease in their positions. Their good attitudes are preserved by the company as a result of this emotion, which encourages them to stay with it. To meet the varied operational needs, the departmental managers design well-structured training programmes.

The reward from any training is to improve profit or decrease costs, claim Laing & Andrews (2011). In contrast to training that is less focused and has a nebulous goal, the potential benefits for programmes that address specific issues or potentially lucrative opportunities are clear.

Objectives of the Study

1. To examine the training system to make appropriate recommendation for more effective training system.
2. To recognize the training needs and effective training methods in order to meet the goal of hospitality industry

Research Methodology

Mail-in questionnaires were used to obtain the data. The surveys were sent to 250 (58.82%) of the 425 hotel groups (authorized by the Ministry of Tourism, Government of India) and were addressed to Training Managers and HR Managers. SPSS was used to analyze the data. Using Cronbach's alpha, the survey's dependability and internal consistency were evaluated. If one variable is taken out of the original set of variables in the questionnaire, this test determines the reliability coefficient (a). Based on a coefficient above 0.80, this test aids in identifying the set of variables that have a high degree of reliability.

Results and Discussion

Respondents were questioned on the importance and application of training and development techniques in order to determine the extent to which Indian hotels did so. The respondents firmly agreed that an organization's commitment to training and development is essential. According to the survey, training and development are crucial for a variety of reasons, which are listed in Table 22.1. The value of "increased availability of employees and staff quality" (90%) tops the list of the range of replies stated.

Table 22.1: Training and Development Practices in Indian Hotels: Ranking and Descriptive Statistics

Training & Development Practices	Importance*			Usage**		
	Mean	SD	Rank	Mean	SD	Rank
1. Induction Training						
Adequate importance is given	5.76	0.66	3	4.18	0.79	25
It is well planned	5.60	0.72	5	4.11	0.78	30
It is of sufficient duration	5.05	0.77	16	4.95	0.76	8
To enable gain self-confidence and perform better	4.14	0.80	30	5.00	0.75	7

(Contd.)

Training & Development Practices	Importance*			Usage**		
	Mean	SD	Rank	Mean	SD	Rank
It protects from costly mistakes	5.20	0.75	12	4.14	0.77	29
Understand general objectives, scope, programmes, problems, policies and structure of the organisation	5.00	0.78	18	5.20	0.75	5
2. On-the-job Training						
To acquire technical knowledge and skills through training	5.42	0.73	6	4.82	0.77	13
Participate in determining the training they need	5.38	0.72	9	4.61	0.79	27
The quality of in-company programmes in your organization is excellent	5.40	0.74	7	4.68	0.77	15
Senior line managers are eager to help their juniors develop through training	5.36	0.72	10	4.64	0.75	19
Improved availability & quality of staff	5.96	0.76	1	5.70	0.71	2
Training takes place either on or off-the-job	5.09	0.77	15	4.13	0.79	28
Satisfaction with performance reviews	5.40	0.72	8	4.15	0.81	26
Line managers provide the right kind of climate to implement new ideas and methods acquired by their juniors during training	4.45	0.68	28	4.95	0.76	11
3. Off-the-job Training						
Enhanced confidence, commitment & motivation	5.10	0.73	14	5.75	0.70	1
Recognition, greater responsibility & pay improvements	4.18	0.77	29	5.42	0.70	4
Availability of training for problem-solving ability	4.10	0.85	31	5.62	0.69	3
Understanding of the skills and knowledge they are expected to acquire from the training	4.95	0.74	19	5.63	0.70	24

(*Contd.*)

Training & Development Practices	Importance			Usage		
	Mean	SD	Rank	Mean	SD	Rank
Employees returning from training are given adequate free time to reflect and plan improvements in the organisation	5.90	0.66	2	4.51	0.76	22
External training programmes are carefully chosen their quality and suitability	4.73	0.78	24	5.10	0.70	6
To change behaviour, attitudes or opinions	5.30	0.75	11	4.85	0.79	12
Off the job training is more preferred by the employees	4.90	0.82	21	4.66	0.80	17

One-way ANOVAs were carried out to evaluate the association between some of the controls and the use of training and development strategies, or in other words, to test Hypothesis. Table summarizes the findings of this analysis and provides the related F-values. This table's findings provide useful information. The average scores of the related control variables are listed in the column labeled "mean scores." In the 5-level Likert scale, it can be observed that all means are higher than 3.

Table 22.2: F-Values from the One-Way Anova on Training & Development Practices Control Variables

Training & Development practices	Mean scores	Category of hotels	Age	Size in capital	Size in empl-oyees	Type of enterprise
Induction training	4.60	4.454	3.125	3.586	4.520	3.433
On-the-Job Training	4.34	4.100	3.782	3.425	3.178	3.704
Off-the-Job Training	5.20	4.749	3.514	3.325	2.085	3.923

Conclusion

The study added to our understanding of training and development strategies used in the Indian hotel business. It has added to our understanding of the elements that affect how effective training and development techniques are adopted. This study discovered considerable variations in how Indian hotels used and valued training and development techniques. The findings show that training and development practices variables are positively correlated with hotel category and business type, however, the findings are somewhat different when it comes to training and development practices factors and hotel age and size (capital or employees).

This is sometimes resulting in the creation of a more strategic, integrated approach to the application and significance of training & development. This study is simply indicative; further research is needed. According to the research, training and development may be more important than previously thought in the coordination of activities for the development of human resources. These findings only make the case for the use and acceptance of employee growth-focused training and development approaches as a guiding concept in human resource development. The implementation and adoption of recognized training and development strategies in Indian hotels appears to have contributed to the changes found in this research. Thus, it would seem that training & development, which had previously played a relatively minor organizational function, is now beginning to take a more prominent place in the human resource development strategies of many Indian hotel organizations.

Future Scope

Future studies should take into account including additional crucial factors that have not been taken into account or omitted from previous studies and are likely to have an impact on the adoption of training & development practices in Indian hotels, such as management support, employee satisfaction and attitudes, perceived information quality, training & development needs, perceived benefits, and implementation and cross-comparison issues.

References

Akinyele, Taiwo, (2007). The impact of Nigerian Training Programmes on Employees Performance, *Research Journal of Business Management,* 1, pp.11-19.

Al-Emadi, Marquardt, (2007). Relationship between employees' beliefs regarding training benefits and employees' organizational commitment in a petroleum company in the State of Qatar, *International Journal of Training & Development, 11*: 1, pp. 49-70.

Alipour, Mehrdad & Salehi, Mahdi (2009). A Study of on- the-Job Training Effectiveness: Empirical Evidence of Iran, *International Journal of Business and Management,* 4(11).

Armstrong (2000). *Understanding training, Human Resource Management Practice.* 8th Edition. Kogan Page Limited, London, p. 543.

Arthur, W., Bennet, W., Edens, P.S. and Bell, S.T. (2003), Effectiveness of training in organizations: a meta-analysis of design and evaluation features, *Journal of Applied Psychology,* Vol. 88, pp. 234-245.

Bacon, N., and Hoque, K. (2005). HRM in the SME Sector: Valuable Employees and Coercive Networks, *International Journal of Human Resource Management,* 16, pp. 1976-1999.

Bartel, A., (1994), Productivity gains from the implementation of employee training programmes, *Industrial Relations,* 33. pp. 411-425.

Baum, T. (1995), *Managing Human Resources in the European Tourism and Hospitality Industry—A strategic approach,* London, Chapman & Hall.

Beaver, G., and Hutchings, K. (2005). Training and Developing an Age Diverse Workforce in SMEs: The Need for a Strategic Approach, *Education Camp; Training, 47,* pp. 592-604.

Bharwani & Butt (2012). *Challenges for the global hospitality industry: an HR perspective, ISSN*: 1755-4217.

Biswas, Malay (2012). *Human Resource Management in Hospitality,* New Delhi: Oxford University Press.

Falola, H.O., Osibanjo, A.O., Ojo, S.I. (2014). Effectiveness of training and Development on employees' Performance and Organization Competitiveness in the Nigerian Banking industry, Bulletin of the Transilvania University of Brasov, Series V: *Economic Sciences,* 7 (56) No. 1.

Kung'u, S. (2011). Assessment of the labour turnover and wastage levels in three to five starrated hotels in Nairobi, Kenya, Kenyatta University.

Laing & Andrews (2011). *International Journal of Human Resource Studies*, DOI: https://doi.org/10.5296/ijhrs.v1i1.860

Mapelu, Isabel Cheloti & Jumah, Lucy (2013). Effect of Training and Development on Employee Turnover in Selected Medium Sized Hotels in Kisumu City, Kenya, *Journal of Tourism Hospitality and Sports—An Open Access International Journal*, Vol. 1.

Mariam, K. (2017). *Factors affecting employee job satisfaction in the hospitality industry in Kenya: a case study of Boma hotels*, Kenya, Management University of Africa.

Ramli, *et al.* (2018). *Work Environment, Job Satisfaction and Employee Performance*, DOI: https://doi.org/10.25105/ber.v19i1.5343

Singh, N., & Dangwal, R.C. (2017). Training Need Analysis Process of Selected Manufacturing Firms in Uttarakhand State: An Empirical Study. *Splint International Journal of Professionals*, *4*(5), 54-65.

Tiwari, Usha (2014). Impact of Training and Development Programmes on Employees Efficiency at Madhya Pradesh State Electricity Board (MPSEB), *International Journal of Business & Management*, 2 (1).

Truitt, D.L. (2011). The effect of training and development on employee attitude as it relates to training and work proficiency. *Sage Open*, 1(3), DOI: 2158244011433338

Index